Sex Work

Sex Work
A Risky Business

Teela Sanders

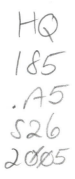

WILLAN
PUBLISHING

Published by:

Willan Publishing
Culmcott House
Mill Street, Uffculme
Cullompton, Devon
EX15 3AT, UK
Tel: +44(0)1884 840337
Fax: +44(0)1884 840251
e-mail: info@willanpublishing.co.uk
Website: www.willanpublishing.co.uk

Published simultaneously in the USA and Canada by

Willan Publishing
c/o ISBS, 920 NE 58th Ave, Suite 300,
Portland, Oregon 97213-3786, USA
Tel: +001(0)503 287 3093
Fax: +001(0)503 280 8832
e-mail: info@isbs.com
Website: www.isbs.com

Contents

Introduction   1

Chapter 1: The peculiarities of prostitution   9
   Visible yet hidden   11
   The dark figure of prostitution   12
   The markets   13
   Makers and takers   20

Chapter 2: Ethnography, sex and the self   23
   Layered access   23
   Earning acceptance   28
   The rhythms of fieldwork   30
   Sex work uncovered   33
   Risky research   35

Chapter 3: Choice, risk and selling sex   37
   Choosing denigration?   38
   Risk-taking and choice-making   42
   A hierarchy of harms   44
   The women   46

Chapter 4: Picking punters   51
   The prostitution trust game   53
   Eyeballing the punter   57
   Remote observation   64
   Testing on the telephone   66
   Assessing on the Net   68
   Screening for safety   70

Chapter 5: Keeping safe   **72**

The normalization of violence   73

Precautions: behind the scenes   75

Deterrents: calling their bluff   80

Protection: if all else fails   87

Resisting violence   90

Chapter 6: Dodging cops   **93**

The legal landscape   93

Policing prostitution   97

Street wisdom   105

Behind closed doors   110

Displacing deviance   113

Chapter 7: Secrets and lies   **116**

Sexual stigma   117

Covering up   124

Location   129

Isolation   131

Variations of the truth   133

Chapter 8: Staying sane   **138**

Negative emotions as motive   140

Emotion management   142

The strategies   147

When emotion management fails   155

Chapter 9: Professionalizing prostitution?   **158**

Rules, rituals and routines   159

Mechanisms of transmission   165

Regulating a risky business   174

Bibliography   **181**

Index   **201**

This book is dedicated to
Dorothy Dandridge,
my grandmother, with love.

Introduction

Working girls[1]

On a dreary Wednesday mid-morning in February, I am visiting working premises with Alison. We stop outside a semi-detached house in an unspectacular tree-lined street with rows of ex-council houses now donning private brightly coloured front doors. Alison and I gather bags of condoms, lubricants and some leaflets on hepatitis B injections that are offered at the clinic, stash them in an unobtrusive white plastic bag and head for the door. This is my fourth visit to this particular house and the women's friendly acceptance means I am looking forward to seeing them. It takes Katrina and Leigh a few minutes to answer, grabbing something to put round them before checking through the peephole. Greeted with a genuine welcome, Leigh, wearing a black bikini and knee-length boots, ushers us into the lounge where Katrina is putting a sarong around her thong bikini. All four of us are in the lounge, curtains drawn over heavy nets, and the heat is stifling. In the middle of winter, wearing not many clothes, it needs to be red hot. Alison and I peel off layers as Leigh strolls to the kitchen to make coffee as we hug Katrina in a 'good-to-see-you-haven't-for-ages' way. This is because Katrina has been off work for several weeks while she had a breast enlargement. She takes us through the operation, as graphic as any medical documentary, and shows us the scars and the new improved 34D that she claims is a must after having children. Leigh returns with coffee and we all relax and catch up. Alison has known these two women for several years and has a strong, open relationship with them. As an observer I am very aware that I am cashing in on their lengthy acquaintance, listening intently to the conversation and occasionally chipping in.

Applying moisturizer to her legs, Leigh tells us with nervous excitement that she is expecting her favourite client – a six-foot fireman – with whom she breaks all the rules and enjoys every second of his company. The doorbell rings, Leigh checks her lip gloss in the full-length mirror, bounds to the door and whisks the client up the stairs. Alison and I never see any clients, just their vague shadow as they walk up the path. A few minutes later Leigh returns to the lounge to hide her earnings and is gone for twenty minutes. Katrina chats with us about how business has been going, the landlord who is trying to put up the rent and, hence, their search for a new property. Our chat is interrupted while Katrina takes calls from prospective clients, giving out directions, and slamming down the phone on time-wasters. Eventually the phone is too distracting so she takes it off the hook, preferring to relay her news. Katrina tells us of a new business venture they are trying out after a client told them about their competitors who advertise online. The girls have had some arty photographs taken together and now have a website where they are promoting specialist services at a higher price. Katrina jokes that she has gone a long way in ten years when she started on the street. Leigh returns just as Katrina's client arrives, a friendly GP we are told, who walks stridently towards the door, doctor's bag in hand, no doubt disguising his reasons for visiting.

We have a chance to catch up with Leigh, who tells us about her impending marriage to her long-time fiancé who knows about her work. She tells how after her marriage she will only do domination services, and will lose the likes of her fireman who simply want the basics. In what seem like minutes, Katrina returns after wishing her client well as she closes the door. She takes off her bra that was uncomfortable and puts on a tracksuit, then collapses into the sofa and lights a cigarette. They have both seen four clients already, it is 2pm and time for lunch and we have other visits to make. Both women make arrangements with Alison to attend the clinic for a full health screening. We say our goodbyes and I arrange to go back next week alone with my tape recorder. Another day in the life of a sex worker, health promotion specialist and an ethnographer . . .

This book is about one aspect of the sex economy, the indoor prostitution markets, in the city of Birmingham, UK, that facilitates the purchase of direct sexual services between consenting men and women. Concentrating on what Glover (1969) terms the 'flourishing professional', this book moves beyond stereotypes of 'the prostitute' to look at the mundane and essentially ordinary activities of the indoor female sex worker. I came to know the sex industry in 1995 when I volunteered with a non-governmental organization in New York City. A small group of women revealed that in the past they had been sex workers and spoke of their previous careers not as a seedy part of their history but of their 'businesses' working out of five-star hotels, the customers (some of whom were famous) and their courtesan skills. Prior to this my only experience of prostitution had been living in a community where women stood on street corners heckling for business, stepping out territories and using the local park to 'punt and score'. It was puzzling how a 'high-class escort' who appeared to make choices to sell sex to men could be part of the same economy where women on the edge of society trade intimate, albeit brief, flesh-to-flesh contact with a stranger to buy a bag of heroin.

This work began as a doctoral research project, '*A Risky Business. How Sex Workers Manage Their Clients, Community and Conscience*', made possible by the Department of Sociology, University of Oxford, and an ESRC studentship (number R00429934537) between 1999 and 2002. The differences between the sex markets led me to question how women experienced the complexities of working in prostitution. Risk, as an inevitable feature of the clandestine activity, provided a useful baseline from which to make inquiries. Of more interest were the relatively unexplored nature of the responses that sex workers made to the risks they encountered, and indeed the rationality of those responses. It became clear that a core question to be addressed is whether women are passive victims of the circumstances of prostitution or whether they understand and calculate their responses to danger. While I do not argue that women rationally enter into prostitution, I argue for rationality in responding to risks. I endeavour to provide an answer by estimating the rationality of those responses and by providing a measure of how women make sense of different types of occupational hazards.

I came to be able to comment on these matters by experiencing hundreds of encounters like the one described above. I occupied a privileged position where I could listen to women, ask questions, watch them at work and speak to them in their private lives. During the research I met many different types of women who had come to prostitution through various routes. Some were in coercive relationships, suffering drug addictions, clinging onto a life that was devoid of direction and hope. Other women were embedded in secure familial and romantic relationships and enjoyed their work after making economic choices to enter the sex industry. Some women went missing during the fieldwork and have not been seen since, yet in contrast, nearly five years on, I am still in contact with a handful of respondents on a regular basis. Women responded to my endeavours in different ways, revealing a rainbow of emotions. On occasions I was shunted out of doors, verbally abused on the telephone and several attempts were made to defame my character and project in online chatrooms and message boards. Luckily, the responses that kept me going were open, genuine, mainly female interactions that reciprocated respect and understanding. Sex workers invited me into their homes, to meet their family, partners and children, to stay for supper and into the small hours. We talked. 'Eastenders', the latest supermarket prices, the challenges of parenting, love, hate, sex and money were the usual topics.

During my time in the sex establishments I met women who sold sexual services, as well as many people whose roles keep the cogs of the industry ticking over. Men featured in the scenery of the study, as clients, photographers, advertisers, dungeon makers, webmasters, security guards, drivers, husbands, policemen, community protesters and drug dealers. Owners, managers, receptionists, health-care professionals, nurses, social workers, team leaders, union members, campaigners, lap dancers, cleaners, beauticians, fellow academics and researchers were mainly women who shaped how I came to know the industry. At the centre of this world were the sex workers, the majority of whom actively managed their work separately from their domestic life and often considered themselves as professionals.

This book is a reflection of an ethnography – one person's interpretation of a social group that relies on the accuracy of thousands of interactions and relationships that are encountered in the undefined 'lifetime' of the project. Consequently, I have been in contact with hundreds of people through various modes of communication throughout the country to arrive at this point. The Safe Project in Birmingham, Carole Lennox and Alison Cook especially, hosted my ideas and naiveté, allowing me to 'hang out' with them for three years. Without their support, belief and friendship, this project would never have got off the ground. The Internet-based work has been a challenge, stumbling on methodological nuances in the early days, treading on toes and alarming university authorities in the course of my explorations. In this regard, I am grateful to Eric Rambler, who continues to watch over me, despite remaining completely anonymous. The role of the Internet in prostitution has only been scraped at the surface and is something to which I hope to return. Also, I thank the UK Network of Sex Work Projects for inviting me to join as an 'academic' member, especially Hilary Kinnell and Rosie Campbell for keeping the community up to date with what's happening and their willingness to share and support this project right from the start.

This monograph has been a long time coming and although they are unaware, the late Richard Thornton (who drummed it into my sixth-form colleagues and I that there was a book in everyone of us), Dr David Parker and Professor A.H. Halsey, inspired me to continue and be proud of sociology. My doctoral supervisor, Professor Diego Gambetta, assisted me greatly in the early days and I thank him for his endless time and perseverance. Professor Anthony Heath, Professor Roger Hood, Dr Carolyn Hoyle and Dr Phil Hubbard were enthusiastic along the way and the support for several years from Green College, Oxford, was a haven. Dr Maggie O'Neill has been inspirational in her efforts to put prostitution into an academic context while remaining unfettered by the stigma. In the transition phase, I am grateful to Professor Richard Sparks, Professor Keith Soothill and Brian Willan for showing optimism. Colleagues at the University of Leeds have graciously given me space and time: in particular John Michael Roberts and Stuart Lister selflessly read and talked about my work. Special thanks are given to Professor Dick Hobbs, who gave me the confidence and vision to turn the thesis into the monograph and, through his own work, showed me how to 'do the business' in this tricky industry. Many thanks to him for reading all the chapters (in their different forms) and taking my work seriously.

My friends have all been shining stars because they rarely asked about my work, but instead dragged me off to far corners of the world, or their own backyard, to remember the finer things in life. Nerys Edmonds, Annie Horne and Pam Riding continue to keep the New York dream alive and never let me forget what the Big Apple tastes like. Particular thanks to Nerys, who never fails to help me see the brighter side, even when two turns of the world look far away. Alison Burrows (and now Gingers' Girlz) have been spectacular in making me put this work into context and never fail to shock me. Aparna Pal, Nicky Jacobsen, Lucy McFarlane and Faye Mellington were and still are always on hand to dance on the decking or camp on a cliff. Old friends, Martin Smith, Claire Maxwell, Caitlin McKiernan and Harriet Churchill, have kept me on my toes and focused wandering attentions. My parents, Monica and Cliff, have been simply the best: unconditional, solid and ready for anything. My sister Katie continues to pull the rabbit out of the bag, and is always close at hand. This book is dedicated to my grandmother, Dorothy Dandridge, a wise old bird, who keeps the home fires burning. I thank her for her continual prayers.

The findings presented in this book move beyond describing the characteristics normally associated with prostitution to explore the breadth of calculated decision making that form the basis of commercial sexual transactions for some sex workers. Scrutinizing both the social organization of prostitution (the deviant act) and the social organization of the sex workers and organizers (the deviant actors) enables a frank discussion of the regulatory elements of the illegal enterprise. In Chapter 1, examples of the contemporary landscape of prostitution in Britain describe what the sex markets look like, how sex is sold and who is involved. Sketching the key characteristics of the markets provides a platform to discuss concepts such as risk, choice, regulation and management in the later chapters. Chapter 2 provides details of the ethnography by describing the process of 'layered access', how I earned a level of acceptance as an outsider, and the special circumstances, such as nakedness, that informed the data-collection process. Chapter 3 begins with a reflection on the debates that place prostitution on a moral and philosophical axiom between victimhood, choice, consent and sexual labour. This provides a forum to discuss the gendered nature of risk in the context of 'risky behaviour' in prostitution. I introduce the fifty-five women who gave formal interviews and provide socio-demographic details to illustrate the backgrounds of those who took part in the study.

In Chapter 4, I argue that the decision to accept or reject a client is a complex process of judging 'genuineness'. Sex workers do not randomly pick clients but impose a strict assessment criterion to decide who will honour the contract. The screening strategies introduce the complex systems sex workers use to prevent violence and robbery. Chapter 5 continues with the theme of keeping safe and establishes that although violence is a common experience for street workers, a significant number of indoor workers in my sample remained violence-free. This is because sex workers create rational responses in the form of precautions, deterrents and remedial protection strategies to minimize the threat of physical danger. Chapter 6 describes how the organization of prostitu-tion is 'deeply influenced by its legal and social sanctions' (Zatz 1997: 300), especially the quasi-criminalization of sex work. State and commu-nity policing of prostitution creates daily obstacles that determine how women go about their business. I document how sex workers in both the street and indoor markets respond to the local dynamics of policing and protesters to avoid detection, criminalization and repercussions on their personal lives.

Chapter 7 considers the threat of 'being discovered' and the conse-quences of shame. There is a paucity of literature on the extent of secrecy in sex workers' lives and how they manage to keep their work hidden. For some, being discovered is prioritized in the 'hierarchy of harms' because it involves serious consequences for personal relationships. Chapter 8 argues that the emotional risks of selling sex are an occupational hazard equal to those already discussed. Building on Hochschild's (1979, 1983) theory of 'emotion work', I describe how sex workers manage their own emotions when selling sex. However, the prevalence of emotion management strategies does not necessarily mean the techniques are successful. Chapter 9 is an accumulation of the findings where I argue that prostitution, although an illicit and illegal economy, is a highly regulated enterprise and that 'social order emerges in this seemingly disruptive environment' (Prus and Irini 1980: 3). An occupational culture exists similar to other mainstream occupations, and is shaped by social norms and sanctions, moral hierarchies and codes of conduct that regulate working practices and client interactions. I argue that there are distinct contradictions between the legislative approach to criminalizing both the selling, organizing and buying of sex while within the industry there are mechanisms of self-regulation at a local and national level.

Note

1 In Birmingham the term 'working girl' was used by sex workers to identify themselves and their role.

Chapter 1

The peculiarities of prostitution

> Criminologists stand to lose little and gain much in the way of sociological understanding if, when studying people dedicated to an illegal occupation, they will overcome their fascination with the 'illegal' part long enough to focus on the 'occupation' part. (Polsky 1967: 100)

Sir John Wolfenden, chairman of the 1957 committee on homosexuality and prostitution commented, 'one of the difficulties we had while the Departmental Committee was sitting was to get a first-hand account of the life and attitude of the prostitute herself' (Anon 1959). While this imbalance has been rectified through individual women telling their story,[1] a weak, but collective voice representing the labour rights of sex workers[2] and academic investigation,[3] the 'true life' accounts of sex workers have largely concentrated on those who work from the visible street market whose lives are marred by exclusion, drug addiction, male coercion and violence. Hearing the voices of women who negatively experience selling sex was a crucial part of a movement towards placing women's domestic and sexual experiences in the public arena, but 'now it is time to clear space, create support for and theorize other stories' of women who make a living through selling sex (Nagel 1997: 4).

By challenging the titillating, voyeuristic lens through which prostitution has often been looked, I focus on the customary and common aspects of sex workers' lives to demonstrate the regulated nature of indoor prostitution markets in Britain. This will be done by combining two perspectives: first, a socio-psychological analysis that places the sex worker at the centre of the deviant behaviour, and second, a socio-structural analysis that brings into view the organization of the deviant act. Sex workers negotiate prostitution as part of their everyday life, yet they do this under enormous pressure because of the special nature of the work they do. This book describes different types of occupational hazards borne out of selling sex for money and the responses women make to minimize risks of physical and emotional harm while at the same time maximizing profit. In doing so, I criticize the empirical emphasis on health-related risks at the expense of recognizing other types of hazards that sex workers perceive as dangerous.

The majority of academic findings on prostitution establish the relationship between physical health, prostitution and 'risky' behaviours. This concentration on disease and drug use not only blurs the whole picture of prostitution but also distorts the realities of prostitution for many workers. Research has neglected the assessment of what women involved in prostitution perceive as harmful and how they conceptualize and manage risk. Where there has been a focus on risk management this has been among women who work on the street (McKeganey and Barnard 1996; Faugier 1994; Hoigard and Finstad 1992) with only a few exceptions taking stock of the risks and strategies adopted by women who work from indoor markets (Brewis and Linstead 2000b, 2000c; Heyl 1979; O'Connell Davidson 1998; Plumridge 2001; Whitaker and Hart 1996).

Ronald Weitzer (2000: 4) in his chapter 'Why we need more research on sex work' argues that 'when it comes to prostitution, the most serious blunder is that of equating all prostitution with street prostitution, ignoring entirely the indoor side of the market'. The concentration on the street market obscures other important occupational dangers that explain sex workers' behaviour and uncovers the fine detail of the social organization of the sex industry. Staying close to the perspectives of the women in my study, I hope to avoid such short-sightedness by identifying how sex workers rank the risks they are exposed to. Addressing West and Austrin's (2002: 491) criticism that prostitution 'markets are very rarely studied in terms of *how* they work and operate' (original italics), this book uncovers the complex nature of the organization of sex work in Britain.

I intentionally avoid the clearly exploitative situations where women or children are confined, coerced or trafficked into selling sex.[4] As Butcher (2003: 1983) notes, by 'merging trafficking and prostitution, the agency of the sex worker is overlooked' and any objective reality is confused with moral ideology. Although I will refer to 'pimping', where a man (usually a boyfriend) controls the organization of prostitution for a woman, this is not a central theme. I also do not explore either sex tourism,[5] or the non-contact markets of the sex economy, such as the production and distribution of pornographic videos and magazines, telephone chat-lines, erotic dancing and stripshows.[6] Therefore, the generic term 'sex work' will in this case refer to prostitution activities where there is a consensual exchange of sexual services for cash between consenting men and women.

Visible yet hidden

The place of prostitution in the city is not hidden from the curious observer. Local knowledge updated by the media and urban folklore provides a roadmap to locate 'red light districts' in major towns and cities in Britain. Although the street market has been a recorded aspect of the social history across the country,[7] the indoor markets are, to a lesser extent, still a noticeable feature of the modern entertainment economy. In the capital, calling cards that advertise escorts and brothels have long decorated telephone booths found near train stations and the pleasure ground of Soho (Hubbard 2002a; Swirsky and Jenkins 2000). In Britain, a steady process of normalization of the 'sexpolitation economy' (Murphy 2003: 307) has taken place as sex shops, access to pornography (see Jacobs 2004), peep shows, erotic films and lap-dancing bars have become an accepted part of the night-time, and to some extent, the day-time entertainment industry, where sexual fantasies can be visualized and realized. The rise of lap-dancing bars, led by American giants Spearmint Rhino, are not only an obligatory part of the stag party that signals an end to laddish frivolity as men head into the constraints of marriage, but are a regular feature of weekend (increasingly for mixed-sex groups) leisure. This 'unbridled ethic of sexual consumption' (Bernstein 2001: 389) is not only for the boys. For the girls, and in particular the hen party entourage, the male striptease and the Ann Summers parties encourage outrageous sexually orientated behaviour that excuses feminine homosociality (Storr 2003).

Alongside what can be considered to be the 'normalization of the erotic' of non-contact sexual services, the availability of direct sexual services is also becoming increasingly tolerated and therefore visible. Premises licensed for 'massage' and brothels are edging closer into the night-time zones of pleasure, resisting their traditional place on the periphery of the city previously driven there by high rent prices, the dominance of corporate offices and multi-million pound pub chains that monopolize prime city space. Sex businesses can be big businesses that boast the financial capital to compete for a place on the entertainment strip. Neon lights, metal shutters, and signs such as 'sauna', 'parlour' or 'bronzarium' suggest something more than a relaxing massage is on offer in the surrounding streets of the entertainment districts. Sex is not only for sale in the city. A recent headline in *The Observer* (18 April 2004) announced 'Sex comes out of the city into middle England', exposing the everyday accessibility of brothels in suburban neighbourhoods. For the novice customer or the enthusiastic hobbyist there are a range of guides that direct men around the country to spend their cash. The most widely read, *McCoy's Guide to Adult Services*, provides a graphic directory to over 400 massage parlours and 500 working women in Britain – a testament to the extent of both supply and demand. In addition, a momentary perusal of sexual services advertised on the Internet opens up what seems like an infinite escort service, where sex workers can be booked online, to arrive at a location of choice for a significant fee.

While the indoor markets flourish, the street market nestles in between the entertainment strip and the no-man's land of deserted office blocks, industrial estates, car parks and derelict scrublands that form the backdrop before suburbia begins. Nevertheless, although it could be argued that indoor commercial sex markets are moving out of the shadows of dark alleys and dingy backrooms, little is recorded about the nature and extent of these markets. Forced by the threat of police interference, the fear of being recognized as a 'prostitute' and the stigma that is attached to 'the oldest profession', most people involved in selling sex do not openly admit their dealings but instead are masters at managing deviancy.

The dark figure of prostitution

There is no comprehensive recording of the number of women involved in prostitution or the number of men who purchase sex because of the 'formidable methodological problems of realistic estimations of population size' (Wellings et al. 1994: 120). The fragmentary evidence that does exist suggests that prostitution is a significant phenomenon in Britain and despite the over-sensitization of academic, media and policing attention on the street market, most prostitution occurs indoors. Historically, records show that in 1859, the police were aware of 2,828 brothels active in London, with as many as 80,000 women working (Porter 1994). Over a century later, Matthews (1997) analysed police records, newspaper advertisements and conducted a telephone survey, to calculate that in London only 12 per cent of prostitutes worked on the street, with a further 4,600 women working from various indoor markets.

In Birmingham, the location of this study, McLeod (1982) calculated that in the late 1970s, approximately 800 women worked in prostitution, and in any one week 13,690 clients bought sex. Kinnell (1991) calculated that in 1987, 1,200 women were selling sex in the city. The sexual health project through which I gained access registered over 700 workers at its health clinic. Similar numbers of workers have been suggested in other British cities. Using the capture-recapture technique, McCullagh et al. (1998: 41) estimated that between January 1994 and December 1995, 557 women worked on the streets of Liverpool. In Edinburgh, the health service SCOT PEP came into contact with 504 sex workers between January and September 2001, of which 212 were street workers (Morgan-Thomas 2003). Taylor (2003), writing about the Mainliners Working

Women's Clinic in Streatham, London, estimates that there are 102 women working the streets in the borough, and a further 150 who work in flats. The figure relied on in the Home Office consultation paper *Paying the Price* (2004: 15) refers to 80,000 people involved in prostitution in the UK. This number is derived from a survey carried out in 1999 by Europap UK of seventeen projects who were each in contact with an average of 665 sex workers. Multiplied by the 120 projects that exist to support women in the sex industry, 80,000 is a somewhat tentative estimate, and I would argue only the tip of the iceberg.

Collating the human involvement in adult prostitution bears little weight on the amount of revenue made through consenting commercial sexual services. Sullivan and Jefferys (2002) report from the state of Victoria in Australia (population of only 4.8 million), where prostitution is legalized in licensed brothels and escort agencies, some 60,000 men spend $7 million (approximately £3.5 million) a week on the industry. In Britain, the Metropolitan Police Clubs and Vice Team have estimated that in the Soho area, £1 million per month is spent on the sex industry. Although all of these figures are tentative, what they signal is that sex work in Britain is a significant industry. Therefore it should not be surprising that the markets that facilitate this commodity are varied and complex.

The markets

The organization of the indoor sex markets has attracted attention from journalists, especially at times of high-profile court cases such as that of Josie Daly, who was accused of running a £7.5 million brothel business from her wheelchair, and more recently, Margaret MacDonald, who was charged with organizing Europe's largest escort ring and sentenced to four years' imprisonment by a court in Paris. More recently, qualitative research has offered new insights into the life of the British entrepreneurial sex worker (O'Connell Davidson 1998), the organization of sex work (Brewis and Linstead 2000a; Weitzer 2000; Whitaker and Hart 1996) and the behaviour of male clients (Monto 2004; Monto and Hotaling 2001). Although there can be no typology of sex workers because of the varied backgrounds of women who work in prostitution, it is possible to suggest a typology of sex markets. While these markets are not mutually exclusive or entirely comprehensive (for instance, there is growing anecdotal evidence that prostitution is increasingly informal in bars and clubs), the markets described below constitute the main prostitution arenas in the British sex economy. Despite the common and fundamental feature of exchanging sexual acts for money, the characteristics of markets vary in terms of organizational structure, working practices and exposure to risk.

Weitzer (2000: 3) highlights the 'reality of *variation* in sex work' is based on '*different kinds* of worker experiences and *varying degrees* of victimization, exploitation, agency and choice' (original italics). He goes on to note five points of digression between the indoor and the street markets based on the social status of the sex worker, the level of freedom women have to control working conditions, levels of exploitation and victimization, psychological adjustments and the impact prostitution has on the community. Sex workers are either self-employed independent entrepreneurs or they work in other people's establishments. The relationship between the establishment and the worker is not the same as the contractual agreement between an employer and an employee in other occupations because in the sex industry, women who work in other people's businesses usually pay to do so. Yet renting a space in a business is not uncommon for mainstream occupations such as hairdressers and taxi drivers who are self-employed but use the umbrella of an established company to gain custom.

The working environment dictates the mode of advertising, the services offered and the legality of the activity. Sexual services are partly dictated by the client's desires and partly by the worker's willingness to sell access to different areas of her body. Lever and Dolnick (2000: 95) surveyed 998 street prostitutes in Los Angeles and 57 per cent said the most popular request was fellatio, while Monto (2000: 75) confirms from interviews with 518 clients that 47 per cent usually buy oral sex. There is evidence that this pattern of preferences is the norm in Britain. On the street, services are usually 'no frills' intercourse and fellatio because 'street prostitutes are usually approached by men who want quick sex at cheap prices' (Campbell 1991: 1372). This can be compared to the elaborate fantasies that are available indoors and the emphasis on a leisurely, intimate experience.

The sex economy in Britain can be divided into six distinct markets. Licensed saunas are officially endorsed by the local council to sell massage; brothels are illegal establishments where groups of women pay to work; working premises are also illegal if several women work together, but women who work independently can work legally; independent escorts; women who work from home; and the street market. Collectively the first five markets will be described as the indoor sex markets in comparison to the street market.

Licensed saunas

Saunas that offer sexual services are often highly organized, commercial sex establishments. Some local authorities license these businesses to sell massage only and require inspections from health and safety authorities and a registration procedure. This system of licensing for massage is not as liberal as other regulation systems such as that in Nevada, USA (Campbell 1991; Hausbeck and Brent 2000) and the formalities in Britain represent something of a charade, as the reality is that the core activity of licensed saunas is illegal. Saunas are located in urban areas, on main streets and among shop fronts and they are fairly stable enterprises (see Soothill 2004b). Their outward appearance can be subtle, above a shop or amidst offices, sometimes only located by telephoning for directions. Other saunas are obvious, sporting neon lights, accompanied by suspicious boarded windows or shutters. The building is often a converted house, with the majority of rooms serving as bedrooms. Often, 'the physical environment in sauna and massage parlours does vary considerably and this does seem to have an influence on the nature and quality of the service encounter' (Jones and Pratten 1999: 40). The decor can range from dark, seedy interiors with few furnishings other than a bed and a shower through to upmarket saunas that provide a jacuzzi, four-poster and other boudoir luxuries. All licensed saunas have a communal area for workers that are unavailable to clients, and a public lounge where customers wait, relax and choose from the menu of services and workers.

Saunas operate from mid-morning until late at night, and those in London usually operate twenty-four hours a day. The number of workers recruited depends on the size, location and image of the establishment. For instance, some saunas in my study had a reputation for hiring at least twenty women at weekends, whereas other, more exclusive saunas have a regular staff of three women on each shift. Among interviewees there was unease about working in establishments that hire a large number of workers because of the competition, especially when custom is scarce. In these environments, distrust of other workers is common, especially where theft of personal belongings, including condoms, was reported to be commonplace.

This market is renowned for 'house rules' and expectations of conduct. May, et al. (2000: 26) interviewed ten managers who established a list of common rules: 'Never employ juveniles, no anal sex, condoms always to be used, no partners allowed in the workplace, no overcharging, no rudeness or unpunctuality, no drunkenness and no clients under the age of 18'. Evidence suggests there is limited use of illegal drugs in off-street prostitution: 'the split between users and non-users was divided almost exactly between flat workers and street workers' (Taylor 2003: 7; also see Brewis and Linstead 2000a: 87).

Based in a middle England town, O'Connell Davidson (1998: 21–2) describes 'Stephanie's', as a typical sauna that involves a complex financial system of fees. Owners receive a 'shift fee' as rent from each worker plus a 'punter fee' from the worker for each client that purchases a service. In addition, a 'receptionist fee' is also paid by the workers to cover the managerial overheads (see Prus and Irini 1980: 65, for an American example). The owner also receives a 'massage fee' directly from each client who enters the building. O'Connell Davidson (1998: 23) calls this 'transparently exploitative' as it is not uncommon for workers to give at least half of their earnings to the owner. To maintain competitiveness, owners impose a rigid price structure for each sex act. However, individuals explained how they made additional cash by negotiating 'extras' such as spanking and fantasies.

The services available in saunas are extensive, ranging from basic sex acts to services including uniforms, role-play, a 'lesbian' show, fantasy and domination routines. At the time of the fieldwork (2001) the prices in the saunas were as follows: £40 for intercourse or fellatio, £60 for vaginal sex and fellatio, a minimum of £80 for fantasies and services with two women. Anal sex was generally not considered part of the repertoire. In London, prices usually increased by £30. Clients are seen for various lengths of time and are offered a choice of rooms. In one sauna I visited, three different rooms could be hired for a minimum of half an hour. A standard room, with just a bed and a shower, cost £10; the jacuzzi room with a double bed cost £15; and the executive suite supplied with a water bed or a four poster bed, a large bath for two, mirrors and equipment for fantasies could be hired for £20. The fee for the room is direct profit for the owner, as well as covering household bills and the manager's salary.

Brothels

Brothels are illegal establishments, usually owned and organized by a man, who recruits female workers. Although they appear similar in design to saunas they are not licensed, registered or inspected by local authorities. Brothels are usually open longer hours and located in residential suburbs. The brothel culture is more informal than that of a sauna: drug use is often accepted and there are few rules. Brothels frequently close down as a result of police interference or complaints from neighbours. Nevertheless, the owner makes profit, with few financial overheads, and avoids cooperation with bureaucracy.

Respondents explained that there are two types of payment systems in brothels. One is similar to the charges made in saunas and the second is based on the number of clients. The owner dictates the price of each sex act and the percentage the worker must hand over. For instance, if a service costs £60, the worker could be expected to relinquish half of this to the owner. These charges are much higher than those in saunas and are supposed to compensate the owner for taking the risk of organizing the illegal activity, for which he could theoretically be imprisoned for procuring, brothel keeping or living off immoral earnings. This market has the highest turnover of staff because the competition is stark and profit is low. Brothels are attractive for women who prefer to work on a casual, flexible basis, as no time commitment is required. Brothels often have a reputation for unscrupulous practices and activities, and are sometimes considered to be a cover-up for crimes such as drug dealing, people trafficking or other organized crimes.

Working premises

Women also work from privately rented premises or their own property. They either work alone or two or three women work together. Those who work alone from their own property operate a legal activity because there is no third party or brothel keeping involved. O'Connell Davidson (1998: 88–90) describes 'entrepreneurial' prostitution using the example of 'Desiree', a self-employed independent worker, who owns a separate property for business. She is highly successful, earning between £1,000 and £2,000 each week, owns two properties and a top-of-the-range-car. Although sex workers like 'Desiree' have been described as 'a very small elite of prostitutes' (O'Connell Davidson 1996: 181), my research found that this type of worker is now part of an expanding market of businesswomen who advertise and organize their work through the Internet.

Working premises, whether privately owned or rented, are usually two-bedroom apartments located in residential areas. The landlord often knows that the property is being used for vice, so charges a high rent (approximately £200 a week). Whittaker and Hart (1996: 404) report how sex workers in London can pay extortionate rents of between £120 and £250 per day to work in dilapidated buildings. Financial investments such as clothes, condoms, purchasing a mobile phone and advertising fees are necessary in the indoor independent sector, which means there are considerable start-up costs (Phoenix 2000: 40).

Unlike saunas, independent workers can choose when to work, and often arrange their hours to suit family commitments or financial need. The services available in this market vary in quality, ranging from standard to luxurious with a price tag to match. For instance, full sex could cost £60 or £200 depending on the setting and the type of experience that is on offer. It is not uncommon for independent workers to specialize in a certain service and invest in fantasy equipment and bondage rooms, so they can cater for a niche market and charge inflated prices.

Escorts

Women operate independently as escorts by visiting men in their own homes or hotels (outcalls), although they can work via an agency. Either way, there is little evidence of soliciting, so escorting is usually free from law enforcement. If an agency is involved they are responsible for attracting and arranging meetings with clients in the same way a sauna manager is responsible for maintaining custom. Both the client and the worker pay a fee to the agency. Here, the escort does not always have a choice over the type of client or hours but they have discretion over the price and negotiate directly with the customer (Salamon 1989). Escorting is often combined with working in other markets or a mainstream job.

For an extra fee, escorts travel long distances to meet clients at their place of choice. If the distance is considerable, clients are asked to pay the expenses by credit card or bank deposit prior to the meeting. Escorts, who meet each other on the Internet, organize 'tours' to other towns where clients have requested their business. In this market, services take place for any length of time during the day or night. Sexual services can be elaborate and women offer to dine out, or accompany clients on holidays or business trips. Escorts charge a range of prices; those who advertise on the Internet charge a minimum price of £150 an hour or £750 for an overnight stay. Those who advertise in magazines or newspapers normally charge by the sexual act, starting at £60.

Increasingly, escorts are using the Internet to advertise their business because it offers an efficient, effective and cost-cutting method of marketing a service for a specific audience. Escorts are ditching the traditional newspaper advertisements and telephone booking system in favour of websites and email. Durkin and Bryant (1995: 180) call this 'computer erotica' and warn, 'just as the computer has begun to revolutionize social life, it may also revolutionize crime and the parameters of sexual deviant behaviour'. The difficulty of policing the Internet gives sex workers the freedom to advertise their services explicitly with little fear of legal repercussions.

From my unsystematic observation of sex workers' websites, the majority includes a picture gallery where prospective customers can view the worker in different poses and outfits, a menu of services and sometimes prices and feedback from satisfied customers. Despite the fees for web design and maintenance of computer software, respondents who had tried several forms of advertising said that the Internet was the most efficient method because it reduced the number of telephone enquiries and time-wasters and also gave them control over the contact they have with potential customers. They explained that advertising solely via the Internet was also a calculated selection tactic to attract middle-class professionals who were willing to pay higher rates and who were probably less interested in robbing or harming them.

Working from home

Rather than pay to work in an establishment, some sex workers decide to work from home. Working from home introduces the risk of being caught by family or creating suspicion among the neighbours. In addition, there is a risk of blurring the boundaries between work and home when clients are visiting a private space as well as increased safety concerns. Therefore women who work from home are often experienced workers who only see a few clients each week and rarely see new customers but instead rely on regulars who have earned trust over a number of years. Working from home reduces overheads considerably and often women do not need to pay for advertising.

The street market

Street sex workers rely on their physical presence to advertise to male clients their availability for hire. They may work in a mixture of industrial and residential areas close to parks, wasteland, cemeteries, industrial estates or car parks. Ashworth *et al.* (1988) specify that the 'red light district' must allow for sex to be advertised, negotiated and administered. The street is a competitive arena where workers mark out public space as their sales pitch, often referred to as the 'beat'. For example, the area in Birmingham is known as a 'walking beat' because women do not stand in one place but continually walk the neighbourhood. This can be contrasted to a nearby town where areas are territorial and scuffles regularly break out over 'poaching' space.

In contrast to those who work indoors, street workers are highly flexible, with little pattern to their work, engaging in sex work on an 'as and when' basis, sometimes only a few times each year (Boynton 2002). Women often work in neighbouring towns and cities, or have 'away days' in London where profit margins are greater. During the fieldwork, minimum charges on the street were £10 for hand relief or fellatio, and £20 for intercourse – considerably lower than the cheapest indoor prices. Sometimes women charged £5/10 for 'extras' such as fondling breasts or kissing on the neck.

A significant point on which the street market differs from indoor establishments is the prevalence of drug use and the inter-relationship between drug and sex markets (May *et al.* 1999: 37; Surratt *et al.* 2004). Findings suggest that women who work on the street are likely to be drug users and that globally the 'crack-related sex trade has deflated the monetary price' of commercial sex (Campbell 1991: 1372). Street workers self-report high levels of abuse and sexual trauma in childhood and experience of the local authority care system.[8] Recent research by Cusick *et al.* (2004) describe how young women are sustained in street prostitution by mutually reinforcing 'trapping factors' such as using 'hard drugs', homelessness and 'being looked after' by the statutory care system. Compared to indoor workers, those on the street are younger and have usually entered prostitution at an earlier age.

The relationship between the street worker and the male pimp has been historically documented (Barry 1979; Faugier and Sargeant 1996; Hoigard and Finstad 1992; Light 1977; Norton-Hawk 2004; Phoenix 1999b; Swann 1998; Williamson and Cluse-Tolar 2002). These studies explore the complex relationships between men who manage sex work and women who sell sex. These relationships are usually defined by drug abuse and violence (Green et al. 2000; May et al. 1999; Porter and Bonilla 2000), leading May et al. (2000: 8) to conclude that in Britain, drug dependency has replaced physical coercion as the predominant form of manipulation and control over sex work. Often, drug dealers control patches or streets and those who work in the area are expected to pay a fee and/or buy, even sell, drugs if they want to remain in the area (Maher 2000; Miller 1995). However, 'street workers are more likely than those working off-street to have a pimp, but a large minority – possibly majority – do not' (May et al. 2000: 8). The street prostitution market does not stand alone but is influenced and meshed with other criminal markets and features of the salubrious street scene resulting in a fluid, changeable but ultimately dangerous climate.

Makers and takers

Within each market there is an ever-increasing number of ancillary industries that profit from the sale of direct sexual services. The physical location of the indoor markets means that there are several benefactors from the secret liaisons between purchasers and sellers. At inflated prices, landlords rent rooms, houses or apartments by the hour, night, day, week or month to individuals or groups of women. Rooms are rented in motels and motorway service stations to cater for the mobile customer, and for the international clientele, airport hotels provide convenient meeting places. Owners of establishments and women who register as a 'hostess' with the Inland Revenue buy the expertise of accountants to manage income, reduce tax bills and balance the books. The safety of the sex industry is the responsibility of men who are employed as door staff to parade outside saunas, as personal minders for women who work alone, or drivers to take women on escorting jobs. Taxi drivers are indispensable to the constant ferrying of people to and from establishments and in between home and work. Similarly, on the street an informal economy of hustlers exchange anything that anyone needs – protection, food, cigarettes, alcohol, needles, a place to sleep for the night, a ride into town (see Prus and Irini 1980).

Inside the industry, sex workers are supported and supplied by an array of enterprizing individuals. Under the auspices of either the 'maid' or 'receptionist', saunas and working premises employ a woman to carry out the day-to-day organization of the business. Maids are often older women, sometimes ex-workers. Whittaker and Hart (1996: 398) describe the maid as a co-worker and gatekeeper who monitors access to the sex worker. The maid assesses clients' behaviour, imposes rules regarding who is appropriate to enter and monitors the client throughout his visit. Jones and Pratten (1999: 40) suggest that the receptionist has two roles: 'information transfer' to potential customers and 'representation' as the face of the business. The receptionist is valued for her telephone manner, professionalism and the ability to deal with 'time-wasters'. Cleaners are employed to maintain high levels of hygiene, supply fresh towels and restock the mini-bar. Beauticians, nail technicians and hairdressers visit women while they are at work and sometimes women check into private clinics for facial surgery and breast implants. A daily feature of the indoor markets are the peddlers who bring their wares (usually designer goods that are fake and/or stolen) to a captive audience. Perfume, cosmetics, alcohol, jeans and trainers, condoms, lingerie, sex toys and children's toys are all on offer, especially in the run-up to Christmas. Commodities inevitably include cannabis, amphetamines, tranquillizers and ecstasy, sometimes for work purposes but usually for pleasure time.

Advertising is another ancillary industry that profits from matching sexual services with the desires of the client. In London, card boys are paid up to £100 each day to trawl the telephone booths replacing cards after they have been confiscated by street cleaners. This continual replacement cycle is of no inconvenience to the printers who charge extra for designing motifs, slogans and images to catch the eye of the tourist or opportunist punter. The traditionalists continue to advertise their telephone numbers in newspapers under the 'personal column' sections, and whether business is booming or slack, some women fork out the exorbitant prices charged by national tabloids that list sex workers' telephone numbers amidst their gallery of bare breasts and buttocks. In the specialist advertising industry, cameramen have the arduous task of photographing semi-naked women in various regalia and dungeon-style rooms to be eventually displayed in pricey top-shelf directories. On the Internet, women invest in webmasters, webpage designers and administrators of websites who update and promote the site. In addition, money is made from chatrooms and message boards that enable hobbyists to discuss their latest accomplishment.

It would be incongruent not to mention the ballooning research, policy-making and service sector that exists because of the sex industry (and here I include myself). Over recent years, prostitution has become a policy issue, with increasing Home Office money designated to creating a certain type of knowledge about this illicit economy, providing a stepping stone for researchers to craft out their careers. With prostitution firmly on the public protection agenda through the Home

Office Crime Reduction Programme (see Hester and Westmarland 2004), a splurge of funding has seen an increase in projects to support (and rehabilitate) street sex workers. This has been met with an increase in empirical data collected about the nature of prostitution. However, such opportunities must be considered carefully, as O'Neill (1996a: 132) warns 'researchers are sometimes seen as akin to pimps, coming into the field to take, then returning to the campus, institution or suburb where they write up the data, publish and build careers – on the backs of those they took the data from'. Although there are epistemological and method-ological ways in which this can be avoided, there is a reality that means the individuals involved at the periphery benefit professionally and personally from an industry that is so often condemned.

Notes

1 For accounts see Cockington and Marlin (1995); Delacoste and Alexander (1988); Efthimiou-Mordant (2002); Jaget (1980); Kempadoo and Doezema (1999); Levine and Madden (1988).
2 See English Collective of Prostitutes (1997); Mathieu (2003); Weitzer (1996); West (2000).
3 Hoigard and Finstad (1992); McKeganey and Barnard (1996); O'Connell Davidson (1998); O'Neill (2001); Phoenix (1999a); Weitzer (2000).
4 See Agustin (2004); Barrett (1997); Bindman (1997); Friedberg (2000); Gulcur and Ilkkaracan (2002); Kelly and Regan (2000); Kempadoo and Doezma (1999); Shrage (1994); Swann (1998).
5 See Brown (2000); Clifter and Carter (2000); O'Connell Davidson and Sanchez Taylor (1999); Opperman (1999); Ryan and Kinder (1996); Ryan and Hall (2001).
6 See Abbott (2000); Barton (2002); Dodds (1997); Liepe-Levinson (2002); Mon-temurro (2001); Murphy (2003); Smith (2002); Storr (2003); Wood (2000).
7 See Bartley (2000); Brooks-Gordon and Gelsthorpe (2003); Finnegan (1979); Harras (1996); McHugh (1980); Walkowitz (1980).
8 Bagely and Young (1987); Barrett (2000); Dodsworth (2000); Friedberg (2000); James and Meyerding (1977); Sanders (2001); Silbert and Pines (1982, 1985); Surratt et al. (2004).

Chapter 2

Ethnography, sex and the self

'Being in is never settled.' (Elijah Anderson 2004)

This study relies on information obtained through taped interviews with fifty-five women and over one thousand hours of observation of the sex industry to 'provide the dynamic, contextualized picture' (Maher 2000: 202) of the indoor markets. I started this research having never visited a brothel and unlike other analysts of the sex economy who have been well placed to critically observe how it works (Chapkis 1997; Kesler 2002; Nagel 1997; Ronai 1992), apart from a few Ann Summers parties and a weekend in Amsterdam, the sex industry was a mythical entity. Initially, I felt bereft of the personal resources that were evident in other valuable ethnographies that describe how researchers have literally lived alongside the groups they studied, partly because their own histories are located within that same culture (see Adler and Adler 1991; Hobbs 1988; Roseneil 1993; Wolf 1991). Nevertheless, guided by the work of others, the task ahead was to position myself within the sex industry: 'immersion in the life-worlds of women working in prostitution through ethnographic research enables the foregrounding of feelings, meanings and experiences from the multiple standpoints of women, and may facilitate the development of "thick" description of lived cultures' (O'Neill 2001: 4). This chapter describes my assisted passage into the illicit enterprise of prostitution, the multiple layers of access, the processes of earning acceptance and the rhythms and the peculiarities of the sex work fieldsite.

Layered access

On reflection, my own biography, or more specifically some acquired skills, were undoubtedly a significant reason why this study was made possible. There were four levels of access that enabled the collection of information about the intricate emotional and physical world of the sex worker. The first level of access was through the formal bureaucracy of the National Health Service that was an official gatekeeper to the sex industry. Although naïve about the sex economy, I was well versed with other areas of women's lives through my training and (brief) practice as a social worker. The links between the social work profession and the emerging work of early sociologists in the Chicago School enabled me to forfeit my role as a regulator of behaviour to that of an observer (see Heap 2003). As an agent of social control, I regularly encountered the victimhood of women in the form of domestic violence, sexual abuse, rape, homelessness, social exclusion and drug addiction. Working with a public statutory bureaucracy in the form of social services prepared me for negotiating access through a sexual health project that was documented as a successful but complex access route (see Sanders 2005, for a review). Knowing the pressures of working in a government agency struggling with the familiar scenario of under-resourced and over-worked as well as the additional burden and repercussions of the stigma and marginalization inflicted on their client group, I approached the sexual health project in the spirit of offering an exchange or what Barnard (1993) and earlier Douglas (1972: 5) term a 'research bargain'.

The notion of offering an exchange with those who facilitate the data collection has been at the core of research in the sex industry mainly because of the potentially exploitative scenario of taking information from vulnerable women. Accounts in the field show that there is often an informal exchange of commodities such as cigarettes, food and small change (see Maher 2000: 212), but increasingly respondents are paid for interviews (Cusick 1998; Lever and Dolnick 2000: 89; Pyett and Warr 1997: 540; Surratt et al., 2004). A popular exchange relationship is built around the service-provider role that is combined with the research process. McKeganey and Barnard (1996) conducted an ethnography among drug-using street sex workers in Glasgow and provided sterile needle equipment and condoms to respondents. This type of service-provider role is advantageous on two accounts: it provides the re-searcher with a legitimate place in unfamiliar and hostile territory and it fulfils the distinct moral obligations of researching a vulnerable group.

Learning from others, I offered to exchange social work and research skills in return for observation opportunities. This convinced the manager and later one specific outreach worker that I had serious intentions. I was allowed unlimited access to the female-only space that was reserved for sex workers and staff at the project, as well as the opportunity to work late into the night on the outreach van. However, it was not only what I could offer but my values that determined whether people accepted me as a legitimate outsider. Primed by others, I was aware of the beliefs I had to set out if I was to be accepted by those in charge. Hubbard (1999a: 233) learned that gatekeepers in the sex industry only comply if the following four principles are evident. First, that the research will produce knowledge to help reduce stigma surrounding prostitution; second, that the researcher has an insight into reality; third, a recognition that prostitution is a legitimate form of work; and fourth, a belief that health and safety risks should be minimized. Only after I had established my moral standpoint was I able to cross the threshold from a total outsider to an outsider who had been officially approved and was worthy of trust.

The second level of access to be conquered was with the health-care professionals who worked on the frontline. As Smart (1984: 153) notes, once official access has been achieved, the researcher has the task of convincing people lower down the professional hierarchy to assist with the research. One such person was Alison, an outreach worker who showed me the ropes, and without whom this work would never have been completed. Alison introduced me to some larger saunas in the city that became key sites I returned to on a weekly basis throughout the ten-month period. Although it was not apparent at the time, the 'open arms' attitude the management showed me at 'Moonlights', the sauna I visited most, was more about their respectful relationship with Alison than anything that I had done. Gaining access to the hidden economy usually began as part of 'a favour for a favour' and then it was left to me to create effective, trusting relationships.

The third level of access I had to secure was with the predominantly female owners and managers of saunas and escort agencies who were naturally suspicious of my requests. Without a trusted advocate there would have been little chance of ever entering a sauna because, as Barton (2002) found when her gender was out of place in a male-dominated strip club, women who were not sex workers were misplaced in a sex establishment. Bosses wanted my word that I would not do anything to affect the reputation of the sauna, or the workers, and that my presence would not interfere with the day-to-day running of the business. After these expectations were discussed, there was often an enthusiasm to 'set the record straight' and dispel stereotypes by demonstrating the routine business ethic that formed the basis of the establishment.

Negotiating the third level of access was tricky because the owners who were not particularly comfortable with the health-care professionals were even less tolerant of a nosey stranger. Therefore the establishments I was introduced to were already selected by the health-care professionals as those that were open to the external eye. Relying on proven snowball sampling techniques to infiltrate hidden groups (Atkinson and Flint 2001; Bloor et al. 1991; Faugier and Sargeant 1997; Kaplan et al. 1987), my passage through the city's indoor sex markets was made possible by informal networks. There was a strong gendered nature to my experience of networking as access relied on female friendships or business circles that existed in a localized, historical context that I was not aware of before I began the project. In a face-to-face context, I could rely on establishing myself as trustworthy by engaging in conversation and actions that enabled gatekeepers to make up their own mind about my legitimacy. Nevertheless, some introductions fell flat and on three occasions I was asked to leave the premises. I had to be mindful that I was asking to be introduced to organizations and people who were often on the other side of the law and it had taken the sexual health project many years to gain acceptance and offer services to the sex workers. Most people connected my role with the sexual health project, so I was aware that my actions had an additional responsibility; if I created ill feeling then it would jeopardize individual relationships with the health service. Relying on this quasi-service-provider role by, for instance, offering condoms on each visit, was an aspect of the research bargain that appeased any sense of intrusion on my part and any suspicion on the part of the respondents.

The fourth level of access was to negotiate relationships with individual women. Unlike McKeganey and Bloor's (1991) optimistic reflections of male researchers infiltrating all-female environments, being a man would have made it difficult, if not impossible, to get alongside both the sex workers and the sexual health project (Cusick 1999: 22; Hubbard 1999a: 232; Sanders 2005). Just as O' Connell Davidson maintains from her participant observer role with an entrepreneurial sex worker, being a woman is essential in some forms of prostitution research, I also felt that being a woman was fundamental to this research endeavour. Many sex workers do not trust men (that is not to say they trust women either), and while 'gender does not guarantee sisterhood' (Maher 2000: 210), as the process of acceptance unravelled, being a woman was a crucial advantage. Yet it was not just about being a woman – sex workers assumed my heterosexuality and a certain degree of personal sexual experience as a way of reconciling why I was interested in prostitution. These assumptions facilitated an exchange of ideas about the nature of sexual behaviour from women who were experts in dealing with men's sexual urges, bodies and of course, their own temptations. During the intimate conversations with women about the differences between sex as work and sex as pleasure, respondents would expect me to engage in some self-disclosure in order to make sense of the experiences they described. Because sex workers knew I did not have sex work as a frame of reference to understand their world, they deferred to my own experiences as a way of exploring their realities. As Hobbs (1988: 9) acknowledges how his maleness enabled him to gain a 'close collaborative relationship' with the working-class men of the East End, being a woman who could talk about and try to understand the dichotomies of using sex to make money became the basis for a trusting, dynamic relationship. In this fourth level of access there was a different type of exchange relationship with respondents. Just as I had explicitly offered to exchange relevant skills with the health managers, I subtly offered the women frank and honest discussions about myself in the expectation that they would respond to my intimate quizzing. It can therefore be argued that just as the access process is made up of different layers, the research exchange or bargaining process takes on a different set of expectations with each audience.

Another aspect of this ethnography was the observation of websites and bulletin boards used by the sex work community (see Sanders 2004b, for more details). The Internet became a virtual fieldwork site in response to the growing trend of female entrepreneurs who had abandoned the traditional forms of advertising in favour of computer-mediated communication. There is a 'virtual community' (Sharp and Earle 2002; Soothill 2004a) of buyers, sellers and organizers of commercial sex in Britain who shape the state of the online sex market. Mostly, I adopted the role of a 'lurker', covertly observing the online interactions between buyers and sellers in chatrooms and bulletin boards. I analysed the content of sex workers' websites and also contacted women via email asking them to take part in the research. In the same way as cold-calling resulted in non-response for others (O'Connell Davidson and Layder 1994: 213), emailing without prior introduction was not a successful recruitment method. Convincing women that I was a *bona fide* researcher via the Internet presented other methodological challenges that meant relationships often had to move from online to offline status before credibility could be recognized (Sanders 2004b). Nevertheless, after substantial negotiations and establishing my credibility in a manner that was reminiscent of textbook-informed consent, several email correspondents agreed to meet in person for a face-to-face interview.

The notion of 'layered access' in the fieldwork process is part of the extensive negotiations that are familiar in studies of deviant activities. Moving from an official organization through the hierarchies of association until the opportunities for observation are reached is a complex process for the ethnographer. The presence of different audiences, who sometimes may be present at the same time, highlights how 'field roles are continually negotiated and renegotiated' (O'Connell Davidson and Layder 1994: 167). This requires skills that Sharpe (2000: 366) describes as 'flexibility bordering on the schizophrenic' to manage the relationships, environments and tensions in the sex work fieldsite.

Earning acceptance

The power relations in the researcher–respondent nexus were ever present as I tried to convince women to spare time to be interviewed or gain permission to hang out in their premises. The researcher is 'subject to an evaluative positioning' (Roberts 2001: 3.2) by the respondent; or more specifically the female researcher experiences 'othering' by female respondents (Pickering 2001) as they politically position the inquirer through various identities. Maher (2000: 213) describes how the minority women she got to know in the drug and sex markets of Brooklyn placed her as 'other' not only by her outsider status as a non-drug user and a non-American, but also by what she was – a self-defined white, middle-class 'square'. Taking advice from the standard textbooks on qualitative research, I attempted to position myself by declaring my status and intentions as a researcher. My status as a postgraduate student from a university may have washed with the bureaucracies of the National Health Service at the initial point of access but the women simply were not interested in where I came from or even the objectives of the study. As long as I was not a journalist, an undercover policewoman, or a spy for a rival competitor,[1] my academic intentions appeared superfluous.

In face-to-face situations informants were more intent on establishing who I was, and my opinions about prostitution and their lifestyles. They wanted to find out as much about my history as I did about theirs. To reach a juncture where we both felt comfortable, potential respondents positioned me through interactions orchestrated to test my ability to deal with their world, to maintain composure and protect their interests. Similar to when Elijah Anderson (2004) finally realized that he had gained an insider status in Jelly's bar when the owner asked him to get a beer for a customer, I also encountered a similar 'positioning' event in a sauna with Emma and Belinda. As my fieldwork diary recalls:

> Today I was propositioned by a client. It has taken three months to happen but now it has, it opened my eyes to much more than expected. I was sitting in Foxy's, with Emma and Belinda. We had been there since 10 o'clock without any clients visiting, when one of Emma's regulars arrived. Even though I had not seen him before I could tell he was a regular by the casual nature of the greeting. The man came into the lounge and sat opposite me on the sofa and proceeded to chat about the weather. This all seemed normal until I noticed that both Emma and Belinda had gone out of the room and were upstairs watching on the CCTV that was firmly focused on the customer and I. After a long awkward silence he confided that he always 'tried out' the new girls, even though Emma was his regular

and if I was free, would I mind seeing him in the jacuzzi room. As planned, I made excuses that I was just a friend and not working. I could hear raucous laughter from the girls upstairs as they listened and watched on camera. Minutes later Emma came down to rescue me and took the client to a room. Belinda came downstairs laughing at my embarrassment, assuring me that it was all on camera to show the manager and the other girls when they came on shift. The confrontation with a client that I had anticipated since I started visiting saunas had uncovered something else. The women had used my status as a 'non-sex worker' to provide their fun and games. (Fieldwork Diary, August, 2000).

Successfully completing tests and trials has been documented as an integral feature of securing relations in the field. Van Maanen (1988: 85) describes his own process of acceptance into a police force in the USA, 'the novice . . . must cross several work boundaries, pass a series of social tests designed to discover something about the prudence, inclinations and character of the person'. Similar kinds of initiation rituals are common in the sex industry but what is unique is that such tests usually raise a few eyebrows from the researcher because they warrant embarrassment and sexual innuendo to prove credibility, seriousness or moral standpoint. In her account of an initiation into a strip club, Murphy (2003: 332) notes that ethnographers quickly shift between 'watching the spectacle' to becoming 'part of the show'. Orchestrated by the male manager, Murphy had to down a cocktail shot from a testube that was held in the mouth of a female topless stripper. She was observed by most of the club and it was clear that refusing such an offer would have been detrimental to gaining access to the male-dominated setting.

The initiation process is crucial as researchers find their footing in worlds where they have little legitimate place. The diary exert above demonstrates how Emma and Belinda placed me at the centre of their slapstick comedy as a way of checking out my character and making sense of my presence in their working environment.[2] Maher (2000: 213) notes 'how the "there" we study does not exist prior to, and independent of, the shared worlds we create with informants'. My relationship with Emma and Belinda was based on a research process that was alien to them and constituted an imposition on their normal working lives. My presence created a new experience for both the researcher and informants that did not exist before or after I left the field. Being part of their humorous banter was an important confirmation that I was partially included in their 'backstage' performance and was, to some degree, accepted into the private aspects of their working activities. However, I never took this familiarization as complete acceptance as I was always defined as a 'non-sex worker'.

The rhythms of fieldwork

'You've gotta have faith, faith, faith' blasted out George Michael from the radio. The kettle was steaming, the washing machine spinning, in a distant room the hoover hummed and the clip-clop of stilettos on the wooden staircase confirmed it was another busy working day in the sauna. This was a large Victorian detached house over three floors and most of the rooms had been converted into bedrooms. Much of the activity centred on the 'backstage' of the kitchen and the adjoining lounge that was only for the workers. As I poured hot water into the collection of mugs for teas and coffees, Kirsty dashed in wanting her dress zipped up, the phone was ringing, Zeta was badgering me with her notebook wanting my daily sandwich order, while the owner, Maureen, was offering me a herbal cigarette promising that 'It's better than puffing nowt' and in the same breath bellowing 'Will someone answer that bloody phone'. The ringing stopped. Melanie was downstairs painting her toenails in the communal lounge where clients wait their turn, relax, watch TV, flick thorough a magazine and pay their entrance fee. She was finishing off her big toe with deep crimson polish as she offered the caller directions to the business in her 'happy-to-help' manner. Within five minutes the humdrum had died down as the women got on with their routines either in the bedroom or doing the cleaning chores. Maureen and I were alone again in the kitchen where, two hours previous, we had started the second session of a taped interview about how she became the owner of a lucrative sauna. We collapsed onto the sofa to pick up where we had left off. I grabbed my tape recorder, signalling the start of the serious questions 'Where did we get to?' Maureen inquired. 'You were telling me about when you offered to buy out your partner and became the sole owner', and off we went discussing the intricacies of managing an illegal business – until the next interruption. (Fieldwork Diary, March, 2001).

Porter and Bonilla (2000: 107) note that interviews with women in the sex industry are made up of broken snippets of information filtered through their working schedules. Interviews were often grabbed in this haphazard fashion, in the spaces women had while they were preparing themselves or their workplace, waiting for or organizing clients, starting or finishing a shift. The fact that the majority of the interviews took place in the workplace meant there were often interruptions. This was normally due to the women answering the telephone to take bookings or pass on details to prospective customers. Heyl's (1979: 5) life history of

Ann, a madam who organized a brothel in a midsize American town, describes how the day-to-day activities of the sex establishment 'seldom provided ideal interviewing conditions', so instead much of the three-year study was conducted over the telephone. Acknowledging the difficulties of conducting interviews while anyone is at work, I decided the workplace was to be at the centre of the ethnography. Hence, on many occasions in my study the interview was stopped or rescheduled because a client arrived. Refusing clients meant refusing money and women were rightly not prepared to make economic sacrifices for a researcher who was not offering financial compensation. Even when clients did interrupt, usually it was for no longer than fifteen minutes and the interview was resumed without further hindrance (seven minutes was the quickest turnaround of a client). Respondents always protected the anonymity of the client and often I was instructed to make myself scarce or pretend to be another 'working girl'. While the respondent completed a transaction I was hiding in a spare room or scuttling from kitchen to bathroom to avoid any confrontation and embarrassing questions all round. Although this process of collecting data was sporadic, these complex interviews provided rich opportunities to witness all aspects of the sex work activity.

The fieldwork was often disjointed, consisting of 'hanging out' with women, drinking tea, watching daytime television, having a natter and doing the washing up. The women sometimes found my strategies of 'research' somewhat ambiguous – and at times so did I. Maher (2000: 232) warns from her own submersion in the street-level sex and drug economies that 'ethnography is a messy business'. Like Nencel (2001), Downe (1999) and Hart (1998), who conducted fieldwork by hanging out in bars, cafes and barrios, the unstructured, uncertain and often mundane hours of fieldwork certainly felt messy, and counting the number of cups of tea I was offered in a day was sometimes the most effective way of evaluating progress. As Nencel (2001: 73) concludes, the fieldwork's rhythm is dictated by the '(un)events of respondents' lives'.

In times of uncertainty about my role I would rely on my previous hat as a social worker, and offered a helping hand by facilitating women's access to health and welfare agencies. Developing the service-provider dimension of the researcher role fulfilled the 'norms of reciprocity' of the research relationship (Adler and Adler 1991: 175). Such actions could be interpreted as self-indulgent or even as manipulative in order to expand the opportunities for observation. However, these instances arose naturally, sometimes out of crisis, and always on the invitation of the individual. Assisting women in their everyday lives manoeuvred my observations from the work setting to the private domestic sphere. Pasko (2002: 51) found that by varying the interview location between work, home and leisure settings with the same female dancers she was able to achieve 'different levels of reflection and retrospection of their stripping experiences'. By spending time with women in different settings, the 'double life' of the secretive sex worker became transparent.

Women were often too busy to be interviewed because of commitments either at work or home. Flexibility was the key and being able to fit in, rearrange, wait, plead, negotiate, reciprocate and be downright persistent became the skills I relied on over the ten-month period. There was little rhythm to my interviews as the complexity of respondents' lives shaped the data-collection process. One interview was conducted over a four-day period in the thirty-minute slot that Beryl allotted for her preparation routine before the working day began. Meetings with Beryl were at 11am, five hours after she had started her day with an hour's housework, preparing school uniforms, pack lunches and breakfast for her four children, and completed the school run, food shopping or bill paying. She then made the forty-five minute drive to her rented apartment in the city where clients visited between 12 and 4pm, four days a week. While Beryl was showering, shaving, drying and styling her hair, deciding on lingerie and dressing, applying make-up and organizing the room, I asked questions. Lapses of time between starting and winding up an interview were not uncommon. Completion of an interview with Kelly, a twenty-seven year old sauna worker with whom I conducted seven interview sessions, did not take place until she returned from a six-week stint lap dancing in Helsinki. Fitting in with women's schedules revealed the transitions made from motherhood to dominatrix and from the suburban community to the shuttered fronts of the massage parlour.

As Maher (2000: 226) perceptively describes, interviews are 'socially defined speech events' that take place within a specific context. Taking only the words from these contexts means that the cultural location of the encounter is removed. Throughout my visits to saunas I became accustomed to spending much of the fieldwork among semi-naked women performing various intimate body preparations on themselves and each other (see Sanders 2005, for a discussion of nakedness in fieldwork). Beryl's engagement in her personal care routine during the interview and her state of undress did not distract the interview content, yet at the same time constituted the context of the speech acts and the experience of the interview for both participant and researcher. It is this context that is lost through the process of retelling dialogue in the written form. While I intend to be convincing in my descriptions, much of the context of 'being there' escapes the written word. Only the words of the interviewees can paint the true picture.

Sex work uncovered

In contrast to some of the refusals and hostilities from individuals and establishments was the overwhelming acceptance, friendship and honesty from some women with whom I formed strong bonds. Having originally met women in their place of work, they invited me into their personal lives – to meet their partners, children, family, friends, followed by expectations to socialize at birthday parties and Christmas celebrations. Considering that one aspect of my questions centred on the dichotomies of disentangling the world of sex as work from the private sphere, invitations into women's private lives was initially considered a resounding success. Contrary to the 'professional distance' (Fetterman 1991: 94) advocated by some as necessary in field relations, I occupied a position that meant I was privy to the domestic life of the sex worker that was previously masked in the professional sphere.

Yet I found that straddling the public and private worlds of respondents was fraught with dilemmas and difficulties. For instance, when Jackie asked me to meet her long-term partner, who for the past three years had known nothing about how she earned money, I should not have been surprised at the collusive role I was quickly expected to adopt. I was 'Tina from the office' and was expected to act like a work-mate, remembering to use real names – a strict taboo in the workplace. I was adding to alibis and living proof of a cover story that protected intimate relationships from the harm of the whore stigma. Mitchell Jr (1991: 108) describes how fieldwork is not 'an autonomous self-directed creation' because the researcher 'is no longer distanced from the action, the discourse, but is implicated unavoidably in its production'. Taking part in the shift between work and home, I also experienced some of the transitions women encounter each time they move from the illicit, deviant subculture of sex work to the normalized domestic sphere. Witnessing and taking part in this transition made me explicitly a part of the process of living a 'double life' where one set of information was legitimate with one audience, only to be concealed from another.

Creating intimate relations with respondents also posed questions regarding the legitimate nature of participant observation. Anthropology and sociology boast a tradition of researchers who have 'gone native' in the sexual field. Erotic and sexual dimensions of the researcher–respondent relationship have been reported in gay and lesbian communities (Altork 1995; Bolton 1995), the nude beach (Douglas *et al.* 1977), the naturist club (Parry 1982) and everyday settings where sexual relations have formed part of the research process (Goode 2003). These cases have brought into question the nature of participant observation and the ethics of engaging in intimate, naked or sexualized behaviour as part of the fieldwork. In my research, such ethical dilemmas became a reality when Astrid asked me to watch her performing a sexual service on a client 'to see how clinical it really is'. Unlike other ethnographers who have little choice but to observe sexualized behaviour in strip shows and erotic dancing (Dodds 1997; Lewis and Maticka-Tindale 2000; Liepe-Levinson 2002; Thompson and Harred 1992), this proposition posed a confusing dilemma about what legitimately constituted participant observation. Maybe I should not have been perturbed by Astrid's invitation but instead should have looked on the occasion as an opportunity to watch what I was asking to be described. After all, as social science students we are taught that ethnography is 'seeing through the eyes of the subject' in order to 'describe the mundane details of everyday settings' (Bryman and Burgess 1994). Having sex with a client was, surprisingly, a mundane and routine feature of the respondents' working lives and seeing the commercial transaction as anything other than this would have been a case of impinging personal values on the very subject I sought to understand.

On the other hand, Adler and Adler (1994: 380) are clear that the researcher is only required to 'interact closely enough with members to establish an insider's identity without participating in those activities constituting the core of group membership'. Yet such clarity did not answer why observing sexual acts was different from observing other aspects of the commercial interactions and the intimacies that seemed inescapable in the sex work setting. The question remained: if participant observation of the commercial sex act was above and beyond the call of duty, then what 'specialness' was afforded to the sexual relationship even though the sex was not part of any romantic, emotional commitment but simply a monetary exchange? On many occasions, women argued that I would never truly understand commercial sex until I had witnessed it first-hand. They were probably right. Confronting such decisions was part of the everyday fieldwork process, as Becker warns (1965: 602) 'no matter how carefully one plans in advance the research is designed in the course of its execution. The finished monograph is the result of hundreds of decisions, large and small, whilst the research is underway.' These dilemmas of the ethnographer are not new, but they were new to me. Often I was caught unaware and would suddenly find myself in a situation, being offered the chance to step away from the periphery and closer to the centre, knowing that the wrong answer could spurn a trusted informant and possibly my reputation within the local sex work community (see Sanders 2005). Much of the ethnography was characterized by these rollercoaster incidents and interruptions, reinforcing how acceptance was only temporary.

Risky research

It can be assumed from ethnographies of prostitution that researching this activity is not a secure fieldwork site. Dangers exist to a lesser or greater degree depending on the market and the researcher's positioning. Maher (2000) categorizes her experience of risk in prostitution research on a continuum of legal, health and personal risks. Legal risks are usually present because there is a possibility of arrest or conviction for procuring as part of the research process. Close contact with the everyday interactions in the street sex and drug markets led Maher to be questioned by police and with few assurances of immunity she was open to criminalization through pursuits in the field. In my fieldwork, spending hours in brothels and saunas that were theoretically at risk of a police raid could have landed me in trouble. My interactions with women on the street were far more likely to be scrutinized by the police and community informers as I stopped to speak to women: sometimes I was present when drugs were bought and sold. This was not intentional but part of the everyday interactions that were an ordinary feature of the subculture and therefore inescapable as an ethnographer.

The practical challenges of doing research in the field have been discussed in relation to dangerous fieldwork settings or subjects of inquiry (Ferrell and Kane 1998; Lee 1995; Punch 1989). Goldsmith (2003: 105) reports from his research in Colombia that fieldwork is often characterized by fear and it is the task of the fieldworker to sift the perceived from the real risks in a violent and insecure society. Personal dangers in the prostitution fieldwork setting can take different forms. O'Neill (1996a) was witness to a physical attack of a sex worker and subsequently appeared in court four times and for taking a stand had her property vandalized. Sharpe (2000) conducted 'street corner re- search'. in a Northern British city and found the presence of the street environment harsh, hostile and depressing, while Miller (1997) recounts the emotional strain of listening to continual stories of violence. At another level the personal risks of researching a volatile society mean that physical harm is to be guarded against. Sharpe (2000) and Maher (2000) both describe how respondents died or were killed during the street fieldwork. Mindful of the dangerous encounters from others and reflecting on the confrontational and aggressive situations that I was involved in as a social worker, my approach to the fieldsite was guided by the potential for danger. I never encountered any overt threats but this was because, first, most of my time was spent in the relatively safe indoor markets; and second, the health-care professionals took their guardianship role seriously, steering me away from individuals and establishments that could bring trouble.

Succeeding at ethnography invariably means emotional investment on the part of the researcher (Hobbs 1988: 10). Liebling and Stanko (2001: 421) describe 'moral turmoil' experienced by researchers who witness violence and harm in people's lives. During the fieldwork period, interviewees experienced traumatic and life-changing events. One woman was drugged and raped in a club, four women had miscarriages, at least three women were injured in domestic violence, one woman had her house burnt down, another had her child taken into foster care by child-protection agencies and several others were in and out of prison. Confronted with the devastation of some women's lives, I had to be clear with myself and those around me that I was not a social worker but a researcher, and although awful to witness, I was relatively powerless in making any difference to individual situations. As Barnard (1992) reflects on her research with street sex workers, there are dilemmas for the researcher because of the competing pressures of moral obligations and research objectives. Among women who had entrusted me with their real names, addresses and true family histories, I felt an extended sense of responsibility. Leaving the field sometimes brought a sense of relief, and returning on a few occasions filled me with dread over what I might find. I quickly learned to become 'thick skinned' (Maher 2000: 211) and act like an 'acceptable incompetent' (Miller 1995: 433) in order to achieve what Smith and Wincup (2000: 342) have termed a 'mutually advantageous relationship'.

Notes

1 For similar accounts see Barnard (1992: 145); Lever and Dolnick (2000); Maher (2000: 211); Sharpe (2000: 366).
2 For a further discussion of the place of humour in the sex industry, see Sanders (2004a).

Chapter 3

Choice, risk and selling sex

There is no standard sex worker. Each woman has her own reasons for working, her own responses of boredom, pleasure, power and/or trauma, her own ideas about the work and her place in it. This work can be oppression or freedom; just another assembly-line job; an artistic act that also pays well; comic relief from street realities; healing social work for an alienated culture. What is at work within each woman that lets her accommodate this situation? Intense denial, infallible sense of humor, co-dependency, incredible strength, a liquid sense of self? The only safe thing to say is that we're all in it for the money. (Vicky Funari, peep show worker, 1997: 28)

It is difficult to expand the debates on the rights and wrongs of prostitution without reflecting on the concepts of choice and risk. In recent times there has been much 'sociologizing' of both these complex concepts in all areas of the social sciences. The key debates around the nature of prostitution have relied on these terms to dissect the contradictions between agency and victimization. Yet often choice and risk are set up as opposites rather than analysed in terms of how an individual's decision-making is bound up with risk-taking or avoidance. In this chapter, I draw on these wider sociological debates to inform an analysis of the gendered experience of women involved in prostitution and the complexities of choice and risk from the sex workers' standpoint.

Initially, this chapter describes the debates regarding the legitimacy of prostitution as either work, exploitation or somewhere in between. The second section describes the nature of risk in prostitution, arguing that subjective outcomes of risk depend on individual biography and the environment of the market. Finally, details about the women who were interviewed for this study are provided.

Choosing denigration?

There has been much controversy and divisions among writers and in particular feminists over the question of whether women enter the sex industry voluntarily or are forced by unequal power relations (for reviews see Gulcur and Ilkkaracan 2002; Kesler 2002; O'Connell Davidson 2002). Some radical scholars consider prostitution as an 'absolute embodiment of patriarchal male privilege' (Kesler 2002: 219) because selling sex for money is always oppressive, damaging and responsible for the objectification of the female body (Barry 1995; Jarvinen 1993; Jeffreys 1997; Raymond 1999).

This argument, which has come to be known as the abolitionist perspective, concentrates on the suffering and victimization of women and argues that because the nature of prostitution commodifies the body there can be no consent. This reading of victimization states that a woman can never be a 'sex worker' because she is turned into a 'sex object' by structural and power inequalities between men and women (Barry 1979; Dworkin 1996; Mackinnon 1982; Pateman 1988). Fuelled by fundamental Christian ideals that consider prostitution as a threat to the moral fabric of society and family structure, the debates surrounding choice or exploitation in prostitution are symptomatic of what Weitzer (2000: 3) calls a 'sex war' of 'sex objects vs. sex workers'.

Others, by contrast, move beyond the sex worker-as-victim model (Walkowitz 1980; Bell 1994; Kempadoo and Doezema 1998) on the basis that such an argument leaves individuals 'devoid of choice, responsibility, or accountability' (Maher 2000: 1) and offers little solution except to eliminate the sex industry. The argument that selling sex should be considered as legitimate work has been established by several scholars (Boynton 2002; Brewis and Lindstead 2000; 2000b; Perkins *et al*. 1991). Chapkis (1997: 67), for instance, explains how some women make an informed 'rational choice' to work in prostitution, rather than a 'free choice', available to few individuals in a society that is structured hierarchically by race, sex and class. Some scholars question whether there can ever be choice or consent to selling commercial sex. For instance, Phoenix (2000: 38) states that there are certain conditions through which women are sustained in prostitution, therefore for some women, prostitution 'makes sense' within their limited economic, social and material conditions. However, as Kesler (2002: 223) summarizes, women may not be presented with a free choice, absent from constraints of opportunity, but ultimately all non-prostitute women who make decisions about entering into marriage or employment do so within a particular set of constraints under the present patriarchal capitalist system.

Such debates are intensified when discussing the situation of women in developing countries who make stark choices between extreme poverty, starvation, the likely infection of HIV and using their sexual bodies to survive (Evans and Lambert 1997; Wojcicki and Malala 2001). Campbell (2000: 479) conducted research with sex workers in a South African gold mining community and concluded that to speak only of sex workers' powerlessness is 'unduly simplistic'. In Britain, the 'feminization of poverty' (Glendinning and Miller 1992) coupled with the rise in female single-headed households juggling childcare, part-time work and living on welfare benefits means that 'the choice of sex work has begun to be seen as rational "resistance", if not courageous choice, in the face of poverty' (Brooks-Gordon and Gelsthorpe 2003: 444). These complexities are expressed in the decision made by the United Nations to favour prostitution as a human right (not wrong) if it is consensual (Raymond 1999).

Sex radicalism views prostitution as action against male exclusivity of sexual control or as an expression of sexual emancipation, exploration and empowerment (Chapkis 1997). Others criticize mainstream feminists for the rigid doctrine that states that providing sexual services oppresses all women, reflecting on the lack of acknowledgement of what sex workers can bring to any analysis of gender oppression. Nagel (1997: 2) and other feminists who work as porn actresses, peep show workers, and sex providers recognize that their certain 'economic and racial privilege' means their participation in the sex trade is by choice, yet there are many women for whom this is not the case. However, this does not mean, as Millet (1971) advocates, that prostitution is an act of self-denigration or degrades all women (Dworkin 1981). Any logic in such an argument would mean that all institutions, including marriage and long-term cohabitation, where there is a sexual monetary exchange would be oppressive. Instead, Nagel (1997: 4) argues against dividing women into either sex workers or non-sex workers, but that exchanging sex for money or commodities is on a continuum.

The prostitution rights movement, while fighting against the unequal treatment of women, regards the selling of sex for money as employment, and contends that those who work as prostitutes should receive equal status, protection and rights as those bestowed on other employees (Jenness 1993; Lopes 2001; Weitzer 1996; West 2000). Some recent sociological thinking on sex work supports the capacity of women to choose how to earn money, given their circumstances. Women make choices within a series of constraints, both personal and structural (e.g. paid employment, limitation of skills and training, benefit dependency, childcare commitments, single parenthood). O'Neill (1996b) highlights the fact that prostitution provides an attractive income for working relatively few hours, and a realistic opportunity to combine flexible working hours with family commitments. 'The "idea of business" is central to women in all sectors of prostitution, irrespective of their backgrounds' (Day 1996: 78) suggesting that some women decide to work in prostitution after calculated evaluations.

Despite the argument that sex work should be considered a form of employment, it is clear from other qualitative research with women involved in prostitution (Hubbard 1999b; O'Connell Davidson 1998; O'Neill 2001; Phoenix 1999a) and from findings in this study, that selling sex is very different from other, mainstream occupations. While there is no room for what Weitzer (2000: 6) terms 'gratuitous moralizing', care must be taken not to overstate discourses that present a normalized view of prostitution that ignores both the negative public image and the damage prostitution can cause to individuals. Few other jobs attract stigma and marginalization to the same extent as sex work. Also, the fact that selling sex, particularly on the street, is criminalized and continually policed by law-enforcement agencies and community protesters increases the stress and stigma experienced when trying to earn money. The striking differences between prostitution and mainstream employment lie in the significant likelihood of being robbed, attacked, raped or even killed. It is on the issue of violence that O'Connell Davidson (1998: 64) draws the comparison of why sex work is not like other occupations. She points out there are other professionals, such as plumbers, sales personnel and estate agents, who enter houses alone to meet strangers, and occasionally we hear of violence or even fatalities. Only in sex work is it prevalent that if a customer is unhappy he will beat, rape or murder the service provider because 'there is no popular moral doctrine which tolerates hostility towards "dirty plumbers" only "dirty whores"' (O'Connell Davidson 1998: 64). With over sixty sex workers murdered in Britain during the last ten years (O'Kane 2002b), prostitution is a violent and dangerous business, marking it out as one of the most perilous ways of earning money.

For other theorists the issues of control and consent in prostitution mean that neither the abolitionist perspective nor the work model adequately explains the real relationship between a female prostitute and a male client. O'Connell Davidson (2002) criticizes the social and political inequalities that form the basis of market relations that underpin prostitution. Questioning whether sexual capacities constitute property that can be legitimately offered as a commercial transaction, O'Connell Davidson (2002: 85) highlights the complexities of labour and in particular sexual labour, as a 'transfer of powers of command over the person'. Arguing from a Marxist perspective, O'Connell Davidson (1998: 9) describes how labour is not separate from the person but through the process of buying labour, the purchaser has direct power over the person. This argument leads O'Connell Davidson (1998: 10) to argue that prostitution is 'an institution which allows certain powers of command over one person's body to be exercised by another . . . he pays in order that he may command the prostitute to make body orifices available to him, to smile, dance or dress up for him, to whip, spank, massage him or masturbate him'. However, the transfer of power is not done in such a way that the client has complete control over the worker (see Hart and Barnard 2003). Relating this argument to a mainstream employer–employee contract, the complexities are evident. For instance, if I were to hire a gardener I would pay for his expertise and manual labour but I do not have total control over his actions because the gardener comes to the job with experience, expectations, standards relating to his craft and his own business ideology. The purchaser/client may have the power to direct the labour but ultimately the labourer/sex worker has control over how they perform the job to meet the buyer's requests. Therefore, I would emphasize that although there are inherent gender and power inequalities in the sex worker–client relationship, it is not conclusive that a sex worker abandons all control over her actions by entering into a commercial sexual contract.

Models of 'victim' or 'worker' have also been criticized because they tend to 'dichotomize agency' (Maher 2000: 1) and ignore the complexity of power and resistance that define the sex worker's experience. Murphy (2003: 308) argues that women who use their bodies to make money are more 'subjects with power than objects of power'. Even where power struggles limit women's opportunities, it does not necessarily mean that women do not have agency over their lives. Wood (2000) also agrees that while gendered power is at the centre of women's experiences in the sex industry, power is not accepted but contested and negotiated by women in their interactions with both external structures and personal relationships, including economic relationships with clients. Reflecting on the somewhat exploitative nature of the sex trade in Uganda, Wojcicki and Malala (2001: 107) note that agency is not necessarily absent even in dire situations: 'Just because women may be depressed and despairing, does not mean that they are not actors . . . Sex workers are not passive victims but rather actively participate in the power struggle that often exists between sex workers and their clients'. The power struggle referred to is a concoction of masculine power expressed through the cultural acceptance of male physical and sexual dominance over women both in private, intimate situations and wider social, political and economic structures. I argue that despite structural and cultural constraints, some sex workers exercise a degree of self-determination over the use of their bodies. This can be seen most distinctly in a micro-analysis of how sex workers understand risk in prostitution and respond to occupational hazards.

Risk-taking and choice-making

Relying on what Douglas (1992) calls a contextual approach that uses qualitative work to explore individual, interactional and cultural aspects of risk, this book identifies how sex workers not only develop discursive practices that demonstrate personal agency but also create rational strategies to stay in control. The dynamics of risk in prostitution are complex but it is only when the '*meso* level of analysis in which local/cultural context and the ordinary confusions of life' (Wallman 2001: 75) are placed at the centre of any analysis of risk, that the relationship between choice-making and risk-taking can be defined. Objectively, risk is a statistical probability of the likelihood of negative outcomes associated with certain actions. Some risks can be associated with certain activities or roles regardless of the response by particular actors. For instance, there is an objective and, in principle, measurable difference in the risk of being the victim of violence in the street market compared to the indoor markets. Despite this calculation, the objective probability of risk is not the only influence on the possible outcome because of what Wallman (2001: 76) calls the 'fuzziness' of the risk experience.

This book describes how the reactions and responses made by an individual combine with the external social, economic and cultural factors that shape the sex industry to determine the outcome of a particular risk. For example, women who work as escorts, visiting men alone in isolated circumstances, all encounter a similar chance of being harmed. However, some individuals will be prone to taking risks while others will avoid risks at all costs, and so take precautions, deterrents and protection strategies to reduce the chance of a bad outcome. Further still, the plight of the escort worker is structured by the illegal and illicit nature of this subterranean economy that remains outside the law and exempt from any work-based employment or civil rights to protection. Trying to decipher sociological meanings of danger and risk, Wallman (2001: 76) states that 'risk as a personal choice "taken" is a far cry from risk as a danger imposed'. Yet in the case of prostitution women may take the decision to sell sex but they do not favour dangerous working conditions that expose them as a vulnerable sexual minority group. The outcome of risk depends on both the individual's assessment and response to the risk as well as the structural and social context of the sex market. Speaking specifically of prostitution, Hart and Barnard (2003: 33) argue that 'risk behaviour in this paradigm is understood as the outcome of a complex interplay between individual and social factors, interpersonal relationships and situations'.

The social constructionist perspective places the rational agent at the centre of risk-taking or avoidance but also pays attention to the social constraints of the environment in which the risks are prevalent. Such an approach avoids criticism applied to models of habituated risk-taking by accepting that risk and risk management are a complex interplay between individual biography, responses to risk and external structures and dynamics. In relation to the sex industry, the presence and response to risk must be understood as a dynamic between individual, social, economic and cultural factors that influence the illicit economy. Applying Best and Lukenbill's (1982: 15) theory of social organization of deviance to the experience and management of risk, the dimensions of prostitution can be understood at two levels. First, the social organization of the deviant act in terms of how the commercial sexual transaction is facilitated; and second, the social organization of the interaction between deviants, or more simply, how individuals organize themselves to minimize risks.

At the first level, the social organization of the sexual transaction is partly determined by the extent to which risks are recognized and responses are constructed. Prostitution studies already describe how the place, timing and details of the sexual transaction, outside and indoors, are specifically chosen to reduce potential threat. At another level, the social organization of certain interactions between sex workers, clients and organizers is structured by risk-reducing behaviour such as general rules and codes of conduct (see Chapter 9). At the same time, the illicit activity is influence by its marginal structural position. For instance, Plumridge (2001: 210) has established that indoor prostitution markets are constrained by structural factors such as an absence of the rights of wage earners, individuals are left with limited autonomy because of the stringent house rules and competition is divisive between workmates. Yet at the same time, knowledge, skills and tasks are created and sustained among individuals to reduce the level of threat and prepare women to avoid risky situations. As Wallman (2001: 77) neatly summarizes, 'the realities of risk management are such that each strategy is compromized by opportunity costs, by other priorities and dangers, and by the actions and purposes of other people'. The social organization of prostitution depends on this fluid, interchangeable relationship between risk-taking and risk-avoidance at an organizational and individual level.

Although women are traditionally portrayed as passive avoiders of risk (Chan and Rigakos 2002; Lupton 1999), women involved in prostitution are placed outside acceptable conceptions of femininity and appear to be risk-taking by the standards of others in the community. The exclusion of sex workers from the protection granted to others is exemplified through public discourses that spell out the appropriate behaviour for female safety. This moral code of safety justifies why those women who do not follow the gendered set of values are asking for trouble and place themselves outside the expectations of public protection (Stanko 1996). The decision to take or avoid risks is not necessarily 'voluntary' but is shaped by the social, economic and political situation that constrains women's lives. For instance, sex workers constantly juggle three preferences: the desire to stay physically safe, the desire to maintain their sanity and the desire to earn money. The outcome of these competing preferences is determined by an individual's propensity to avoid or take risks as well as the inherent gender power relations.

Douglas (1986: 30) suggests that perceptions of risks tend to be less realistic than the actual danger in an attempt to make their immediate life situation more acceptable. Plumridge (2001: 210) speaks of how sex workers acknowledge risk but at the same time dismiss potential harm through a self-image of the 'fearless protagonist'. Contrary to this I found that interviewees were experienced in judging their circumstances and were relatively accurate in their perception of and response to the threat of harm. As Warr and Pyett (1999: 305) suggest, 'perhaps living with high levels of danger has the effect of normalizing risk for [these] sex workers'.

Consideration must be given to whether the focus on risk in prostitution is over-sensitized because of the deviant, intimate and unregulated nature of the industry. Scambler et al. (1990: 123) proposes that certain aspects of prostitution are over-emphasized because of their illicit nature and the excitement factor connected to sexual deviancy. Scambler highlights that there is a 'paradox of attention' applied to prostitution: the mundane everyday interactions are ignored in favour of the deviant nature of sex work. This paradox accounts for why certain types of risks have been studied while others have been sidelined. The basic features of prostitution, namely a woman engaging in serial sexual relations with an extensive number of men, focuses attention first on sexual health and then, given the precariousness of deviant occupations, other physical 'bodily risks' (Monaghan 2003: 12). The perspectives of the women and, hence, more subtle yet equally important risks have escaped the attention of researchers. Just as Polsky (1971: 100) studied the hustler, I approached the sex industry from the perspective that although the relationships surrounding prostitution make it an illegal activity, sex work is a regular job for some women and deserves similar attention to how sociologists have studied other occupations.

A hierarchy of harms

The premise that risk in prostitution is related to health or drug use is a bias in the literature that ignores the realities of selling sex for many women. For women who make the daily transitions from the private, personal sphere to the clandestine underworld of the sauna, brothel or escort agency, health is only one of many risks that are guarded against. I argue that sex workers construct a 'hierarchy of harms' which prioritizes certain types of dangers depending on the perceived consequences and the degree of control individuals consider they have over minimizing the likelihood of a risk occurring (Sanders 2004c). Sex workers describe how they rationalize their approach to health risks as an individual responsibility. All of the indoor workers I interviewed were staunch advocates of using condoms for all commercial sex acts and considered the condom to be an integral part of their working routines (also see Cusick 1998; Day and Ward 1990; McKeganey *et al.* 1992; Sanders 2002). While women described the threat to their health if a condom broke, slipped off or, even worse, a client forced unprotected sex, all of these events were relatively unusual. For these reasons, sex workers considered health risks to be one of the more controllable aspects of their work. Armed with the correct medical information and preventative measures such as regular health checks and so forth, the relationship between risk and sexual health is an area sex workers in my study felt they could control and therefore did not warrant continual re-evaluation.

Instead, other subtle risks were given more attention and strategic intervention. The potential physical harms from violent clients was considered an unpredictable occupational hazard to be guarded against in each commercial transaction. Assessing the likelihood of physical harm from clients was a difficult judgement call and although many women had never experienced violence at work, there was constant concern about the possibility. Reducing the likelihood of physical risks was prioritized through a complex system of precautions, screening, deterrents and remedial protection. Individuals constructed their own tactics to avoid a bad customer and some women rarely accepted new clients, preferring to stick with those who were 'tried and tested'. Owners and managers took a serious approach to the potential threat of violence from opportunistic clients and gangs who specifically target saunas for robberies. A nasty incident in a sauna could ruin the reputation of the owners, spark intrusions from the police, discourage regular customers and generally cost the business financially.

Despite the prevalence of violence and the complex responses created at an organizational and individual level, violence was not the overwhelming concern for sex workers. Risk was not only considered on the basis of tangible harms. Often women said that they could recover from physical injuries but there were other kinds of occupational dangers that would bring irreparable loss in their personal lives. The emotional and psychological consequences of selling sex are a hazard equal to that of physical violence and health-related concerns. Emotional risks were prioritized because the chances of 'being discovered' was considered to be somewhat out of their control. The likelihood of a family member witnessing a sex worker in an environment such as a sauna or hotel could be minimized by choosing specific geographical locations and types of markets carefully but much of whether women were 'found out' was left to chance. Women felt that often they had little control over the emotional risks in prostitution, and therefore these pitfalls were to be guarded against over what has been considered in the literature to be more obvious harms. When asked about the preoccupying dangers in their everyday lives, sex workers referred to the emotional implications of their work because, unlike physical harm, the emotional consequences of selling sex do not stop when a woman leaves the sauna. Emotional risks are not confined to the place or hours of work, but are to be guarded against always: at home, in private and even when prostitution is a distant memory. The remaining chapters in this book show how sex workers construct their understanding of risk in relation to their personal situation and prioritize risks depending on the perceived consequences or outcomes.

The women

The intention of this research is to understand the lives of women who had made an economic decision to provide direct sexual services for men in exchange for money. The fifty-five women I interviewed defined their involvement in prostitution as voluntary, they were all aged eighteen years or over and British citizens. They were all able to choose how to manage many aspects of their occupation. The parameters of this research are set by the types of markets that make up the indoor commercial sex industry and this is the population from which the participants were chosen. Alongside observation and formal taped interviews, 'guided conversations' (O'Neill 1996a: 132) in the form of informal chatting with sex workers constitute an important part of the data collection. In all 230 people were contacted, most of who were women engaged in selling sex. Of those that were interviewed, twenty-three worked in saunas, ten worked in rented premises with another worker, eight worked alone in rented premises, four worked from home, five worked from the streets, three were owners of establishments and two were receptionists.

Selectivity and representativeness

Tackling the issue of representativeness, Maher (2000: 29) reasons that 'the search for typicality continues to plague both sociologists and criminologists' and that such a search is dangerous in the sense that it 'obscures what the anomalous or the marginal can reveal about the centre ... and perhaps most of all, strategies of resistance'. Roseneil (1993: 179) rejects value-neutral expectations and describes how and why she has 'no problems taking sides'. I make no claims that this ethnography is a general reflection of all women involved in prostitution in Britain but I do claim that it is a truthful account of my observations during the fieldwork. The three specific criteria that determined the selection of interviewees (minimum age of eighteen, British citizenship and 'voluntarily' working) meant that from the outset the focus was on just one group of women in a specific locality. Nevertheless, within this narrow selection the aims of the study dictated that a cross-section of participants was necessary. The women interviewed were part of a much wider sex work community and most of their peers had similar working experiences and lifestyles as those reported here. The interviewees are certainly located within the same structural, economic and social systems as other sex workers. On these premises, the sex workers who describe their daily encounter with the subliminal world of the sex industry are representative of other women who, like them, are up against similar risks, opportunities and constraints.

Age and residence

The age range of respondents who sold sex was 18–52 years, while the oldest interviewee, who owned a sauna, was 55 years. The mean age of workers, 33.5 years, reflects the general older profile of women who work indoors. Twenty-eight participants lived with a romantic partner and thirteen of them said they kept their prostitution secret from their partner. Sixteen women were in relationships with men but lived alone, and eleven described themselves as single. Forty-eight women grew up in the West Midlands. Fifteen had histories of physical or sexual abuse in childhood and problematic family relationships. Seven of these women had been in the care of the local authority.

Ethnicity

Although the majority of the sample was white European (45/55), six women described themselves as Asian and a further four were African Caribbean. This was a fairly representative reflection of the local population and the cohort of sex workers who visited the sexual health project. I am aware that not enough questions were asked about the experience of ethnic minority women who were in the sex industry, their relationships with each other and issues of inclusion and exclusion within the sex work community. There was no obvious exclusion of ethnic minority sex workers as women appeared to unite because of their acknowledged and shared stigmatized identity as sex providers. However, specific attention is needed to address the subtleties of the racialization of sex work in relation to the organization of prostitution.

Education and formal labour participation

Forty-one of the fifty-five participants had left school at the age of sixteen with few qualifications and had entered manual, unskilled or semi-skilled jobs. Three women had left school before the age of sixteen either voluntarily or had been expelled. The other eleven women had gone to college immediately after school to do various vocational qualifications (hairdressing, social care skills and catering). Of these eleven, five women completed professional nursing training (two specialized in psychiatric nursing) while two others took first degrees at university. At the time of the study, three women were currently working towards a university degree. Virtually all of the interviewees had previously worked in mainstream jobs that were usually unskilled, manual 'feminized' work such as cleaning, catering or caring. Looking after the elderly and infirm featured in most respondents' (and the researcher's) career histories, along with bar work and catering.

Motherhood and reproduction

Forty-one women had eighty-five children between them, with an average of two children each. Of these forty-one, twenty-one described themselves as lone parents. Two women had had their children cared for by the local authority, but at the time of the study, all of the mothers were caring for their children, sometimes with the help of grandparents. Thirteen of the fifty-five women disclosed that they had had abortions, often when they were in their teenage years. However, anecdotal experience suggests that the number is probably much higher. Women recounted many experiences of miscarriages and at least four of the interviewees had miscarriages during the fieldwork period. Most of the women who had been working in prostitution while also having a family discussed various periods of absence from prostitution while they were pregnant and caring for a new-born baby. This period of time ranged from three months to three years. Of the twenty-one women who described themselves as lone parents, they all confirmed that they had entered prostitution to provide financially for their children. Often this was as a result of the father leaving the relationship and not providing maintenance for the child. Women found themselves in economic desperation and for those who had not been accustomed to a life on welfare benefits, the dramatic reduction in quality of life was too severe, and prostitution was considered a financial solution. The entire sample identified themselves as heterosexual, although several women reported having same-sex sexual experiences.

At the time of the fieldwork, I met at least three drug-using street workers who were at various stages of a pregnancy and still working. There was a strong moral discourse among the other women that this was not only unhealthy for both the mother and the unborn child but also self-deprecating and cashing in on the perverted fantasies of some clients. Of the fourteen women who did not have children, two were currently undergoing fertility treatment, three others had decided not to have children, while the other nine said that they were too young or not ready to be mothers although they expected to have children in the future.

Prostitution career

For this group of women, the average age of entry into prostitution was 23.1 years. This is older than that found in other studies because of the concentration of indoor workers in the sample (50/5). Thirty-three respondents had worked in more than one market. Sixteen of the fifty workers had experience of the street; however, only five workers remained in this sector while the other eleven had moved to indoor markets. This suggests an upward trajectory from street to off-street prostitution. Thirty-four women had worked in licensed saunas and twenty-three remained in this market. Six women had worked from home, ten participants previously worked alone from flats and a further twenty-one had worked in brothels. At the time of the interview, twelve women were working in more than one market. This was often a combination of working in a sauna or working premises during the daytime and taking escorting work in the evenings. Women either worked through escort agencies or independently by placing an advert in the local newspapers.

Drug use

Reflecting the characteristics of indoor prostitution, there was limited drug use among the sex workers in this study. Only four women confirmed they were using heroin and/or cocaine and all of these were currently working on the street. Among indoor workers the use of 'recreational drugs' such as cannabis, amphetamines and stimulants was tolerated but not usually as part of the working repertoire. Three distinct patterns of drug use were noted. First, drugs such as ecstasy, amphetamines and cannabis were associated with leisure time and non-work activities such as socializing with friends, dancing in late nightclub venues or relaxing with a romantic partner. Therefore, recreational drugs were generally not introduced to the indoor work scene because women wanted to stay alert and in control when they were with clients and not experience the emotional exhilaration or mellowness they associated with 'taking pills' or 'smoking spliffs'.

Second, women who tended to use recreational drugs were generally under thirty-five. Many women in the indoor sex markets are older than this and often there were generational divisions between those who thought drug use acceptable or 'normalized' and those who thought that illicit drug use was deviant at any time or place. This reflects a much wider division in society regarding the use of substances as a normal part of youth lifestyles and the growing trend to use 'dance drugs' (Parker *et al.* 2002). Many of the participants had grown up in the 1980s when rave music and Acid House was transforming how young people spent their leisure time (Muncie 1999). This group still considered themselves part of a youth culture and frequented nightclubs and early-morning chill-out venues in the city, where recreational substance use was a regular part of the socializing ritual (Malbon 1999).

Third, the use of recreational drugs within the indoor sex establishments such as saunas, brothels and rented premises depended on the quality of the establishment, the image the owner wanted to portray, the type of clientele and the atmosphere of the working environment. Saunas that employed up to twenty women were often less fussy about imposing strict regulations and turned a blind eye to the use of stimulants at work. Some participants reported that amphetamines were used at work as primers to gain confidence with the clients, handle the competitive atmosphere, as well as stay awake on night shifts. Owners and managers of these establishments were often less interested in how the staff conducted themselves as long as the business was running smoothly, avoiding police intervention and making profit. In contrast, other saunas prided themselves on 'clean', drug-free workers and 'respectable' clientele. For these establishments, drug use became a yardstick for measuring the legitimacy and reputation of the business.

Chapter 4

Picking punters

The buzzer in the sauna rings in short bursts. The sex worker who is not entertaining jumps from the barstool to study the television monitor. The close-circuit camera television above the door shows that the client on the other side is a man smartly dressed in office clothes. He carries a briefcase, is clean-shaven, relaxed and standing confidently as he waits for the response. The man would be welcomed in without question if it wasn't for one glaring suspicion in the mind of the sex worker. The reason for the hesitation is that the man is African Caribbean. The rules of the sauna are that black men are only welcome if they have visited before or can be verified as trustworthy by another worker. The woman recognizes the man but is not quite sure. All her colleagues are unavailable to ask and the receptionist is new and doesn't recognize him. The woman speaks through the intercom: 'Hello love, have you been here before?' The man no doubt has been through this process before and so supplies the required information that identifies he has been vetted by the sauna before: 'I came about a month ago and I saw Pandora'. The sex worker felt at ease, as Pandora had worked in the sauna for several months. However, just to be sure she asks the man to describe what his previous encounter looked like. The client gives an accurate description of Pandora and he is let in. (Fieldwork Diary, September 2000)

Sex worker and client are not automatically matched by their common interest of one selling and the other buying sex. This chapter challenges the stereotype that the commercial sex liaison is haphazard by describing how some sex workers subject prospective clients to a complex selection process. Other studies mention how women in prostitution use 'selectivity' (Prus and Irini 1980: 59) to 'screen out' clients based on past experiences or intuition (Barnard 1993; Campbell 1991: 1371; Dunhill 1989b: 205; Maher 2000: 160). In Glasgow, McKeganey and Barnard (1996) found that clients are selected on the basis of subjective clues: guidelines for mannerisms and body language which women perceive to be suspicious. However, much of this research draws on the street market where there is a distinct time pressure to attract a client and move away from the prying eye of the police and protesters as quickly as possible. With the exception of Whittaker and Hart (1996), there has been little detail regarding the extent and nature of the screening systems that indoor sex workers adopt as a crucial strategy to avoid harm. This study found that in the indoor markets there is less pressure to choose clients quickly and therefore sex workers screen more thoroughly. In addition, individuals rely on colleagues, technology and the physical structure of the building during the selection process.

Forty-two of the fifty-five interviewees said that they rely on their instincts when deciding whether to accept or reject a client: 'I always go with my instinct. I can always sense if a customer is funny. If I have got vibes as soon as I open the door I won't see the customer, I won't risk it' (Katrina, working premises). Women describe these feelings as 'gut instincts', 'sixth sense' or 'intuition': 'I haven't really got any rules ... you have to go with your own instincts' (Seema, sauna). The same women said they refuse customers when they feel negative reactions that they cannot explain. They could not elucidate why, but something told them the person would be trouble: 'I have turned down a lot of money from gut instincts. Then you know if you felt like that again, when I had that instinct, I wouldn't see them. You know who to trust by your instincts' (Kelly, sauna).

Mary explained how relying on instincts is not unique to prostitution but can also be acquired from other jobs: 'I have instincts with people, like any job. When you are working on a bar and you look at people and think he is going to be trouble or he is all right.' Although biography played a part in the skills associated with judging customers, sex workers are also taught on the job. Two owners said they teach employees to follow their initial feelings: 'I always say to my girls if in doubt do nothing. Don't open the door if you get that feeling, that instinct, then don't do it' (Sylvia, sauna owner). Michelle operates an escort agency and offers similar advice: 'I say to any girl, if you get a bad feeling on the phone, say you are fully booked or say you don't want to see him. Don't go through with it.' Until now, there has been little attempt to unravel or explain the crucial decision-making process that many workers make every time they 'do business'. Through conducting probing interviews and my own observation, I set out to explore what lies behind these gut reactions.

The prostitution trust game

Before I explore the screening strategies, it is important to explain why assessment is so important in prostitution. As Warren (1999: 1) states 'trust involves a judgement, however implicit, to accept vulnerability to the potential ill will of others ... When one trusts one accepts some amount of risk for potential harm in exchange for the benefits of cooperation.' The sex worker's decision to accept or reject a client can be cast as what Bacharach and Gambetta (1997) have defined as a 'basic trust game'. Here, I will adapt this frame to the case of prostitution as a way of understanding the selection process. The nature of the purchaser–provider relationship is based on two strangers meeting for an intimate sexual exchange, both taking risks without knowing the outcome. Where commercial sex is surrounded in illegality and attempts are made by the State to silence, remove or ignore the interactions of sellers and buyers, other processes and activities are constructed to create, monitor and maintain trust. As Claus Offe (1999) argues, trust can produce social coordination where State regulation threatens or destabilizes the capacity to achieve desired social and economic interactions.

In the current British context, there is a low expectation of trust for both parties in the prostitution trust game, yet they need to cooperate to achieve their desired goal. The client takes a chance by paying for a service before receiving it: the quality of the service could be poor, or worse, he could be robbed, injured or arrested. For the worker, the trust game is an explicit calculation of costs and benefits and the outcome depends on whether her judgement is right or wrong. If her decision to accept a client is right, then she gains financially. If she refuses and the client is genuine, then she makes a financial loss. However, if she chooses to accept and is wrong, the costs could be robbery, rape, physical injury and possibly death. In trust-building, behaviour takes on special meanings because both parties are aware of the stakes, as there is mutual knowledge of what each player wants to achieve.

The sex worker starts from a position of distrust until proven otherwise. The decision to accept or reject a client is based on a judgement of his genuineness or trustworthiness. This is not necessarily a moral judgement on his character but clarification that he has the qualities to fulfil the commercial contract. Interviewees describe a genuine client as a man who completes the transaction without breaking the negotiated contract by paying the agreed price before the service without argument or bartering, and who will conduct the sexual transaction without risk to the worker's personal safety. A client is considered trustworthy in relation to the contract if they display certain characteristics. Indeed, 'trust is a belief built upon perceptions or images of the characteristics of others' (Offe 1999: 49). In this chapter, the terms 'trust' and 'genuineness' are used interchangeably to refer to the qualities necessary to honour the contract. Respondents explained that the contract could be broken in the following ways:

- A client agrees a contract, pays, completes the sexual transaction then takes back the initial payment by force (robbery).
- A client agrees a transaction, pays, and then carries out non-contracted sexual acts against the woman's wishes (sexual violence).
- A client agrees a contract then physically attacks the woman (physical violence).
- A man enters the sauna with no intention of purchasing, observes the woman, makes excuses and leaves (time-waster).

Posner (2000: 19) explains that in the commercial relationship the best associate to yield cooperation over a period of time will be those with 'low discount rates'. The low discount rate in the prostitution trust game refers to clients who have no intention of breaking the contract, while others are tricksters pretending to be good customers (high discount rates). The former are 'good types' (those who will cooperate and complete the transaction) and the latter are 'bad types' (those with harmful intentions). The sex worker who is aware that there are good and bad types, sets out to select only genuine clients by assessing their behaviour. Gambetta *et al.* (2001) describe this process as an intuitive application of signalling theory. Before the theory is applied to the sex industry, it is useful to outline two problems that sex workers encounter when screening clients. First, 'mimics' are those who appear as good types but are really bad types aware of the signs that good types display. Second, some of the traits that the sex workers assess are observable while others are not.

Mimicry and traits

There are three players in the prostitution trust game:

- The sex worker (truster) who decides whether a client is genuine or not based on the information she observes or can further acquire.
- The genuine client (trustee) must reassure the truster that he is trustworthy especially when he shows a negative sign (for example, being young).
- The mimic who is motivated to rob and/or attack but displays signs of genuineness to trick the truster.

The mimic is a customer who appears to be trustworthy but in fact has dangerous intentions. Frank (1991: 207) describes how it is difficult to tell when someone is lying and believes that there will always be those who can successfully fake behaviour and achieve deception. The mimic understands the prostitution trust game, especially the signs displayed by genuine customers. For instance, for a mimic to gain entrance into a sauna the man must convince people he has traits that are desirable. By acting polite, appearing well-groomed and negotiating calmly, the mimic can win the trust of the unsuspecting worker by engaging in behaviour that is easy to copy. For sex workers who accept cheap rather than costly signals, the mimic can trick his way into a sexual transaction, only to commit harm. The time-waster is a special kind of mimic. There are no defining characteristics of the time-waster, so he is difficult to detect. O'Connell Davidson (1998) describes how 'Desiree', an independent worker, guards against time-wasters by charging an entrance fee to all visitors. Therefore, even if men decide not to purchase, they have not had a thrill for free. Although time-wasters are usually non-threatening, this form of mimicry must still be managed.

The trust game is complicated because some traits are observable while others are not. As certain traits or intentions are not observable, the truster must rely on other signs because of 'types of *actions* [that] signal the extent of trust' (Offe 1999: 47, original italics). For example, the sex worker cannot directly observe 'wealth' but must rely on signs that make this quality known. A man who is well dressed in a suit or designer clothing, wearing gold jewellery and driving an expensive car, displays enough signs to convince a sex worker he is a good type. The signals that sex workers look for are often what Posner (2000: 21) calls 'conspicuous consumption' or 'cultural competence'. Sex workers accept observable traits as signals of genuineness because they believe that a mimic would not possess these traits or that a mimic would not go to such tiresome lengths to display positive traits when there are workers who do not screen, so can be easily tricked. When the trustee's properties are unobservable, other actions or behaviour are considered such as past performance, a good reputation and recommendations from an already trusted client.

The trust game becomes difficult when the trustee (client), who may not have the financial resources to pay, purposely displays the signs of wealth through mimicry (borrowing a suit, wearing fake gold, stealing a flash car). Those who aim to trick workers into thinking they are genuine will display observable properties that they do not really have. Therefore the trust decision for the woman is whether the signs are genuine or fake: 'an appropriately costly signal can prevail in equilibrium as long as observers believe that anyone who sends the signal belongs to the good types' (Posner 2000: 21). The rest of this section applies one aspect of signalling theory, the 'costly to fake principle', as a formula to understand the communication between the sex worker and the client.

The costly to fake principle

Zahavi and Zahavi (1997: xiv) state that 'in order to be effective, signals have to be reliable; in order to be reliable they have to be costly'. Sex workers judge the genuineness of a client on the types of signals he sends and on the extent to which those signals are costly or cheap. Posner (2000: 19) explains:

> To distinguish themselves from the bad types, the good types engage in actions that are called 'signals'. Signals reveal types if only the good types, and not the bad types, can afford to send them, and everyone knows this. Because a good type is a person who values future returns more than a bad type does, one signal is to incur large, observable costs prior to entering a relationship.

The sex worker knows that only a genuine customer can afford to display certain signals and therefore she will only take specific behaviour as a signal of genuineness. One example is that only honest clients can afford to offer information that makes them vulnerable (e.g. company email address, home address, credit card number, full name) because they have no intention of foul play. Those who intend to harm would not be prepared to release sensitive information because they know that they are not genuine good types, and that if they break the contract they could be found and punished. Therefore, sex workers who realise the trust game look for reliable signals based on the costs involved in displaying the behaviour or information. This process of assessing behaviour for the 'best type' has been described as the 'handicap principle' (Zahavi and Zahavi 1997: xiv) or the 'costly to fake principle' (Frank 1991: 523). For the male client who genuinely seeks a non-threatening commercial transaction, displaying costly information allows him to verify that he is a good type. The worker assesses the reliability of the signal by how costly it is and is not satisfied with easy to fake behaviour (e.g. politeness, presentable appearance, paying up-front), so will look for signals that are costly.

The fieldwork identified four mediums of screening based on the type of communication through which the client first presents himself: visual assessments during face-to-face contact; assessment over the telephone; checking by remote methods (peephole/cameras) and via the Internet. The remainder of this chapter describes how communication takes place between a sex worker and a client in the prostitution trust game. I will demonstrate how the costly to fake principle can be used to explain some of this interaction, although not all.

Eyeballing the punter

Goffman (1983) describes face-to-face social interaction as the most important form of 'interaction order'. All the sex markets provide an opportunity for face-to-face visual screening at some point in the negotiations and forty-six of the fifty-five interviewees said this type of screening is the most frequently used assessment tool. This section describes a range of traits that are assessed face-to-face.

Demeanour

It has been reported that doorstaff in the night-time economy, who have the task of preventing violence, look for 'individuals whose appearance and demeanour suggest trouble' (Hobbs *et al.* 2003: 122). 'Trouble' for sex workers also refers to violence, but in addition they are interested in identifying those clients who may not pay, or will demand obscure sexual fantasies, have unbearable hygiene problems or resist wearing a condom. To this end, physical appearance is one of the first features of assessment: 'I look at their appearance. If someone looks shabby and horrible I won't see them. I look at their body language and how they carry themselves' (Aliya, sauna). Sex workers judge certain appearances with caution in the same way doorstaff turn away skinheads, men with large tattoos, bruised eyes and scars as types that may cause trouble (Winlow *et al.* 2001: 544). Respondents in my study, like table dancers (Ronai and Ellis 1989: 280) believe that men who appear unkempt are less likely to be a wise economic partner. Men who hide their face by wearing dark glasses or a hood are not accepted unless they display other, positive signals.

Sex workers place value on conventional observable traits that determine status, wealth and social class. For example, clients who reveal or look like professionals (policemen, solicitors, teachers, and doctors are popular clientele) are expected to honour the contract as their occupational status is taken to be a sign of trust. This is because professionals and the middle classes are considered to be less inclined to rob or attack a sex worker as the repercussions could be substantial. The working classes are also subject to similar screening related to occupational integrity and class-based expectations of behaviour. Ten respondents said that men dressed in Royal Mail uniforms, British Telecom overalls and builders' scruffy clothes are afforded trust as they are likely to be 'honest' men on their way home from work or visiting during their lunch break. Also, there is a possibility that men could be traced by their company uniforms, so those who wear company logos are more likely to be concerned about future payoffs. Therefore occupational status and identifying features such as uniforms are a costly signal that only those who are genuine can afford to display. For the safety-conscious sex worker, trust is assessed through informal knowledge and networks. In the same way that doorstaff create 'rational informal admittance policies' based on 'indicators of trouble' (Hobbs *et al.* 2003: 125), sex workers look for 'indicators of trust' before deciding to accept a client.

Posner (2000: 22) warns that traits based on appearance may be unreliable because the costs of changing appearance are not great: 'When the signal consists of conformity to manners, clothing styles, and linguistic trends, people are vulnerable to the con artist, who exploits people because his unusual skills and idiosyncratic tastes enable him to mimic signals more cheaply than ordinary bad types.' Women realize that mimics could easily acquire clothes and a convincing appearance: suits are cheap to buy and obtaining a uniform is not difficult. Screeners do not assess the genuineness of a stranger on the basis of appearance alone but probe for other signals that are not observable.

Attitudes such as politeness, friendliness, and respectfulness are properties that some interviewees associate with genuineness:

> If someone calls me the wrong name I will not take an appointment. If they go into detail about the service they want they will be refused. People who know what they want and have done this before are straightforward and are not too picky when they contact you (Natasha, working premises).

However, several anecdotes highlight just how cheap to mimic these signs are. Those who have been tricked by men displaying respectful attitudes devise other ways to test the attitude of a client. Neesha often uses the street to attract customers and describes a test she uses to assess who will be a genuine partner:

> I will stand there and I will refuse every man who stops by me and refuse to get in the car. If they hurl abuse at me then I know I was right not to get in that car. If they come back round and are laughing and being sweet then you can suss them out more and I will get in the car. If I get a feeling that they are just trying to play it clever then I will not get in that car. I give them a little test, then tell them the prices and see how their attitudes are towards me. Then if they are all right you can get in the car. If they lock the car door then you need to get out of there as soon as possible as you know there will be something not right. When you are driving that is how you get to know them.

Neesha refuses all new clients, as she believes that the humiliation of being rejected by a 'prostitute' standing on a street corner brings out the true attitude of any man. It is the client's reaction to her refusal that is the deciding factor. Taken together, attitude and appearance are powerful observable traits that inform the sex worker's decision-making but traits must be carefully considered as they are cheap to mimic. Deciding what signals are genuine and what is mimicry is the task of the observer.

Ethnicity

Thirty-eight interviewees describe ethnicity as a sign they consider when assessing genuineness. In the sex markets I observed, it was easy to identify a general belief that white men will honour the contract while black men (sometimes Asian men) will not. In Brooklyn, Maher (2000: 187) found that sex workers preferred European American men because they were considered to be less violent and have the resources and inclination to pay. In my study, some women from all ethnic groups rejected black men, in particular men of Caribbean origin. Saunas and brothels often adopted rules of entry based on ethnicity that were dictated by the management. Therefore, the behaviour of the black client was rarely considered as the rule of 'no black men' was mobilized before negotiations began. This section explores the complex reasons why the majority of participants believed that genuineness could be evaluated by skin colour.

The first explanation for excluding certain ethnic groups was that men should not be trusted because there were intrinsic reasons why they would make unwise customers:

> We would never see black men. They are cheeky and they are arrogant and they want everything for no pence and they will take up the whole hour. They are sly and they will look around and see what is in here and they will see you in the street and shout you down (Astrid, working premises).

> I won't do no yardies or no Jamaicans. Ninety-nine per cent of the girls down Coventry are the same. I can say it is hard for a black man, except if they are from the African continent, to pick a girl up. We are not sure if they are pimps or not. And that has been like that since I went out on the streets (Amy, street).

Stereotypes that underpin this exclusion relate to images of black men as pimps who exploit women through prostitution to gain financial rewards. Exploring the 'racialized' identities that are reinforced in prostitution, O'Connell Davidson (1996: 189–90) describes how the racial boundaries between white women and black men determine some relationships in the illicit economy: 'It is not uncommon for street walkers' pimps and sauna owners to tell "their girls" to turn down black punters on the basis of the "racist" assumption that all black men are pimps and thus potential competitors.' Connotations of black men dealing drugs and participating in dangerous criminal activities are commonplace: 'We never entertain black guys. That is personal choice as well, because they would set you up' (Margaret, working premises). Such attitudes are evident among flat workers in south London: 'black and foreign men had been banned from buying services because owners, maids and working women feared violent effects of crack use from this client group' (Taylor 2003: 7).

Offe (1999: 50) argues that the dominant basis for individual trust is experiential: 'Out of *past experience* develops a *present* orientation concerning the anticipation of *future behaviour*' (original italics). Previous experience accounts for the second reason why ethnicity is a popular screening strategy. Sex workers who exclude black men said that they did so because they have had experiences that suggest these men are an unwise economic transaction both in terms of profit and time. Some respondents claimed that the sexual stamina of a black man is such that sex work is made a time-consuming and exhausting proposition and therefore not financially profitable: 'They have got too much stamina and they would take the piss basically' (Margaret, working premises). Beryl had worked throughout the indoor and street markets over a twenty-year period: 'I definitely won't do black people. That is on the preference that they will take too long, I have tried it . . . I will be honest with you that I have had a couple and they take too long, forget it. They just work me too hard and I can't be bothered with it.'

Others who refuse say that in their experience this group of men tend to be violent, attempt to rob them or the establishment: 'The sauna excludes black men because they say you cannot differentiate between a pimp' (Sarah, sauna). On the street, Neesha reports a similar attitude:

> As for the black men they are a definite no go. Out of the black clients that I have done I have only had four good clients and they have always been regulars. The rest have tried to take off, rob ya, beat ya, tried to pimp ya – that's why it is a no no to black men.

However, the exclusion of black men is not applied unconditionally. Seema highlights how she rejects them not because they are black but because they display specific signs that spell trouble: 'I would not let a black man in if they had chaps on [heavy gold bracelets] or if there was something wary about him, then I would not see him. To fool them I ask for a membership card and they leave.'

African-Caribbean men are also excluded when sex workers have partners who are black. Tied to the issue of secrecy and working in prostitution without close ones knowing, of the twelve workers who had black partners, ten refused to accept black clients: 'Some women who live with black men won't do black men because they may find out. What happens if they [the client] are someone your man knows or he comes in as your man's friend one day?' (Julia, works from home). Krystal agreed: 'The black guys do not want other black guys knowing their business. Even if he knows you are working, you ain't gonna be doing no black guys.' To prevent being discovered working in prostitution, most women with black partners refuse all black men as a safeguard against potential identification and the ramifications on her partner's reputation and her personal relationship.

Black men are not excluded if they can display signs that are too costly to mimic. For example, if a man in a suit, clean shaven, late 30s, carrying a briefcase, with a polite, well-spoken accent came to the door of a sauna, the wealth of positive signs (appearance, clothing, class status, profession, age) would counteract the negative sign of blackness:

> I don't accept black men, but there are a few that are allowed in here which the girls have got to know. You can normally tell on the camera what kind of client he is by how he is dressed. You do get some that come up from the university and they are very nice people and that's OK, but it is the black men with the caps on who we obviously don't let in (Sylvia, sauna owner).

Being known as a regular client can offset the general rules of rejecting certain men:

> We are not allowed to have black men in here and I am the only person who does black men. When the black men come to the door they will ask for me as that shows they have been here before (Sarah, sauna).

Twelve interviewees did not use ethnicity as a screening strategy: 'You have to work on your instinct, no matter what race they are. You get bad people in all races . . . I am not going to ban someone just because of the colour of their skin' (Petra, working premises):

> You get good and bad in all colours. You can't make decisions like that. I have had some big rastas with long dreads, and they have been really nice. Some would look at them and say black guys – no – but some of them you can just tell and you get to judge the character (Anita, working premises).

Anita is African-Caribbean and Leanne is Caucasian and both have had romantic relationships with black men. They felt that ethnicity was useless as a benchmark for judging whether a client would honour the contract because in their experience men from all ethnic groups had broken contracts: 'I have not had a bad experience at all. I mean I probably have had more bad experiences with white than black clients' (Leanne, working premises). Where ethnicity is excluded from the screening process, other signals (re-identification, recommendations, age and status) were prioritized.

Age

Face-to-face contact enables sex workers to assess the age of the client. Participants generally refuse young men in favour of middle-aged men, or if the customer is young then they will probe for other signs: 'When it is someone younger I do get really wary. I think I feel safer with older guys' (Dora, sauna). 'I don't do young people because I am old. Young guys are hard work and the older businessmen, they are just great and no contest' (Anita, working premises). Bacharach and Gambetta (1997) describe how the trust game involves decisions based on theories that categorize people, such as: young men are more likely to be violent; professional men are more likely to be wealthy. Reflecting findings in academic studies (Cookson 1996; Tatum 2000; Tomsen 1997), sex workers often connect young men to violence, drug use and alcohol consumption: 'You can tell if someone is drunk so you wouldn't let them in' (Seema, sauna). Young men are also suspected of having other motives because workers cannot understand why men in their late teens are buying sex when convention suggests they can attract a woman in a nightclub.

Age difference is a problem with some interviewees who have teenage children: 'I have got two kids, one is eighteen and one is twenty and that age group has a different relationship to me now' (Rita, working premises). Those who did accept young men looked for other signs of their suitability as clients:

> I had a client come in here the other day and he was only young, and he looked like a little trouble maker with a little woolly hat on and I thought here we go. I got him in the room and his attitude wasn't my type of attitude, so I told him the price of the room and he gave me the money straight away. I dealt with him like that. He turned out to be OK but a lot of people would have looked at him and thought no way he is too young (Letisha, sauna).

Here, Letisha looked for positive signs of 'payment up front' to offset the negative sign of youth. This example highlights the fact that workers do not always apply universal rules but make individual judgements based on a calculation of negative and positive signs.

In contrast, middle-aged men are favoured because they are normally well behaved and request a straightforward service: 'The old ones, they respect you and it doesn't enter your head that they might do something' (Krystal, working premises). The trait that older men are less violent than younger men was important in the screening process and informed all aspects of how commercial sex is organized: 'When I advertise in the contact mags I do advertise for mature gentlemen cause I don't really want to see young men' (Kirsty, sauna). Dunhill (1989b: 205) also found that sex workers prefer clients who are older. Middle-aged men are considered gentle, generous and likely to return: 'The ones in their forties are the best because they are quite easy and they pay' (Sammy, sauna).

Re-identification

Just as Adler (1985: 103) found that drug smugglers preferred to do deals with associates who 'had proved their trustworthiness and reliability', in my study the strongest signal of genuineness was if a client was known as a 'regular'. 'Regulars are a lot safer as you get to know the customers and you get to trust them' (Amy, street). The definition of a regular varies: some define a regular as visiting several times a week, weekly, or whenever they are in Britain on business. What is clear is that regulars successfully complete several transactions:

> Most of them are regulars who have been coming here for the six years that this place has been open. This place is mainly for regulars and we do not get any passing trade which means that it is much safer than other places (Diane, sauna).

> It is safer with regulars because you can trust them ... When I see customers that I don't know, I won't do them, even if I am roasting and I am in pain because I ain't got no drugs and I am broke, then I will not do them. I would rather wait the extra twenty minutes for a regular customer (Annie, street).

One sauna explicitly encourages regulars by organizing a membership scheme with a loyalty card; after visiting ten times they receive a free service. Whittaker and Hart (1996: 408) suggest that regular clients are less dangerous because, to some extent, they are a known quantity.

Being known as a regular is a sign of re-identification. Observable traits trigger the re-identification game: the face or voice, a tattoo or car reminds the screener that this man has successfully (or unsuccessfully) completed transactions. This signal has a history dating back to when the man was unknown and subject to the initial screening test:

I always wanted to do escorting. I have just started. I have only done a few. I would only do it with regular clients from the sauna not with someone I didn't know. The clients that I have seen are regular clients I have known since the time I have been working – two, three years. So it is not someone who I would meet tomorrow. I wouldn't do it, I would feel so frightened and scared I wouldn't. I ask them to meet me outside the hotel so it looks like we are old friends. We are really, because we have known each other for a long time (Aliya, sauna).

Being a regular is a costly sign to fake. Impersonating a regular client is virtually impossible because of the physical and financial investments, yet it is an easy sign to display for a trustworthy client. Yet being known as a regular is not foolproof as regulars can change their motives over time and become opportunist attackers: 'I have had clients for years and years and years. But you can still get hurt by your regulars. They do say these murderers are normally someone you know' (Wilma, sauna). Petra recounts a bad experience with a regular:

We have had quite a few nasty experiences; one was in London when I was robbed by three men at gunpoint and knifepoint. That was a regular and he has been coming for six months. It did change how I worked as it makes you more on guard. I never expected a regular to hold a gun to my face.

Depending on the market, it is not only the sex worker who constructs screening strategies as there is often a chain of screening agents such as the receptionist or doorman, who uses visual screening before the client reaches the worker. The success of screening depends on the experience of the other agents and their competence in making decisive judgements.

Remote observation

TS: 'What do you look for when you go to the door'?
Neesha: 'What they have got in their hands, where the hands are, whether or not you can see their face on the camera, how many of them is there, what colour they are. No groups are allowed in as they are too dangerous' (Neesha, street but occasionally works indoors).

In the indoor markets, although face-to-face screening is the most prolific strategy, remote visual observations often happen at the same time. Prior to the client entering the building they are screened through peepholes or close-circuit television cameras (hereafter, CCTV) for other warning signs. For example, CCTV is used to observe who is at the door: 'Most of the girls are sensible enough to watch the cameras before they open the door' (Mary, sauna). Using this method, screeners look for very specific types of risks.

Groups

Sex workers normally refuse men who come to the door in groups. The number of men that constitute a group is defined in relation to the number of workers who are present at the time. The reason why groups of men are not accepted is because workers believe they should never be outnumbered: 'I personally would not let a group in. If I went to the door and saw a group of five young lads I would not let them in' (Seema, sauna). Using CCTV or peepholes, screeners try to observe how many people are standing behind the door, although this is tricky: 'One bloke will come to the door and you open it and then the rest barge in' (Sammy, sauna).

It is not unusual for a group of men to present themselves at saunas or arrange appointments for escorts to visit hotels. These situations are usually accompanied by boisterousness, peer pressure and a strong 'lad' culture of drinking and machismo:

> You get large groups of men booking in at a hotel and one of them can book an escort for the whole group and it is not until you get there that you see there are loads of men and just a couple of you and they are expecting a party. I have known women to hide in the toilets with the lights off to pretend they are not there. There are lots of tricks that they can play. The men do not realise that this is business and that you are doing this for the money (Rachel, sauna).

A common tactic for diffusing a group is to split them up, organize a queue or let them in two at a time: 'I have worked in places where if they come in a group you can let two in and the rest have to stay outside' (Belinda, sauna). The fourteen respondents who work alone refuse to entertain more than one man at a time. As with the majority of signs, screeners realise that it is relatively easy for impostors to present as trustworthy clients: 'You can look on the camera and if someone really wants to get in then they could . . . They will stand behind somebody or they will send someone to the door who looks like the kind of person that you are going to let in' (Mary, sauna).

Suspicious behaviour

Both doormen and sex workers consider young men and alcohol as risky features of the workplace (Monaghan 2003: 18). Interviewees report that

CCTV is particularly handy for checking if clients are under the influence of illegal substances: 'Sometimes you get suspicious about men who are acting strange and you think they are on drugs. Usually you can tell from the way they are acting. Then we will just pretend that we are all busy which saves any hassle' (Diane, sauna). Men who show signs of fidgeting, restlessness, strange facial expressions and agitation are suspected of drug use and therefore refused entry. Men who have spent the evening drinking in the city centre often proposition workers in saunas situated on the main entertainment strip. Visibly drunken men are refused because they are likely to become agitated and cause a commotion, especially when they cannot get an erection because of drinking too much.

Some respondents consider men carrying bags to be a liability. Although women accept that the bags could be full of shopping, items for work or clothes if men are travelling, bags are generally treated with suspicion. Women fear weapons or cameras could be hidden inside:

We are really suspicious of men who bring bags with them and if they don't tell me what they have got in the bag then I will ask if I can have a look inside and if they still say no then I will not let them in. At the end of the day it is my safety and the other girls around me it is their safety as well ... There are always clients who have got a grudge against working girls and there could be a bomb in a bag or anything (Sammy, sauna).

Some workers recognize that bags are suspicious but use other measures to reduce the threat of exposure or attack:

I look on the camera and if they have a bag I always want to look in and if they don't let me look in then I won't see them I am just really wary about men with bags – because I am thinking why are you bringing your bag if you have a car outside? (Dora, sauna).

If they have got bags I throw towels over them and I tell them why I am throwing towels over them. The 'News of the World' brings cameras in bags and you do not even know (Sarah, sauna).

Testing on the telephone

Traditionally women first come into contact with clients via the telephone. Even though the phone can filter out signs of untrustworthiness, interviewees explain how the voice can be revealing: 'Doing this business you do get to recognize a lot of voices as you are relying on the phone all the time' (Michelle, owner of escort agency). This section explains how workers in my study extract information from a short telephone conversation, which they use to assess whether the man is genuine.

Attitude

To leave the impression that they are trustworthy, callers must display a range of qualities in the initial telephone conversation. A straightforward approach (asking for an appointment without going into detail of the service required or the price) is considered a genuine request. Polite language and a respectful tone suggest the caller is safe enough to move onto the visual screening stage: 'You can normally tell by the manner of their voice on the phone what they are like. When you have been in business a long time you pick up on a lot of things. You check the things they ask you' (Anita, working premises). The terminology used by callers is scanned for signs of their attitude towards women who work in prostitution. Respectful, experienced clients refer to sex workers as 'ladies' or 'girls' and any ill-manners leads to immediate rejection: 'Their attitude is the first thing you look for. If they call me "whore" then you tell them to fuck off basically as you have to go on first impressions' (Julia, works from home).

Having observed maids, receptionists and workers answering calls during sixty-three visits to saunas and seventy-three visits to working premises, it became clear that there are unwritten rules regarding the information disclosed over the telephone. Sex workers are vigilant for callers who may be undercover police officers or council officials, so specific details of prices and services are not usually revealed. Genuine clients are expected to be aware of these norms and therefore not ask compromising questions. When callers do ask such details, the listener becomes suspicious. Indeed, if a caller asks for a service without using a condom then the normal response is to sharply finish the conversation. In this case the client is not necessarily untrustworthy but his preferences for unsafe sex is incompatible with the general code of conduct.

Checking consistency

Using other sources of information, indoor workers can check the identity of a client even if he is a stranger. This checking involves a triangle of telephone communication: the trustee (client) gives certain details to the truster (sex worker or agency) who then checks the information with a third party (hotel receptionist, directory enquiries, colleagues online). Amy worked on the street when I first met her but started escorting at the end of the fieldwork period. She learnt methods of checking from an experienced colleague: 'You check out if he is genuine when you phone back the hotel and ask for the room number and to confirm the customer's name.' Cleo had visited clients in their homes for over ten years and explained how verifying information is simple: 'Phone up directory enquiries, give the name and the address and if the phone number corresponds to the details then you know it is right, they are telling the truth and they can be traced.'

Sex workers constantly update their resources and use technology to prevent clients cheating. One escort posts advice to others on the message board: 'I now subscribe to a couple of search sites and if a client does not appear on the electoral role as well as the name, address and phone checking out, I would not take the booking to visit him there.' These reliable signals are examples of the costly to fake principle. Women believe that a bad customer would probably not go to the trouble of providing fake details (name, address, credit card number, landline telephone number) which could be verified with independent sources for the single purpose of tricking a sex worker into arriving at the house or hotel. If the information is correct, screeners take this as a reliable sign because only those who have a vested interest in future payoffs would disclose information that could be used against them.

Assessing on the Net

Observations of websites and message boards show that women who work from the Internet rely on face-to-face screening when they finally meet their client, but up until then rely on email and Internet sources as the main method of screening. Five respondents worked exclusively from the Internet, while a further eleven advertised through websites. Women analysed the language, style of writing and attitude expressed through an email to assess whether a client should be seen face-to-face.

Compliance

Escorts test a client's honesty by the level of cooperation displayed in their email messages and later, over the telephone. Lowman (2000: 995) describes how 'the structure of the escort trade is such that the clients often have to identify themselves in the course of conducting business leaving evidence of their identity'. If a client refuses to provide certain details before the meeting, or shows behaviour that is not tolerated, the possibility of an appointment is terminated. Men who request a meeting yet are not willing to part with sensitive information are immediately seen as a 'bad type' because clients who are genuine offer the required details. Emails that include explicit descriptions of sexual fantasies and unsafe practices are automatically rejected: 'Some are time wasters asking for oral without and stupid business. I just don't reply' (Leigh, working premises). Esther, a successful escort, sheds light on the email screening criteria:

> Of the emails that I get there are fifty percent that I automatically bin because you can tell a lot by the way someone phrases an email. If someone goes into too much detail in the first email or some of them you can tell it is kids messing about on their dad's computer. You become a good judge from the way they phrase their emails as to whether it is the type of customer that you want. Some are too young or will go into really graphic detail. It allows you to be a lot more picky. You have got to have the confidence to be able to sit there and think well I would rather lose the money than see this person.

As part of the screening process, the worker carefully plans when to reveal her address (after all, this could be her home). To limit the number of people who are aware of the address from which she works and to ensure that the client intends to visit, he must pass a compliance test. Clients are told to make their way to a certain landmark, road, or phone box and make a final call before the address is given:

> I don't give my address out to everyone. I would rather know that they are on a nearby road and then you know they are genuine. I always say to them when you get to a landmark give me a call and I will tell them where to come. I don't give a lot out on the phone (Laura, working premises).

> I never give out my address. I always tell them to phone me when they are in the area and then when they get to a certain place they can ring me up and make an appointment and they are normally here within the next five minutes (Margaret, working premises).

Although this does not determine whether the client will honour the contract, sex workers calculate that if the client arrives in the geographical area, this at least shows he is not a time-waster.

Reputation

Denton and O'Malley (1999: 520) note that 'a good reputation is equivalent to a stack of character references in the illicit economy'. Establishing a reputation is a central feature of trust-building in the client–sex worker relationship. Assessing a client's reputation and identity via websites and message boards is an important screening strategy for Internet-based workers. Screeners gather information by reading 'field reports' written by the client about his previous commercial sexual encounters (Sharp and Earle 2003). The five participants who exclusively used email explained how they value these reports as reliable signs because they reveal the probable safety of a client, whether they are known to colleagues and their preferred sexual acts. Sex workers believe field reports are too costly for a mimic; successfully completing a sexual transaction, registering and posting a field report on a popular website would be costly (on average £150 an hour). Also the website that hosts the field reports encourages the sex worker to write comments, which lessens the chance of false information.

In the day-to-day operations of an escort agency Michelle responds to workers' queries online: 'I can verify some clients. A lot of clients will say that you can check me out with Michelle – she knows me. I don't really know them from Adam but I know that they are OK with the girls. The girls can use that as backup.' Sex workers who are entrepreneurial in their approach to the business create thorough and complex systems to check, monitor and record customers. One respondent explained how she uses a 'client action plan' to troubleshoot emails that are problematic. When a certain type of behaviour is displayed in an email, for example, not committing to an appointment, the client will receive a standard predetermined response. This worker holds an active "banned list" and all names, email addresses and telephone numbers, along with any identifying details are recorded, filed and consulted each time a new client makes contact. Checking the genuineness of a client is facilitated by the asynchronous nature of the Internet enabling sex workers across the globe to communicate on such issues of safety. One respondent recently emailed me to explain how a sex worker from the USA had contacted her after a client had given her name as a referee. The reciprocal exchange of information, facilitated by the Internet, is now a feature in the management of commercial sex at a global level.

Screening for safety

Sex workers take measured decisions about which clients to accept or reject and do not always make random selections. Certain traits act as reliable signs that only a genuine client will display. Not all behaviour becomes a signal; behaviour needs to be costly to display – more costly for good types to display than for bad types. Sex workers compile a range of different sorts of information in order to build a mental map of which men are more or less likely to honour the contract. Theories of behaviour as well as assumptions of dangerous places and faces inform the screening process. These processes that create perceptions of who is safe and who is not are evident in women's general understandings of the likelihood of being a victim of crime: 'A common approach used by many women to combat and manage their fear of crime is to engage in a process of cognitive mapping. This involves women determining who and where the perceived threats to their physical safety are located' (Chan and Rigakos 2002: 754). Emotional responses, experiences and preferences determine who is considered genuine and feeds in to the 'validated knowledge' (Offe 1999: 47) that people use to make decisions about who to trust.

What is not explored here is the role of the client in the screening process and the wider regulatory mechanisms of the commercial sex exchange. As highlighted in the extract from my fieldwork diary at the beginning of this chapter, customers, particularly those who may obviously display distrusting signs, are aware of the screening process. Within the context of illicit sexual behaviour, the moral economy of obligation underpins the commercial transaction. Trust is built on moral obligations that propel the client to conform, while repeated transactions with the same client leads the sex worker to rely on 'experiential trust' that becomes a self-stabilizing expectation. This interactional process relies not only on the sex worker observing behaviour over time but also that the client consistently perceives the obligation to honour the contract. Yet how the client comes to know the 'rules of the game', the extent to which their behaviour is determined by these expectations, or whether they carry out their own screening strategies, remains unclear.

What is known is that screeners also have to contend with mimics who trick workers by displaying signs that appear genuine. To guard against mimics sex workers do not accept only one positive sign as proof of genuineness. Zahavi and Zahavi (1997: 32) note that a combination of signals can be used to communicate information and judge behaviour. With reference to the courtship rituals of birds, they state 'the female can [then] use several criteria to assess the male'. As there is no definitive sign of genuineness in the prostitution trust game, sex workers must look for a range of behaviour that conveys reliable, costly signs. Only then is a client accepted and invited to negotiate business. Some workers have the luxury of taking only very positive signals, which contributes to why they rarely make mistakes or experience harm. Other environments are more precarious, providing the perfect conditions for mimics to fake signs. For some sex workers who have not learnt that there are signs separating good customers from bad, or simply decide not to observe and evaluate signs, other mechanisms are used to manage risks. The next chapter describes how some sex workers also rely on precautions, deterrents and remedial protection to apprehend danger.

Chapter 5

Keeping safe

> Women actively manage 'crime' through our strategies of safekeeping, and these strategies and the discourse about them are overwhelmingly dominated by women's acknowledgement of the potential for men's violence . . . Risk is not about modernity and the ontological insecurity people experience. For women it is about misogyny and the continued perpetuation of women's oppression through fear of crime and blame for their situation. (Stanko 1997: 488/492)

Alongside the traditional emphasis on health risks and drug use, violence has received considerable attention in the recent expansion of research on prostitution. Now there is an accumulated literature that records the extent and nature of violence towards a group of women who are sexual minorities because of their commercial activities. The introductory section of this chapter outlines the recent literature drawing attention to the different levels of violence across the markets. The findings from my study are used to argue that despite high levels of violence, sex workers are not passive recipients of male aggression in the workplace but actively address the risk of violence. Reflecting on ethnographic and interview data, I argue that rational responses are strategically created at an individual and organizational level to manage the risk of violence in the form of precautions, deterrents and remedial protection strategies. Resisting violence is described as a defining feature of the social organization of prostitution that affects the manner in which markets are informally regulated and experienced for both providers and purchasers of commercial sex.

The normalization of violence

The high prevalence of violence against women who work in prostitution is reported widely.[1] Along with taxi drivers and police officers, prostitution is one of the most dangerous professions (Lowman 2000: 987). Despite the growing evidence, Barnard *et al.* (2002) state that 'the lack of systematic data on the prevalence, nature and extent of violence against prostitutes in the UK perpetuates the general invisibility of this problem, which in turn hampers the likelihood of effective institutional and social responses to client violence'. These researchers undertook a large survey of sex workers across three British cities (Leeds, Glasgow and Edinburgh) to establish the prevalence of violence. Of the 240 women surveyed, 63% (151) had experienced client violence in their lifetime and 37% (89) had experienced violence in the last six months. Church *et al.* (2001) report, from the same survey, significant differences between markets: 81% (93) of street workers had experienced violence from clients, compared to 48% (60) who worked indoors. This study is one of the latest to document violence against street workers in Britain.[2] Benson (1998) found 98% (49) of street prostitutes experienced some form of violence at work, while Kinnell (1991) reported that seventy-five interviewees experienced 211 violent incidents during their careers. Many women in prostitution have a catalogue of violence, robbery and rape experiences (see O'Neill 2001: 90–3; and Phoenix 1999a, for accounts).

Although many of the violent incidents are from customers, perpetrators are often boyfriend-pimps (May *et al.* 2000: 18; Norton-Hawk 2004; Williamson and Cluse-Tolar 2002), drug dealers and passers-by. The targeting of sex workers as a sexual minority group has a significant impact on morbidity. Without police records, Kinnell (2004) still identified that seventy-three sex workers had been murdered between January 1990 and December 2002. In Britain, sex workers are twelve times more likely to die from violence than other women of a similar age (Ward *et al.* 1999) while in the USA, data from a cohort of 1,969 women over a thirty-year period demonstrated that 'active prostitutes were almost eighteen times more likely to be murdered than women of a similar age and race' (Potterat *et al.* 2004: 782).

In my research, sixteen of the fifty interviewees who were sex providers reported violent encounters from clients. Fourteen women had been physically beaten; seven women had been sexually assaulted or raped; five women had been robbed at knifepoint; three women had been robbed at gunpoint; three others had been confined against their will; and another two had been drugged. In their own words, the stories were terrifying: 'I have been raped out on the street, kidnapped . . . you name it' (Neesha, street but occasionally works indoors). 'I got robbed twice ... they hit me over the back with a metal bar ... first I got threatened by two guys with knives, then they come back again ... with a gun' (Kirsty, sauna). 'When I was just under eighteen, this guy kidnapped me, a big massive bastard he was. I was trapped in this house for two days' (Beryl, working premises). Although all of those who had been victims now worked inside, at least half of these attacks took place when they were working on the street. It is likely that the experience of violence among the interviewees is much higher but respondents did not disclose their experiences because of embarrassment or fear of being considered an amateur or unskilled in dealing with violence. The fact that sixteen women reported multiple episodes of violence suggests that there is a significant likelihood of experiencing violence in the sex industry.

Lowman (2000) theorizes the different types of violence against women in the sex industry and makes a distinction between situational and predatory violence. Situational violence occurs during a dispute in the transaction and as a resolution the client resorts to violence. Women retold stories of how clients had turned aggressive over disagreements about the quality or type of service or the financial agreement. This type of attack is not premeditated but as Lowman argues, this behaviour is presupposed by a belief that women should be controlled by physical mastery. In contrast, predatory violence is premeditated and has a specific motivation such as revenge, expression of hatred or monetary gain. The violent incidents that happened in saunas as a result of robberies were often premeditated rather than opportunistic. A pattern was noticeable whereby a client would previously purchase a service without hindrance, then return, usually with accomplices, armed with guns or knives: 'I was robbed by three men at gun point and knife point. That was a regular and he had been coming for six months but this time he brought a friend along and we had no idea' (Petra, working premises). Premeditated physical and sexual attacks occur when men maliciously target women who sell sex with the intention of serious harm. The screening strategies described in the previous chapter highlight that although women are clued up on the types of men who may break the contract, premeditated violence is difficult to detect, and therefore poses a greater threat.

Thirty-four respondents, all of whom worked in the indoor markets, had never encountered harm through prostitution. Nevertheless, even those who remained free from work-related violence gained knowledge of the risks and took appropriate safety measures. The influence of the risk of violence on the organization of the workplace has been recorded in mainstream occupations: research on the sociology of policing in the USA (Manning 1977) and Britain (Holdaway 1983) establishes that officers are routinely open to danger. Brewer (1990: 658) notes from his study of the Royal Ulster Constabulary (RUC) in Northern Ireland that all officers do not equally experience the threat of violence but that paramilitary threats depend on the geographical area of different forces. Just as the danger posed to RUC members is not of equal proportion, sex workers are not at equal risk of violence because the likelihood is different for each market (Pyett and Warr 1997: 544; Raphael and Shapiro 2004).

It is the unpredictability of danger that causes great anxiety and influences how women organize and conduct business across all markets. Again, there are parallels between prostitution and the police force: 'it is not the reality of daily violence with which they [RUC officers] have to contend but that of dealing on a daily basis with the knowledge that there is a faint possibility of encountering violence' (Brewer 1990: 659). The threat of violence has 'the same uncertain, on-going yet distant quality' that it could happen at any time, but often doesn't (Brewer 1990: 659). An evaluation of the potential dangers enables sex workers, as do the RUC officers, to 'render the threat manageable' (Brewer 1990: 659). However, both police officers and sex workers are well aware that should the event happen the severity of the occurrence would be such that survival skills are necessary. What this chapter contributes to the knowledge of violence and protection in prostitution is that sex workers respond to potential harm in three different ways: precautions, deterrents and remedial protection.

Precautions: behind the scenes

All of the interviewees use precautionary measures as the first stage of risk management before face-to-face meetings, taking telephone calls, emails or walking the street. O'Connell Davidson (1998: 64) notes 'women who have never been attacked often attribute this fact to their routine enactment of certain precautions, while women who have been attacked blame themselves retrospectively for having deviated from their own self-imposed safety procedures'. Precautions are not necessarily separate from deterrents or remedial protection, and change as women acquire more knowledge and adapt their working style as a result of mistakes. An important feature of precautions is that such measures are often not conscious but just part of how women learn to be successful and stay out of harm. Amy had worked in various markets for twenty years and did not screen clients but accepted all men that stopped her. She relied on her experience to escape danger: 'I have had ten incidents in all the time that I have worked since twenty-one, and I have managed to escape from every one. I suppose it is just luck really'. By examining

Amy's working practices it became clear that to prevent business transactions going wrong she practised a set of precautions and her track record was not down to chance. These strategies were evident in other women's repertoires.

General working rules

Working practices that guard against violence and robbery can be found across all markets and form part of a common code of practice identifiable among the sex work community. Steadfast rules guard against robbery such as always taking the money before providing the service, hiding it or stashing it with a third party: 'I let them in, take the money off them, tell them to get undressed. I go out of the room, get my condom and put my money away and come back in the room and do 'em' (Tracy, working premises). Indoors the 'pay first, service after' was obligatory unless the client was very familiar.

The sexual encounter is considered to be the most dangerous point of the transaction and therefore there are 'social norms governing the expected frequency of intercourse and the variety of approved sexual acts' (Heyl 1979: 202). Thirty interviewees explained that sexual positions were chosen with care to prevent the client using their physical strength or gaining psychological mastery over the situation. A sexual position where the client is on top of the woman is unsatisfactory for the safety-conscious worker: 'I always get on top because I feel safer' (Tracy, working premises). Leanne and Krystal explain how their sexual practices are designed to prevent an attack:

I never let clients on top of me. Most girls they think it is easier to let them be on top but no way, they could do anything. When you are on top you know that you have got their arms and legs, you can lean down and head butt them or bite them. You get some that get on top of you and try and smother you. I always make sure that my own arm is by my throat so at least I know I can use my other arm to force him off me. And you can always kick them in the bollocks anyway. You have to try and get them in the position you want (Leanne, working premises).

When you walk through that door you are in control, not them. I do not do any position that I do not want to do, in fact they don't even get the choice because I will say; "Right, lets start with a bit of doggy then", or I'll get on top. I have done all sorts but I don't do the missionary position' (Krystal, working premises).

Proactive tactics to reduce the likelihood of harm become ingrained and an implicit 'routine activity' of the job (Hart and Barnard 2003). Guided by safety, sex workers decide what items of clothing to remove. None of the street workers contacted during the fieldwork reported taking off all of their clothes often because they have to run from a dangerous client, the police or their boyfriend/pimp and being half-dressed impedes their getaway. Just as doormen remove earrings (Monaghan 2003: 17), jewellery such as long chains are usually not worn at work, as they can be used to strangle or tempt an opportunist thief. Not a kinky fetish but a strict safety precaution, eighteen interviewees said that during sex they never take off their footwear: 'I always keep my boots on. I never work without my boots because I know I can kick, so there are little things I have to keep on so I know I am safe (Leanne, working premises). These ordinary features of the sexual negotiation demonstrate the level at which sex workers respond to the potential risks in the trade and through 'methodologies of control' (Manning 1977: 103) dominate the work space.

Physical precautions are complemented by psychological strategies to prevent clients acting aggressively. Workers displayed a constant jovial and friendly manner with clients, which was more than a customer-relations exercise but a precautionary tactic to prevent hostility and aggression. An example of what O'Neill and Barbaret (2000: 133) call 'gentling', Leigh described how the client is often nervous or embarrassed, which can sometimes manifest in hostility. To defuse these emotions, Leigh started her routine with a joke or funny anecdote to ease the tension and make the client laugh (see Sanders 2004a). Equally, conversations with clients are carefully selected:

> You have got to use your own mind to turn it around and be super nice. You maybe having a shitty day and you get to a point when you could easily snap at a client. The one thing I try not to do is to insult someone sexually and demean them. It is irresponsible as you are leaving them in a position where they could attack you or another woman ... I try and make a man feel good about what he has got or I try and find a nice feature – his legs or his feet (Sarah, sauna).

The importance of verbal skills in potentially violent situations is also reported by Hobbs et al. (2003: 139–41). They describe how some doormen consider themselves talkers rather than hitters and take the 'sensible negotiated democratic option'. Sex workers in my sample learned to communicate with clients strategically and negotiate clients' emotions, moods and body language as part of the preventative repertoire.

Women who visit men in hotels and houses adopt specific precautions to prevent a violent incident occurring, or when it does, to make sure they have support. Escorts usually only visit upmarket hotels on the understanding that the chances of being harmed are limited in hotels that have their own security and charge high rates for rooms. Geographical areas that are known to be risky are also avoided: 'None of the girls are allowed to go to the estate as it is where the druggies get housed so it is a no go area for working girls' (Michelle, owner of Internet-based escort agency).

Safety in numbers

The majority of respondents favoured collective work environments rather than working alone:

> I do work on my own but I share the actual house with someone else who works, but we both do our own thing and both have our separate telephone lines. We just really share it for a safety aspect and of course to share the costs (Margaret, working premises).

Sex workers often changed markets to increase safety and considered teamwork as an assurance against risk. For instance, thirty interviewees began prostitution by working alone as escorts and only eleven of them remained in this market:

> I used to do some escorting to begin with . . . it is dangerous, the most dangerous type of work compared to here [sauna]. Here you are in an environment where there are other people around you and you can say no if you do not want to see someone. Only once did I have a bad experience and that was when I was escorting. It was one of the reasons why I stopped escorting and came to work here. I went to a hotel room to see a man whom I had seen a fair few times before. When I got into the hotel room he locked me in . . . I just talked and talked my way out of the situation. I left after that and never went back to the agency (Eleanor, sauna).

At this stage in her prostitution career Eleanor prioritized secrecy over security, which meant that she was vulnerable when visiting men alone. Although women are often alone with the client while performing the service, thirty-eight of the fifty sex workers said they would never work in an apartment or house alone as the level of vulnerability is vastly increased:

> Astrid: Working inside is much safer. For a start, you always work in two's, you stick to your golden rules like we always have some one sit with us.

Krystal: We never work on our own. I have done it but that is only with old old clients that you have had for years . . . They know that there is always someone in here.

Astrid: Like she popped out and I said that she was in the other room, and I made this story to make sure they always know there is two of us here.

Like the majority of others workers, Astrid and Krystal insist that because they see several strangers a day, precautionary measures are paramount to staying alive. Astrid clarified this when I asked why she told potential clients on the telephone that she was the maid. Astrid explained that most indoor establishments use this precaution to give the impression that there are several people present. Those who opt to work without colleagues usually have another trusted party nearby. Explaining her security measures when she visits hotels, Dora said: 'My friend actually came up to the room with me, and I told him that my friend was there and he didn't mind.' Trustworthy clients are sometimes used as chaperons and, as Wilma suggests, this can be in return for cheap services: 'I used to work on my own but Fred has sat with me. He is like a friend but we met him as a client. He takes the rubbish, gets the lunch and does whatever he can. We give him really cheap doubles.'

Saunas provide a team environment where protection can be easily mobilized:

In the sauna you have got advantages in that you have got other girls so you are protected. You have got the back up in that you can refuse a client. If you are in a working flat and the client comes to the door you can't say that all the girls are busy or that you can't do them – go away. It [a sauna] is safer than a flat (Sarah, sauna).

Similar to a 'look-out' on the street, if the worker has not emerged within the allotted time, the receptionist or colleagues checks on the situation: 'The girls generally look after each other. If you looked at the clock and you knew the girl had been in there for some time you check . . . you knock the door' (Annabelle, sauna). Also as a safety precaution, sex workers offer a 'double' service so they can physically work together (Brewis and Linstead 2000a: 282). When women are new to prostitution, working together is a safe option as well as an opportunity to learn skills:

Leigh: We work together as it is much safer and I would never work alone.

Angela: I have only worked on my own for short spaces of time and I would not do it again. There was always someone in the house when I worked. There was someone who worked downstairs as well and when I was on my own I would have the cleaner come up and sit with me. You are so much safer in numbers.

Working together appears to be ubiquitously important as a deterrent and a protection strategy. The combined threat of violence and the legal position of prostitution forces sex workers to rely on each other. There is a natural emergence of tight-knit working relations and an occupational culture based on the anxiety of threat magnified by the exclusion from formal protection.

Deterrents: calling their bluff

As an alternative to or alongside a comprehensive assessment of the client, the worker can rely on discovering whether a client is sensitive to deterrents and the fear of recrimination. Deterrents are a different kind of protective strategy as they rely on the client observing the worker and establishment. This set of strategies is unique because women try to persuade the client that the costs of breaking the contract outweigh the benefits. The sex worker must indicate the disadvantages to the customer if he should break the contract, and, for the deterrent to be effective, the customer must also be sensitive to repercussions. Due to the nature of prostitution, sex workers inevitably engage in transactions with some dangerous men, so deterrents suggest to an untrustworthy or opportunistic client why it would be unwise to act.

Pimps: relying on reputation

Whether such an individual exists or not, the most frequently used deterrent is the threat of repercussions from a pimp or boyfriend (also see Epele 2001: 168; Phoenix 2000: 27). Ten respondents said that if a customer turns aggressive he might be persuaded not to act violently because of the fear of the consequences. Astrid refuses African-Caribbean men when they come to the door. When the client questions why, she replies: 'I say, well my big black pimp is sitting across the room with me and he won't allow it.' This is not the case, but it prevents the client taking his grievance further. Neesha has learned that using the threat of a boyfriend lurking around the corner normally works even though in reality she has no such protector:

I tell them that I have got a man who watches me and he will take the registration number and he knows where I take the punters. I tell them that if I am not back within a certain amount of time then he is coming looking for you and he will beat you and he will phone the police. I put fear into them from the beginning so they know what they are up against.

Women who were very unlikely to be in a pimping relationship often relied on the fabricated threat of a boyfriend-pimp to warn off customers. Neesha explained that because she had been pimped before she could use this local knowledge and status to prevent others manipulating her:

Two girls tried to get me robbed by this bloke [a local pimp], thinking that I was this new girl on the beat. Once he followed me up the road and questioned me but I told him I know who you are and you are a pimp. He was asking who I knew and I told him, that I know names and I remember reg numbers. I told him I have been out here for years. They try and take you over if they think you are new.

In prostitution there is a long history of an informal system of 'street justice' to punish male clients who have broken contracts, which may account for why this deterrent is a popular strategy.

Drivers, doormen and receptionists

As both precaution and deterrent it was commonplace for third parties to accompany an escort: 'You never go on an escort unless you have an escort yourself' (Krystal, working premises). Katrina expands:

If you have a driver they will knock the door and introduce you to the client. They will show them that you are not on your own and that you are with a bloke and he is not moving until you come out. You can check that everything is OK and that there are not ten mates hiding upstairs. Then you go outside to the car and tell them that it is safe and when you are due out and if not then they should come and knock the door. We always tell them on the phone that we are bringing someone else.

Respondents said that drivers have previously been employed as taxi drivers, policemen, professional or amateur boxers, bouncers in night-clubs, or soldiers. Natasha and Suzanne operate independent businesses with their long-term romantic partners who act as a chaperon:

With outcalls people will arrange to see me at their chosen location and Ben [partner] will drop me off and I will give him a call when I have finished and he will come and collect me ... My partner is outside watching when every client arrives and I call him to tell him everything is OK (Natasha, working premises).

My husband used to drive me to them [houses] to make sure I would come out in an hour. He used to sit and he would wait and see the person's face ... If it was a house then he would wait and see what house I went to and wait there ten minutes to see if I was coming out then he would come back in an hour (Suzanne, escort).

Although it was not evident in the markets I observed, workers recalled how establishments in London and other major cities employ doormen to check clients entering the building. Doormen who work at the entrance to saunas, brothels and working flats act in a similar role to bouncers in a nightclub (see Hobbs *et al.* 2003). They survey the men that come to the door, refuse entry to those who look suspicious and evict rowdy revellers:

I had been there six months and I got to know the bosses really well and I said I have got a very good friend he drives girls round for a living. All the girls here had decided to give him a £10 each out of their money and he would sit with us until five o'clock (am) and because of me we were the first place to have security. He used to come in and he used to help with a few little mishaps (Astrid, working premises).

Skills in assessing situations, and presenting an intimidating physical presence are essential attributes for doormen (Winlow *et al.* 2001). Doormen are recruited informally, often because of their aggressive reputation and connections to drug dealing, pimping and other organized crime. However, not all of the protection mechanisms are sophisticated. Kirsty sometimes arranges for clients to visit her at home and described her security as trained for attack: 'I am very safe at home as I have a big Rottweiler to look after me.'

Hired security is invariably male, whereas the role of maid, receptionist or manager is a female occupation. Seven of the eight saunas I visited employed a female receptionist or manager, while a quarter of working premises employed maids. The maid is an important safety measure: 'Protection comes from the maid. It is always good to have a maid rather than work on your own as you have someone there if something happens. When they come to the door they see straight away that there is two of you' (Aliya, sauna). Beryl, who worked from the Amsterdam-style windows during the 1990s in the Balsall Heath area of Birmingham, now works from rented premises with a maid. She explains how the maid should be streetwise with knowledge of self-defence:

Maids are important. They are there for safety. You had to have a maid who knows what she is doing and how to kick blokes out. We always let them know that she is the maid so they know there is always going to be two people. In a flat with two people less trouble is likely to happen as they know that one can call the police.

The maid acts as a deterrent by demonstrating to the client that the worker is not alone, as well as reacting when a situation becomes difficult. Beryl recruits maids who are capable and experienced at dealing with aggression, as well as being physically intimidating. Her current maid previously worked as a bouncer in a nightclub and is experienced in dealing with aggressive behaviour.

Monitoring the mundane

Owners of establishments and sex workers employ various strategies to monitor the client. In the indoor markets safety dictates the physical organization of the building. Saunas are protected by fences, gates, locks, chains and see-through windows to improve the security (Campbell 1991: 1371). Seven of the eight saunas I visited had been structurally altered to improve security. Two saunas were designed so visitors were locked in and could only leave when an employee unlocked several doors. In one sauna, visitors were vetted inside an iron cage before they were allowed access: 'It is very rare that anything happens in here as the cage after the door puts them off. Once they are let in here the door is padlocked and they are not getting out. Sometimes they wonder what it is all for' (Sammy, sauna). Inside the licensed sauna the physical environment is constructed so that the client can be surveyed while he is in the building. Clients are only allowed in certain spaces, namely the communal lounge and the bedrooms. There are usually rooms that are strictly 'women only' spaces so that the men are contained in areas where a receptionist or manager can monitor their behaviour. Often in the communal areas close-circuit television cameras (CCTV) are installed to watch and record the visitors.

Covert monitoring of the meeting between a client and a worker take place in different forms. If an escort visits a hotel, client's home or a client visits her home, a popular procedure consists of 'checking in' with a friend or arranging for friends to call at a set time: 'I always tell my best friend where I am and to ring me within twenty minutes of me getting there' (Anita, working premises). Covert monitoring systems use secret codes or passwords to indicate that the transaction is not going smoothly and that assistance is needed: 'When Billy [husband] calls we pretend he is asking me what I want for tea. If I say sausage and beans he knows I'm in trouble' (Tracy, working premises). Other times sex workers use overt methods of logging the meeting with a third party by making a call in front of the client and passing on details of where the meeting is taking place, the expected length of the meeting and if available the client's name or car registration number. This acts as a deterrent as the client is aware that a third party, who could be nearby, is privy to the liaison.

Sex workers in all markets improve their safety by using CCTV. Cameras were installed in all eight saunas included in this study to dissuade untrustworthy clients and opportunists. Those who rented premises from modern apartment blocks already had the use of cameras on the entrance door. Polly and her maid made the monitoring process obvious: 'We let them know if we are a bit dubious when they come in by saying "Oh, you didn't look like that on camera", so they know they are being monitored.' Despite using technology as a deterrent, interviewees said that cameras did not always discourage trouble and that some individuals with criminal intentions could not be prevented from acting dangerously.

On the street, women also use deterrents that take advantage of technology. Annie explains how she chooses the location for administering a sexual service with care and she will only take clients to public areas where CCTV is in operation:

> I always take them to places where there are cameras. I don't normally point them out unless they are going to start to be funny then I will say to them that there are cameras out there and it is all being filmed and if they don't want business then to drop me off. I normally take them to the hospital, as it is all camera-ed there.

In Sheffield, CCTV was installed in a 'red-light district' as a community safety initiative to discourage street prostitution but instead the extra lighting and cameras encouraged women to use the location to advertise and negotiate with clients because the safety measures were considered a deterrent to potential attackers (Hopkins 1999). The use of CCTV as a community safety strategy has been well documented in the literature (Bannister *et al.* 1998; Norris *et al.* 1998), especially to deter 'antisocial behaviour'. The use of CCTV by sex workers highlights the contested nature of community safety initiatives. In the absence of formal protection from the police despite high levels of vulnerability, sex workers adapt the security resources originally provided to discourage their behaviour. Unintentionally, what is considered by law-enforcement agencies to be an effective tool for surveying communities and reducing unwanted behaviour, CCTV actually facilitates illegal sexual behaviour. This is an example of the resourcefulness of sex workers who manipulate the physical environment to keep themselves safe while they remain outside the realms of legitimate protection (see Hubbard and Sanders 2003).

Assertiveness, aggression and attitude

The thirty-four sex workers who had never been attacked or robbed attributed their violence-free working experience to their assertiveness: 'We didn't have any trouble at all. The clients couldn't do anything because the girls were very strong-minded. Nothing happened in that sauna because the girls were always much more stronger than the clients' (Aliya, sauna). The constant threat of violence has made the reflexive personality an important skill if a sex worker is to avoid trouble. In the same way that sex workers diffuse potential hostility by presenting a "self" which manufactures care' (O'Neill and Barbaret 2000: 133), they also use an aggressive personality as a deterrent. Controlling the initial interactions requires a display of behaviour that can appear somewhat brutal. O'Connell Davidson (1998: 95–6) notes how sex workers are 'imposing women' who can intimidate a man into honouring the financial contract:

I go in the room and I am scary and make them frightened. I am nice at the door but as soon as I get them in the room I turn on them. I look directly at them and ask them what they want. They often say full service because they are frightened of saying anything else. When all the money is sorted out I start being nice, but I am cold to begin with (Leanne, working premises).

I take a deep breath and walk in, I have a strong personality. Even though I am nervous I try not to show that I am nervous, as then you are not in control. I am really confident. I just give them instructions and tell them what to do (Dora, sauna).

It is not only in a face-to-face context that assertiveness is a deterrent. Anita explains her telephone response to new callers: 'I always say I am well built, six foot and older. That puts a lot of men off and if they are a bit psycho then they think that I might be a woman who can handle herself.' This display is reminiscent of Goffman's (1959: 13) concept of the 'front' (manner, appearance, facial expressions, bodily gestures, posture and speech) as part of an individual performance. Sex workers adopt expressive equipment in the form of assertive personalities and brave, often boastful statements, express a fighting resilience: 'If someone comes in here giving me grief they are going to get grief back, simple as that. It is either him or me and it ain't going to be me' (Letisha, sauna). Maher (2000: 95) notes that on the street, sex workers presented themselves as 'bad' or 'crazy' as a survival strategy in a volatile world, while Hart and Barnard (2003: 36) describe how an 'active display of confidence' is a strategy of control. Combining assertiveness with self-assurance diffuses situations and redresses the inherent power dynamics in the client–sex worker relationship. Sarah explains how she used her strong character to prevent a client breaking the contract:

> I always have a plan and think about scenarios that could happen. It would be me or them and I would have no problem thinking about the consequences. A man came in here and turned quite nasty and he wasn't going to pay me. I simply told him that he must pay me as we had a business transaction and if he does not pay me then I would throw him out of the window. I wasn't being dramatic, I meant it. I really meant it. I was quite capable of damaging him and I would have had no hesitation. He paid me.

The 'skills talk' sex workers display centres on their expertise in screening clients, specialist knowledge relating to the market and vigilance skills to outwit the customer. Anecdotes like the one below from Leanne were plentiful during the fieldwork; they had a familiar content that reported how quick-thinking reactions diffused a potentially violent situation:

> There was some trouble once when six guys came to the door. I wouldn't let them in and I was giving them a load of grief at the door. I was trying to get into their mentality. They would be sarcastic about working girls being dirty and I said no it's your mother who is dirty. And they have gone you are all right you are, and I said 'have you got any draw [cannabis] or what' and I thought get onto their level because I bet that is what they are into – smoking drugs. And they were like 'yeah yeah we'll bring you some' and they went. By talking to them on their level, you have got to get into what they are thinking. If you had said move away from the door I am calling the police it would have made things worse.

Sex workers have to react in unexpected situations that could result in their losing out. When Petra became involved with an antagonistic client, rather than react aggressively she decided to debilitate the client to regain the upper hand:

> I was in the sauna one night and this bloke was drunk and you know when they are drunk they want to go on forever. I said no your time is up now. He got very abusive so I picked up his clothes and threw them out of the window. Well he couldn't do nothing and

he begged me to fetch them – but only after he had given me all his money in his wallet.

Sex workers implicitly pass on skills by engaging in this form of talk with each other to illustrate that they are in control and possess the attitude and fighting skills to protect themselves. The dominant ideology that claims that women are passive during sexual negotiations is considered a risk in sex work, so to compensate bravado and assertiveness are implicit in the routine.

Protection: if all else fails

Remedial protection is the final stage in managing the risk of violence. Sex workers rely on skills and techniques to protect themselves when a client attacks. For women who choose not to screen their customers or who are constrained by their working environment, remedial protection is the only option.

Doing violence

Sex workers engage in a range of tactics, behaviours and attitudes to display their 'bodily capital' (Wacquant 1995) and 'competent working bodies' (Monaghan 2003: 18). Carrying weapons was popular across the markets and is an example of how a strategy can be a precaution (in case of an attack), a deterrent (if shown to the client) and protection (self-defence): 'I always carry a blade with me just in case' (Cleo, works from home). Sauna workers reported using kitchen utensils, baseball bats, lighters and bleach in self-defence. Denton and O'Malley (1999: 528) note that there is limited literature on women 'perpetuating violence as a business strategy' because there is an assumption that women are the victims of violence. From their study of female crack dealers, Denton and O'Malley explain how women also act violently, rely on reputations of criminal families and know how to protect themselves or contract out a debt of violence. Likewise, Astrid, Beryl and Leanne are not afraid to use brute force against any violent client:

> We have CS gas here and everything and I wouldn't be afraid to use it. We have an alert buzzer and in the bedroom we have a pickaxe handle. And if I had my way I would kill someone if I had the chance (Astrid, working premises).

> This guy he has pulled my hair and I have gone and head butted him right there and then. I would have killed him, I would have. If

I could get away with sticking a knife around my boot I probably would, but I would end up going to prison I know what I am like. I have been to prison before. I am not going to prison again. Well I have done Thai boxing for years, I can fight so I know I have always been able to look after myself (Leanne, working premises).

You have got to put up a fight. I mean I have had a gun at my head and the knife and been strangled before I came in the flats. I remember this one guy he parked his car and he came straight for my neck and he was strangling me. Later when I saw this guy do it to another girl I was out there kicking the car and smashing the window. And when this guy got another girl I knew where he was taking her so we jumped in the car with a couple of us and we had the bastard. He was getting it (Beryl, working premises).

Knowing how to fight and escape from a situation are survival skills that sex workers learn through their working experiences as well as other life experiences. Anita says 'I was dragged up not brought up and I know how to look after me'; while other women revealed abusive relationships with partners, fathers and stepfathers. Leanne attributes her fighting spirit to her past experience of bar-tending:

I have been able to look after myself, men do not frighten me and I have had loads of fights in clubs before. I stabbed a man in the hand before . . . I stabbed his hand into the bar, stapled him right through the hand. There was a drunk. He was being sarcastic to me . . . he grabbed my hand and stubbed a cigarette out on my hand . . . I walked past and elbowed him and the glass smashed in his face and cut all his mouth . . . The next thing you know all the lads have seen it and they are smashing his head to bits . . . there were people with ears missing. It was a really bad fight. So I have always worked in rough pubs.

There was a noted difference between how indoor and street workers talked about physical danger. In their 'danger talk' street workers showed a form of fatalism – the risk of physical harm was considered part of the job, something that should be taken account of but should not prevent them earning cash (also reported by Surratt *et al.* 2004). Policing research has also detected a similar attitude among officers who routinized and normalized the threat of work-related danger (Westley 1953). In contrast, many indoor workers who remained violence-free recognized the vulnerabilities of their profession but did not always consider themselves *necessarily* exposed to the risk of violence because of their comprehensive and largely successful strategies.

The ambivalence of police protection

Research suggests that the reality is that most sex workers are often not assisted by the police when they fall victim to violent crime and rarely report incidents (Barnard *et al.* 2002; Wojcicki and Malala 2001: 105). Hostility towards the police is not unfounded, as the police, law courts and criminal justice system have a history of discriminating against women involved in prostitution (Kennedy 1993: 144–54; Smart 1995: 58). Differential treatment of sex workers can be seen in contrasting police attitudes (Pauw and Brener 2003) and the unfavourable reporting of the murder of prostitutes compared to that of 'innocent' women (Smith 1989). Sharpe (2000) and Roberts (1994) suggest that sex workers do not report incidents to the police because they are not treated in the same way as women who do not sell sex. Campbell and Kinnell (2001) note further reasons for non-reporting are that women believe the allegations will not be taken seriously, they will be arrested for prostitution-related offences or that the court will not secure a conviction.

In my study respondents gave mixed reactions to making recourse to the police as a form of protection. Those who had been previously assisted by the police spoke of their effectiveness and non-judgemental attitude. Six respondents confessed that policemen were among their clientele, but usually it was officers from another force. This meant policemen who were clients could not directly provide protection, but advice and information were exchanged during commercial interactions. Nevertheless, the majority of interviewees recounted negative encounters with the police and considered them untrustworthy:

> Being raped is a working girl's nightmare because if you go to the police they are going to go 'well you fuck for a living anyway, so what's wrong with one more dick up ya?'. They may show concern at the time but you know they are laughing at you. They are not going to do the same as if it was for a woman with a family in a good job. They are not going to chase them [the perpetrators] for a prossie (Kelly, sauna).

Others were reluctant to involve the police because they were under pressure from management not to expose the activities of the establishment: 'I wouldn't [call the police] because it would compromise management and I wouldn't do it because it is part of the conditions of working here' (Sarah, sauna). As others have argued, the place of sex establishments outside the law exposes women to violence and cuts off the normal channels of justice. The criminalization of brothel-keeping and procuring dissuades owners of establishments to engage with the police when serious violence and robbery are committed on their premises. Reporting violence to the police was also avoided in case activities were made public. Angela was raided at home and charged with brothel keeping. The police played an active role in making the prosecution public and media attention resulted in her marriage disintegrating and the subsequent pressure from neighbours forced her to move house. Now Angela refuses to involve the police because of the insensitive way they handled the situation. Instead, she uses precautions and deterrents to prevent untrustworthy customers visiting her premises.

Resisting violence

The available options for keeping safe in the sex industry are determined by the constraints or opportunities that women face in each market. This chapter illustrates that sex workers are not passive recipients of violence at work but even when clients are indiscriminately accepted, workers rationally calculate ways of reducing the likelihood of harm by adopting a combination of precautions, deterrents and protection mechanisms. In conjunction with the screening strategies documented in the previous chapter, there are four alternative combinations of protective working styles:

• Women who adopt all four strategies: precautions, screening, deterrents and protection.
• Women who take precautions and screen clients but do not devise deterrents or remedial protection.
• Women who create precautions, deterrents and protection but do not screen due to the limitations of the environment.
• Women who take few precautions but rely on remedial protection.

Precautions, deterrents and remedial protection are not singular categories separated from the overall process of managing risks. Strategies cross-fertilize; precautions need to be in place so that responses can be triggered if a client breaks the contract. Equally, some forms of remedial protection such as weapons and hired security are also used as deterrents. A core set of precautions exist across the industry that constitutes a set of 'occupational norms' regarding safety practices. Yet despite such strategies the structural place of prostitution in society means that there is an inevitable degree of violence and victimization.

What Lowman (2000) calls the 'discourse of disposal' towards prostitutes is perpetuated not only by media stereotypes and salacious reporting (Walters 2003) but is evident throughout our indifferent culture. For example, in 2002 a popular video game, 'Grand Theft Auto', featured the player cruising the streets to pick up prostitutes for sex, then faced with a set of choices the player can either thank, attack, rob, drive over or kill the prostitute. In Australia the game was considered to incite violence to such an extent that the prostitute was removed from the video before it went on sale.

A 'tolerance of brutality' (McLeod 1982: 66) towards women in prostitution is perpetuated by what Lowman (2000: 1004) calls the 'quasicriminalization' of prostitution that marginalize sex workers in four ways. First, prostitution is outside the legal structures and therefore individuals are responsible for their own victimization and safety. Second, prostitution remains part of an illicit economy where brute force and exploitative relationships flourish in an informal primitive market. Third, the system encourages prostitution to merge with other illicit markets, especially the drug trade. Fourth, women are 'alienated from the protective services' and have little recourse through legitimate channels. Intolerant government policies are responsible for not tackling the issue of violence and safety in prostitution: 'the law and law enforcement prevent those engaged in prostitution from adopting strategies that would decrease their vulnerability' (Church *et al.* 2001: 525). As Gilbert (1990, quoted in Archer 1994: 313) states, where the law is weakly represented and there are few other inhibitors to resist violence, then dominant relations become determined by individuals. The role of power between male clients and female sex workers can be understood through what Archer (1994: 313) calls the 'Lord of the Flies' view; as exemplified by William Golding's novel, 'take away the civilized rule of law, and human beings will revert to a power struggle based on the ability to use force'.

The majority of indoor sex workers in this research were exceptional in keeping themselves safe because although violence was a real occupational hazard it was also a relatively rare event. However, remembering that at least sixteen of the fifty interviewees experienced violence at work suggests that screening, precautions, deterrents and protection sometimes fail. As McKeganey and Barnard (1996) remind us, safety strategies give women the confidence to continue working but do not guarantee that they will never encounter client violence. These findings must be contextualized in the wider premise that all women have a heightened sense of sexual danger and 'fear of crime', so therefore create 'an elaborate set of precautionary strategies' to manage everyday interactions (Stanko 1990: 176). Sex workers are an extreme example of how all women adopt 'rules of caution' (ibid.) to minimize harm in the home, sexual harassment at work, taunts in public and censorship for what they wear. Stanko (1997: 488) describes how knowledge of self-protection is *'situated, locally-produced'* (original italics). Sex workers perceive risk in relation to their position as sex providers to men and, like all women, the rhetoric of policing advice and gender expectations state that they are responsible 'for sorting safe from unsafe men' (Stanko 1998: 67). In the absence of any legitimate recognition, labour rights or even equal citizenship rights, what Radford (1987) terms 'self-policing' is a crucial tool for sex workers who have little option but to actively manage the risk of violence every time they 'do business'.

Notes

1 For example, in the USA (Busch *et al.* 2002; James 1974; Kurtz *et al.* 2004; Maher 2000; Miller 1993; Raphael and Shapiro 2004; Silbert and Pines 1985); South America (Downes 1999; Nencel 2001); Canada (Lowman 2000); Europe (Hoigard and Finstad 1992; Mansson and Hedin 1999); and South Africa (Wojcicki and Malala 2001).
2 See Barnard (1993); Campbell and Kinnell (2001); Day (1994); Day and Ward (2001); O'Kane (2002b); Sanders (2001).

Chapter 6

Dodging cops

> The prostitute – perhaps more so than any other figure – represents an identity whose 'place' in the city has always been fought over and whose presence in the public gaze remains subject to moral disapproval, regulation and control. (Campbell *et al.* 1996: 176)

This chapter describes the legal landscape and policing practices that determines the place of prostitution in British society.[1] The police response to the law influences the risk of arrest, criminalization and imprisonment for street sex workers while the chance of State interference is much less likely in the indoor markets. Community activists demand the removal of prostitution from 'their' neighbourhood, intensifying State policing. In turn, the control of so-called nuisance behaviour is devolved to private agencies, organizations and individuals. In response, sex workers across the markets develop strategies to minimize income disruption while at the same time staying one step ahead of the law. This chapter reviews how the laws, policing and strategic responses by sex workers shape the visible and hidden markets of commercial sex. Using Birmingham as a case study, I explore why intense resources targeted towards street prostitution have had little effect. Unlike other chapters in this book, here I give equal attention to the street and indoor markets in an effort to convey the contrasting emphasis on criminalizing certain types of prostitution.

The legal landscape

Prostitution sits at a unique juxtaposition because although primarily a consensual private behaviour, commercial sex is often considered a social evil, a social problem or a public protection issue because it contravenes the 'normative rules governing sexual behaviour' (Heyl 1979: 202). The morality of prostitution crosses the legal system when social norms, such as appropriate gender relations, appear to be threatened. As Peelo and Soothill (2000: 131) evaluate, 'legal systems work not only to protect individuals and prosecute others in order to maintain "law and order", but they also define the boundaries of what, in a complex and fragmented society, are the agreed social values and symbols which we decide to protect'. The place of the law in a consensual (hetero) sexual interaction has historically been questioned, the act of selling sex in Britain is not illegal, but as Day (1996: 75) neatly summarizes 'it is legal to *be*, but not to *work* as, a prostitute' (original italics). The law restricts how prostitution is organized and controlled so that the only legal form of prostitution is one woman, working alone, in a property she owns without explicitly advertising or financially supporting another person. In addition to the vagrancy laws that governed prostitution in the nineteenth century (see Self 2003), there are currently some thirty-five offences related to adult prostitution (Travis 2003) and with a review of the law currently underway, this could either increase or decrease. For now, the laws that govern prostitution were established over fifty years ago and are based on four distinct philosophies: first, punishment for those who 'offend against public order and decency' or 'expose the ordinary citizen to what is offensive' (Wolfenden Report 1957: 8); second, a concern with public sexual health (Mahood 1990; Sprongberg 1997); third, prevention of the exploitation or coercion of women; and more recently, the criminalization of men who purchase sex (Brooks-Gordon forthcoming; Campbell and Storr 2001).

The Sexual Offences Act 1956 made it an offence to procure a woman into prostitution, for a man to live off the immoral earnings of a woman or control her activities, and includes brothel-keeping as an offence. It is commonly accepted that these measures encouraged women to take to the streets, while the preceding Street Offences Act 1959 criminalized loitering and soliciting in a public place, 'sweeping women off the streets and into call-girl flats' (Self 2003: 8) as they were lured by the prospect of private, commercial enterprise. Sex workers cause offence in public because they are regarded as 'potential sources of disorder and violence', improperly using public space, and are heralded as an example of immorality and decay (Maher and Dixon 1999: 491). Social attitudes not only publicly condemn women but the term 'common prostitute' is still used in court, remaining the only offence that allows previous convictions to be discussed and where the only evidence necessary for a conviction is from two police officers (Bindman 1997: 3b).

In 1982, the abolition of the use of imprisonment as a punishment for women arrested for soliciting could have signalled a move away from the castigation of sex providers. Yet at the same time, fines for soliciting increased and women were imprisoned for non-payment. Heidensohn (1985: 47–52) argues that the courts operate a 'double standard' in regard to sexual behaviour, controlling and punishing women but not men, and that the courts are excessively punitive towards women who deviate from the norm by not conforming to acceptable standards of femininity, heterosexuality and monogamy. Such calls for equal justice may have shifted legislation to focus on the purchasers of sex, but the strength of social disapproval (or hypocrisy) coupled with entrenched legal and policing practices towards prostitution have done little to remove the double standard.

The 1985 Sexual Offences Act saw a shift in the focus on *who* was the 'problem' in prostitution by criminalizing kerb-crawling for the first time (Matthews 1986). Providing no immunity for sex workers, criminalizing buyers only encourages the sex worker to identify a client and move from the streets as quickly as possible in case they are both arrested. Criminalizing the purchasers of sex continues under the Criminal Justice and Police Act 2001 where kerb-crawling became an arrestable offence, rather than a summons to the magistrates' court, leading to an increase in prosecutions to 856 in 2001 (Criminal Statistics for England and Wales 2003: 55). Legislating against *both* sex workers and clients may appear to equate them in law but this is only a thin disguise for ignoring the social conditions in which prostitution occurs and the absence of rights to safety, protection and labour for the women involved.

Attempts have been made to introduce the American preference for the re-education of clients through 'John's Schools' (Bernstein 2001; Monto 2004) or 'prostitution offender programs' in Canada (VanBrunschot 2003). The Kerb Crawler Rehabilitation Programme was set up in 1998–9 by West Yorkshire Police as a pilot initiative to actively change the behaviour of men arrested for kerb-crawling. Described as an educational day programme, the activities and philosophies of the seminars were underpinned by a radical feminist belief that prostitution constitutes violence to all women. This prompted a response from a group of researchers, policy-makers, activists and sex workers who challenged the kerb-crawling programme because of its dehumanizing portrayal of clients, continual criminalization of prostitution and 'short-circuited thinking' about the place of prostitution in society (Campbell and Storr 2001: 103). Abandoned shortly after, solutions to reduce the demand side of prostitution are under review as it is clear that removing or 'rehabilitating' individual men is not an effective crime-prevention model. A strong abolitionist philosophy could see a continuation in the criminalization of both sex workers and clients in a similar fashion to the Swedish model (Bindel and Kelly 2003; Gould 1999).

Motivated by a 'moral panic' directed towards the sex advertisements in telephone boxes in London, prostitutes' calling cards were described by Westminster City Council as a serious crime and disorder problem affecting residents, schoolchildren and visitors to the area (Hubbard 2002b). Reactionary national legislation to a localized concern saw the Crime and Police Action Act 2001 outlaw sex advertisements in a public place; an example of what Hubbard (2002a: 359) describes as a mechanism to 'regulate the visibility of illicit sexuality'. This intention was later confirmed in the Sexual Offences Act 2003, where a new offence was established against sexual behaviour in a public place. Under this most recent Act, prostitution law was modernized to apply to both male and female sex workers and the Act strengthened the laws against managing, controlling or recruiting individuals into prostitution, with new offences relating to brothel-keeping with up to seven years' imprisonment.

The most significant legal development for women involved in prostitution, especially street workers, has been the Crime and Disorder Act 1998, which introduced Anti Social Behaviour Orders (hereafter, ASBOs) to be used against those who persistently offend in a certain neighbourhood. Intended to 'protect communities from alarm, distress and harassment' and modelled on young people who cause aggravation, street workers have become a primary recipient of ASBOs. Initially a civil process, the police or local authority must establish that the individual has a pattern of offensive behaviour before a geographical curfew is served. If an ASBO is breached the matter then becomes criminal with the possibility of a five-year custodial sentence. By the time the fieldwork ended in Birmingham, nineteen sex workers had been served ASBOs for persistent soliciting and two women had been sent to prison after breaching the Order. These prohibitions have been severely criticized by legal experts because they are 'not only ineffective but also discriminatory in application to street sex workers' (Jones and Sager 2001: 873).

Contradictions and loopholes in the legislation give rise to the majority of literature suggesting the law on prostitution in Britain is outmoded, biased against providers of sex and lenient on those who organize, buy, control and coerce women (Edwards 1997). The law could be used to assist sex workers to continue to work against HIV and in the interest of public health by addressing their 'right to work with the law's protection from harm, be it rape, violence, robbery or other violations' (Butcher 2003: 1983). In the absence of such protection and rights, in 2001, 2,847 individuals were found guilty of prostitution-related offences and a further 740 were cautioned (Criminal Statistics for England and Wales 2003: 55). At the time of writing there are no Home Office guidelines on policing prostitution. Instead several subjective factors, most noticeably the ideology of the local chief inspector, appear to influence the probability of law enforcement.

Policing prostitution

The application of law to the activities surrounding selling sex is not consistent over police force, time, geographical space or workplace (Benson and Matthews 2000; Campbell and Kinnell 2001; Day 1996: 82; Sharpe 1998). Policing approaches to different markets manifest a spectrum of theoretical and moral positions that influence how individuals experience the law. In Britain two models of policing prostitution are in operation. The indoor markets are generally tolerated through a *laissez-faire* approach whereas on the streets, as Reynolds (1986) theorizes, a control model is applied to suppress conspicuous prostitution through active law enforcement. Relying on the stories of the street sex workers I contacted during the 280 hours spent on the outreach van, alongside extensive observations indoors, insights into the relationship between legislation, policing and the consequences of criminalization on sex workers' professional and personal lives reinforce the centrality of policing as an occupational risk that increases vulnerability.

Soliciting on the street

The manner in which the street is policed has a significant bearing on how the enterprise is organized: 'The distinguishing features of street work lie in not only where the work takes place (i.e. the streets) but also in the issues of risk, protection and control' (Phoenix 1995: 71). McKeganey and Barnard (1996) note that in Glasgow the changing definition of a 'working area' is at the heart of everyday negotiations between the police and street workers and that women are never sure of the geographical boundaries where they can work free from arrest. Respondents in my study found that the inconsistencies in policing were difficult to manage:

> On a Friday night, and the first night in ages, the police were everywhere. Not panda cars but vice and I got pulled because I was on warrant, but I gave this address [boyfriend's] and they let me go and said to be careful as they were everywhere. So in the end I thought it was not worth working so I walked off up the road to get a taxi, planning to go home. Got in the taxi and got nicked by vice. They would not even accept that I was going home, they had me for loitering. They said the taxi wasn't prebooked. Different coppers from earlier, but they said they watched me walk up the road, but if they had they would have seen me get out of the first police car. Then the copper started to push me and I went mad at him. They took me to the police station and I refused to give details because I was on warrant ... So I was locked up in the cell and I was there

for hours and hours . . . Couple of hours later they let me go and I was out back at work . . . .You can just never tell how they are gonna be (Neesha, street but occasionally works indoors).

Although street workers I met during this study did not complain about the role of the police, they said policing intensifies hazards in several ways. First, policing increases the risk of arrest and the chance of obtaining a criminal record that has repercussions in the straight world. If repeatedly prosecuted for soliciting then an ASBO and potentially a custodial sentence becomes a possibility. Several women I contacted had been arrested over thirty times; examples of the revolving-door syndrome of fines and arrests, a thin veil for a street licence fee (Kennedy 1993: 152). Second, the presence of the police results in women changing their work routine, namely reducing screening strategies and accepting an increasing number of strangers because regulars are dissuaded from visiting the area. This consequence is particularly apparent in London, where the Metropolitan Police Vice and Clubs Unit monitors street sex offences over twenty-four hours in the West End (see Brooks-Gordon and Gelsthorpe 2003). Third, the camaraderie and shared code of practice, such as the price of sex acts and information sharing, weakens under the external strains of police pressure and community action. This increases competition and divisions among a group of women who gain bargaining power with clients when cooperating as a collective unit.

In addition, one of the main aims of the policing strategies is to displace the illicit activity to another geographical area, moving the problem from one locality to the next. The outcomes of displacement are far reaching, as Maher and Dixon (1999: 503) found among heroin users: 'intensive policing may also produce harmful forms of social displacement [and] produce more, rather than less harm'. A consequence of policing a group of vulnerable women, often paralysed by polydrug addictions, coercive and violent pimping relationships, is that they disengage from services that offer alternatives and assistance. For example, Pitcher and Aris (2003) report on how street sex workers were cautious to engage in an arrest referral scheme because of a lack of understanding from the agencies involved about the issues they experienced.

Displacement also occurs because offenders are deterred from one source of criminal activity to another. 'Crime shuffling' (Pease 2003: 956) is a predictable consequence of policing women who are excluded from earning money in mainstream employment because of convictions, limited skills and training and disorganized lifestyles. Displacing a crime can encourage other types of acquisitive crimes. When purges on soliciting silence the strolls for a matter of days or sometimes hours, it is likely that street workers become 'criminal diversifiers' (Dorn and South

1990), making money through other tricks, preferring shoplifting, forgery or dealing in drugs or stolen goods.

> You might not see some of them, some of the older ones, and they vanish for months on end. I mean one of the girls I haven't seen for ages and she came back out the other day and she said she had been shoplifting – she had gone to have a change – but she is back out there again (Amy, street).

Policing street prostitution is an example of a crime-prevention philosophy developed in the 1990s, placing community safety and problem-orientated policing at the forefront of 'order maintenance' (Reiner 1992: 212). Written into the Crime and Disorder Act 1998, community safety implies that all individuals are at equal risk of crime. Community policing that targets sex workers as the causes of disorder are contradictory as this group of women is one of the most vulnerable, victimized groups within the community requiring specific interventions to keep them free from harm. Community safety policies do not spread so far as to protect sex workers because they are considered to be the cause of disorder and insecurity in the very streets they live and work. Goldstein (1990) notes how problem-oriented policing is favoured when the public demand that police resources are channelled into activities they define as problems, essentially 'shifting ownership of crime prevention strategies' to the community (Pease 2003: 968). Selective members of a community are given resources to address a localized 'problem' which essentially serves to determine those who are inside the legitimate community while labelling and excluding those who are considered disruptive, undesirable and nefarious.

Street prostitution has historically been a focal point for neighbourhood tensions across the country, with high-profile clashes reported in Chapletown in Leeds, Streatham in London, Manningham in Bradford, St Paul's in Bristol and Balsall Health in Birmingham. Phoenix (1999a: 23–4) evaluates how the construction of the problem of prostitution returned to the emphasis on public nuisance with the rise of vigilantism, suggesting that by 1994 most cities had a campaigning group that used the visibility of prostitution to voice a general fear of crime and concern for personal safety. Hubbard (1998) describes the historical backdrop to community protests in Birmingham and the success of the original Balsall Health 'Streetwatch' activists that removed the Amsterdam-style window prostitution, making the streets a 'space of *alienation*' for sex workers (Hubbard 2002b: 373, original italics). A classic example of geographical displacement, street workers moved just two miles north to the leafy, middle-class suburb of Edgbaston (where this fieldwork took place), prompting a second wave of ongoing, intense community action.

Community action groups campaign for prostitution to be removed from 'their' streets for several reasons. Benson and Matthews (2000: 247) describe how residents complain about litter (particularly used condoms), noise and extra traffic from kerb-crawlers, while Birmingham residents felt that prostitution made their areas unsafe, attracting unscrupulous people, drug-related crime and street robberies (Hubbard 1998: 272).

McConville and Shepherd (1992: 92) claim that neighbourhood groups are ineffective and unorganized. Contrary to this, at the time of the fieldwork, Streetwatch was a scheme that engaged in active, organized observations through nightly patrols: 'We residents have put in 25,000 man hours over the last four to five years to combat prostitution. We have picketed the girls and the condom van . . . We don't want the work to be undone now' (*Birmingham Evening Mail*, 26 February 2001). Tactics adopted by the residents centre on humiliation by picketing women while they worked, taking photographs of individual women and car registration numbers of kerb-crawlers, in addition to using the media to voice a specific moral agenda. Lobbying local politicians and councillors for safer streets receives publicity and funding from local and national crime-prevention sources. The two policemen I spoke with confirmed that their jobs had been created as a result of the persistent complaints from residents. Over a sustained period of at least three years, regular residents' meetings were held along with leafleting campaigns to encourage support and active membership. A 'working partnership' exists between the police and residents, who are given powers to take on an overt informer role as key agents in the policing process. One inspector commented: 'We work as a team with members of Streetwatch, who have their own patrols monitoring the area and logging car registration numbers, which are then passed on to us' (*Birmingham Evening Mail*, 8 May 1998).

The rise of the Streetwatch initiative can be understood through what Garland (2001: 124) describes as a 'responsibilization strategy', heralding a radical change by governments to 'extend the formal controls of the criminal justice State' by enlisting agencies, organizations and individuals to reduce and prevent crime. Relying on citizens' sense of duty, moral conscience, private and personal resources, skills and labour, the State spreads the responsibility for crime control to those who have allegiance to the community. Consortiums of private and civil law enforcement agencies work in partnership or act as substitutes for official policing of certain activities that are deemed too trivial or time consuming for police attention (Poland and Fischer 1998). Community action directed at sex workers is reinforced by local forums that normalize the governance of marginal identities and sexualities in urban space. At the time of the study the 'Birmingham Street Prostitution

(Partnership) Action Group' involved over twelve separate local authority and voluntary agencies ranging from environmental services, licensing, social services, the magistrates' courts and the police. No longer exclusively policed by the State, the actions of a relatively small number of women became the focal point for new policies and resources that promoted old ideologies of exclusion and marginalization.

Community protests have not always been within the boundaries of peaceful campaigning. Hubbard (1998) and Campbell *et al.* (1996: 39) report vigilantism that street workers in my study were familiar with, especially on the Balsall Heath beat in the 1990s:

> If ever I went out and the vigilantes were out or the media I would just go back home ... half of the vigilantes were hypocrites because they were punters themselves. Well a few times they would try and push you about. A mate of mine, they would batter her with sticks and things and they were always giving verbal abuse. Or you may be crossing the road and they would put their foot down on the car and you would have to run (Cleo, reflecting on street experiences).

At the time of the interview Annie felt particularly harassed by the protesters because she lives and works in the area:

> I will be walking up the road with my daughter and they will stop me. I say to them at night when I am on my own and I am dressed in mini skirts then they have got a right to stop me but not at three o'clock in the afternoon, with my baby in the push chair with about six carrier bags. I mean am I really doing business in that state? They still stop me.

Police resources, community campaigns and multi-agency forums, all of which gain wide media coverage, give the impression that street prostitution in the city involved an army of uncontrollable, immoral and dangerous women who spend most of their day causing a disturbance by soliciting in public. The reality is that in Birmingham as few as fifty-three individuals have been arrested in any year (personal communication) and national figures for all prostitution-related offences rarely exceed 3,000 individuals per annum. Caught up in the anti-social behaviour rhetoric of New Labour crime-reduction philosophies, sex workers are made to pay the criminal consequences of the demands for commercial sex. The use of ASBOs on pimps and clients has been minimal compared to the regular use of these prohibitions against sex workers.

Tolerating the indoor markets

The indoor commercial sex markets are policed very differently from the streets. Benson and Matthews (2000: 253) conclude from a National Vice Squad Survey that police ' . . . are reluctant to spend time regulating the off-street trade. Half of the squads did not proactively police off-street prostitution and only intervened in response to public complaints.' They found 90 per cent of vice squads spend only 0–10 per cent of their activities policing indoor prostitution, compared to a significant propor-tion of time and resources allocated to street prostitution (Benson and Matthews 2000). Sharpe (1998: 135) researched the Divisional Enquiry Team in Hull and identified that officers gave low priority to prostitu-tion, rating drug offences as more deserving of resources. Chapkis (2000: 182), Larsen (1992: 13) and Zatz (1997: 278) also suggest there is selective policing of indoor prostitution compared to concentrated policing of street prostitution in North America. A Home Office report confirms that policing indoor prostitution in Britain is subject to compromise:

> Although it is illegal for such premises to offer sexual services, police regulation is generally minimal and intervention will occur only in response to a police complaint. A recent case in the South West saw a judge throw out pimping charges against several massage parlours on the grounds that there was an 'unwritten rule' that parlours would only be prosecuted if a complaint had been made against them – leading to a reasonable expectation that a well-run operation would not attract police attention. (May *et al.* 2000: 9)

Respondents expressed a strong belief that indoor establishments only attract police attention as a result of complaints from neighbours. Although there has been anecdotal information since the fieldwork that saunas have seen an increase in raids from immigration services who arrest sex workers with a view to deportation, there still appears to be minimal State intervention in the indoor markets. Contrary to expecta-tions, alerting the police to illegal activities can forge effective relation-ships, as Astrid testifies:

> We had a copper come here and he said there has been a complaint. Not off any of your neighbours, not off none of your clients, off a woman. I said to my friend 'I told you not to say what you said'. This woman she rang up and asked 'What type of place is this? It has come up on my phone bill'. A jealous wife. What does she say [pointing to her colleague] – 'its a bleeding a whore house' – so she had got on to the old bill. So when the copper come here he said we

have had a complaint and I will go back and say I don't know what you are on about. My friend sat chatting to him and he said he didn't care what we were doing.

Over the past decade, the police in the study area had grown increasingly tolerant of indoor commercial sex activities if the business is kept discreet. The following anecdote from Mary, a thirty-eight-year-old sauna worker, demonstrates the relaxed attitude often shown by the police:

> We had this client come, I was working at Moonlight's. The way it works is that you would book them in and then when you got into the room you would talk about the personal services. He said well I don't want a personal service, I just want a massage. And I said well you can't just have a massage I need to make my money, you know the score here, don't act so ignorant. He said well it says in the paper massage. I said well it says in the paper, brand spanking new car for sale but when you get there it isn't that, so don't believe what you read in the paper. So he said I want my money back and I said you can't. He said well I'll phone the police, and I said go on then. And he said the police will be here in a minute, and I said well you are not waiting in here for them you can wait outside. He goes outside, marching up and down the street. The phone rang and it was the police, they said is Mr Jones there and I said he was outside. They were laughing. He said did he not get his personal service, I said he is outside. The copper said shout out of the window, 'Mr Jones the police are on the phone would you like your wife to be informed of where you are?'. So I opened the window and shouted it . . . and he run up the road.

The jovial attitude of the police had not always been the case, as several years earlier three sauna owners had been prosecuted for brothel-keeping and raids on saunas were commonplace:

> Years ago you would just wait to be raided but it ain't like that now. With the police it used to be like a pattern and you would get raided all the time. I think now if there is any girls taking drugs then there is trouble and there will be a raid (Wilma, sauna).

> The police know about me, they are aware. You see, what used to be the commercial vice has been disbanded now and it is down to the local police station. So any time the local police decide to do a purge or whatever then that's it, but I don't think they know much about it to tell you the truth. I think that unless they get complaints

103

from the neighbours or you are causing a nuisance I don't think they are going to bother you (Maureen, sauna owner).

Like street workers, those who work indoors are also subject to disgruntled residents who use an alternative set of tactics to make their disapproval known. Although other European cities such as Oslo have seen a rise in anti-massage parlour organizations (Skilbrei 2001), the tactics applied to indoor workers in Britain are underpinned by the philosophy of 'naming and shaming' individuals to agencies such as housing associations, social services, the media, the police and, most devastatingly, sex workers' families. The following extract, taken from a message board discussion between escorts, highlights the threat of exposure:

> Some malicious neighbour sent posters to every neighbour in my cul-de-sac and it was accompanied by my photos which at the time had my face on. All the street got a copy (apart from myself) in which the title of the letter was headed 'Neighbours Against Prostitution'. They even printed the web address! I actually had the police at my door asking if I knew what my neighbours were saying about me . . . I have moved away by about 10 miles, so new start.

In my study, Angela, who had been in the business for twenty-five years, revealed how she was prosecuted for brothel-keeping after neighbours reported her activities. The criminal consequences of a small fine were incomparable to the embarrassment and shame caused by a front-page cover story:

> I got busted when I worked from home. I was all over the newspapers. At the time I was working from a council estate with another woman, and we were busy so there was always men coming and going. The neighbours got upset and grassed on us. . . . I got a fine but it was not that that was the problem. It was the papers that dragged me through it. So I had to move after that as there was no way I could live near the people that had done that to me. The family didn't know as they lived outside the area . . . The worst thing was having to move out of my home.

The repercussions from community complaints are exacerbated by the fact that many women operate in secrecy and, as described in the next chapter, the risk of 'being discovered' calls for a separate set of risk-management strategies.

Street wisdom

In the same way that drug markets quickly adapt to sustained police presence (Maher 2000: 90), so women still continue to work the streets despite the pressures from the State, police and community. In attempting to map the rational responses to occupational risks, a central question then is how street workers manage the risk of arrest with the necessity of maintaining a physical presence on the street in order to advertise their availability. This section highlights the processes through which street workers modify their working practices and adopt new strategies to combat the restrictions associated with the police and protesters.

Staying power

During the intense policing activities, rather than stop working the streets there was a notable change in working patterns. Women arrived on the streets much later (around midnight) and worked into the dawn to avoid arrest and also minimize the risks of criminalization for the clients (Campbell and Storr 2001: 99, also report this). Taking clients to deserted parks, alleyways and car parks, away from passers-by (that could assist if there were an emergency), increases the likelihood of violence and robbery but decreases the chance of arrest. Others complain that the police presence deters regular customers who are trusted clients. This means that women take on an increasing number of strangers who have not been through the screening system and are potentially dangerous. The decision is stark: risk criminalization or an increased exposure to violence.

Persistent surveillance encouraged approximately half of the street workers I met to combine the street market with the security of an indoor establishment. Anthea explained that an increase in police presence made street working economically inefficient and when asked why she had begun working from home, she replied:

> Because of the police. There is a hot hot purge going on and you are either being arrested or being run off the beat. So, not only do you have to pay your babysitter, you go down there which is petrol or taxi, and you can't do anything because of the police. If they tell you to move then you have to move.

Four of the five street workers who were formally interviewed said they had gradually reduced the number of hours they were on the streets as they made relationships and arrangements with indoor workers. For example, Annie described herself as a street worker even though she increasingly took men back to her flat or went to their house to perform the service. Two routes of mobility are used to avoid criminalization and harassment: women continued to use the streets to attract clients but performed the service at an indoor location, or they secured permanent work indoors (often a rented establishment with others), only venturing onto the street when business was quiet. Over time the police presence could substantially change the organization of the markets creating a cheaper, unregulated indoor market at the bottom of the hierarchical structure because such a market would maintain the characteristics of the street, in particular the close association with the drug market.

Geographical mobility

Ironically, displacing behaviour as a central objective of crime-prevention policies provides the conditions under which sex workers can continue to use the streets to sell sex. Virtually all of the street workers I spoke with used geographical mobility as a tactic to avoid arrest: 'Everyday arrests, imprisonment, fines and police raids led women to move within the industry to minimize their risks' (Day and Ward 2001: 230). Street workers no longer work in one area but move between a number of established 'red light districts' in the region, leading to what one police officer has described as 'national displacement' (Benson and Matthews 2000: 249). Within a thirty-mile radius of Birmingham, there are several street beats. By frequenting beats covered by various police forces, women were less likely to become familiar faces to officers or protesters.

Experienced workers who had witnessed various types of community protest over the years were aware of the intimidation tactics. Perceptively, women mirrored the methods of monitoring, observing and pooling information used by protesters to inform their own strategies of resisting control:

> I work in the daytime to avoid the vigilantes. They are normally in the Streetwatch van, and when I see them coming round I jump into the bushes until they have gone. They usually drive round a set route and you know if they drive one way that you have got fifteen minutes until they come back. You either walk the opposite way or you get a client and move off. The best thing to do is find out which way they are going and walk the opposite way and then get a customer as quickly as possible. Then I am away with the customer for twenty minutes and then they have not seen me as I have been in a car. Before I was out there every day but I have cut it down and work from the phones (Amy, street).

> When we go up there whether it be in a taxi, car, whatever, we look round and see if the vigilantes are out and so we know where they

are and then we know what corners we can and cannot work. Or we go home. We come out when they are there and work round them. They have got to spot you first. As soon as they spot you they will come after you. Sometimes they are polite, or they will just stand there and take reg numbers. The best thing to do is spot them first and always keep a look out for them (Neesha, street but occasionally works indoors).

These quotations suggest that timing is a key tactic for avoiding detection. All interviewees said they did not arrive on the beat haphazardly but made rational calculations about how and when to arrive. They check which agencies are present in the area before deciding where to work and some workers scan two or three beats before calculating the least risky. For the cautious worker, certain times and days are chosen on the assumption that the police will be otherwise engaged. Weekend evenings are popular, as are evenings when local football matches are played (Boynton 1998: 46). Celebratory dates in the calendar (e.g. New Year, Christmas, Bank Holidays) are favourites for the occasional worker who hypothesizes that not even the most determined protesters would patrol on Christmas Eve.

Avoiding identification

To avoid arrest or attention from protesters, street workers adopt strategies that mask any association with prostitution. Women work on the premise that once a face is connected with prostitution then there is little chance of avoiding arrest. Alibis, cover stories and back-up plans are created in response to inquiries from police or protesters. For Annie, the fact that her family live on the beat provides a plausible story for her presence:

I try and not get into trouble as once they know that you are a prostitute then they will be arresting you every time you go on that beat. But if they recognize you, but not as a prostitute and you have not got any previous [convictions] then they will stop and check you out. They will check that you are going to a friend's house, even take you there and ask the person if they were expecting you. But the vigilantes can't do that as they haven't got the power. But the police have taken me to my husband's house to ask if I am expected and he is like 'Yeah, she is my wife'.

Other ways women avoid identification as a prostitute is to disguise their intentions by not conforming to the traditional dress code. Several respondents said that since the residents and police combined forces, they no longer wore clothes that identified them as prostitutes (for example, leathers, thigh boots, high heels, stockings, red lipstick). To blend in with passers-by, clothing is mundane, avoiding bright colours, elaborate or feminine styles. In fact, often it is hard to imagine how clients identify workers as they wear casual, unrevealing tracksuits or jeans.

It would be reasonable to expect that the cost of a disguise would be a reduction in the number of clients. Probed as to how they attract clients without explicitly advertising their bodies, it became clear that workers who use a disguise rely on other signals to attract custom. Louise described how she arranges to meet her regulars by telephone before she goes to the street and attracts new clients by using eye contact, body language, and lingering at a certain point (telephone box, bus stop, etc.). Street workers also said that it was the customer who made the first signal by slowing down and making eye contact, while those on foot directly ask if the woman is 'looking for business'. Workers in Edgbaston demonstrate that stereotypical clothing and bodily exposure are not a necessary advertising feature of street prostitution, as there are other signals that match the client to the worker.

'Keeping 'em sweet'

Despite the calculated strategies to avoid the police there is a strong belief that a cooperative working relationship with individual officers can guarantee a reduction in the rate of arrest. Some officers are broadly sympathetic to street workers. For example, Anthea reports that the police never arrest her as they know she is a single mother trying to put herself through college. Neesha was pimped by a well-known criminal and given protection by the police while the man was on trial: 'When they realized that I was not on drugs or nothing and that I was being pimped they were sweet with me and never arrested me but helped me when I needed it.' Neesha went on to describe why she did not want to be known as a troublemaker:

> You will need the police one day, because it is dangerous. You will need them because you are being harassed by clients who won't leave you alone. You could need them because you have been done over or you could have a pimp on your case. It is best that they know who you really are rather than a fake name as it is not sure that you will come back alive. If they don't know who you are then they may not help you.

There was a strong belief that no one could outwit the police, so abiding by the rules was the only sensible strategy:

The police, they were all right. I learnt if you run from the vice, if you run from them they get you straight away. So the rules are you don't run from the vice you just have to come in. I run from them once and when I stepped out they locked me up because you ran from us they said. You get done then and they are not giving you bail (Katrina, reflecting on street experiences).

When arrested, workers are tolerant towards the police in order to make the experience less fraught and as short as possible so they can be released and return to the streets to earn money. Despite being harassed by the police, interviewees did not hold a grudge:

Don't avoid the police, keep 'em sweet and talk to them ... It is important to have a good relationship with them as you have got to use them to your advantage. Let them think they are doing their job but you are doing what you want as well. I have walked out of a hotel, made a wedge, going home waiting for a taxi and walked straight into old bill and they stopped me and I told them all about it and they were like 'we are in the wrong job'. You have just got to be safe with them, and show that you are going to be safe with them and they will be all right with you (Anthea, street).

Dunhill (1989b: 206) also notes a 'functional camaraderie' between street workers and the police to the extent that the police will negotiate a convenient arrest time, taking into consideration personal situations such as childcare and existing fines. This reciprocal relationship between law enforcer and street worker is based on the need for the police to establish some level of 'organizational penetration' in to other criminal networks (Billingsley *et al.* 2001: 25). Working relationships between sex workers and the police were confirmed by two officers who clarified that because street prostitution is intrinsically connected with drug-related crimes, the only route to the male dealers was through female street workers. Some of the respondents acted as 'participating informers': they were already involved in a crime, often prosecuted for certain offences, but also informed the police on serious activities in return for benefits such as lenient sentencing.

Although mutually beneficial relationships are strategically adopted to minimize arrests, prosecutions and fines, there are obvious costs: namely the willingness to be arrested, move on or disappear on the instruction of the police as well as taking on a 'supergrass' role. Despite these reciprocal relations, street workers are still reluctant to report incidents of violence. O'Kane (2002a) found among 110 street workers across eighteen British towns that 69 per cent had not reported any attacks to the police. This could suggest that street workers only engage with the police when they are unwillingly brought into contact with the criminal justice system, rather than seeking out official protection for their own needs. This raises the question about whether the relationship genuinely benefits sex workers because 'deals are struck up which the women are under every pressure to comply with, in a situation where all the power is on the police's side' (Dunhill 1989b: 207).

Behind closed doors

Even though few indoor workers experienced arrest or prosecution this should not imply that they do not guard against potential State or community policing. In the same way that violence is an ever-present threat yet does not frequently occur indoors, the threat of police intervention is always apparent. In my study, women who operate from indoor establishments devise systems to avoid detection on a similar scale to street workers. The following strategies, adopted to avoid arrest or disruption in the indoor markets, were the most popular.

Disguise and discretion

Sex workers in saunas and brothels risk police intervention if the business becomes transparent or a neighbourhood nuisance. Therefore, the most effective strategies attempt to disguise the activities. Respondents who work alone from their homes or working premises create fictitious job descriptions as a decoy. The increasing popularity of home-working is a handy disguise:

> This is the most public place I have lived and I sit out there and meet people as they come in. Whether they [the neighbours] have worked out why I am having visitors I don't know. I have told my landlord that I am a counsellor. I thought it through before, and realized that they are going to see people so don't pretend that they are not. So just give them another reason for seeing them. So people think I am a counsellor and it is quite feasible (Melinda, works from home).

Concerned that the number of male visitors will raise suspicion, entrepreneurs try to conduct their business routine in a way that prevents their household appearing different. With this in mind, Ali decided to accept only two clients each day at her home while her children were at school. The rest of her time is spent studying for a degree and caring for her children:

> I am very discreet and I do not work that often. It is not like I see twenty people a day, it is only about one or two a day and I have

got a very large family and they are always coming to the house. A lot of my neighbours are working during the day so they would never notice what was going on. So it is all very discreet.

Having a large family is a useful disguise when several men visit residential premises. Louise, a nineteen-year-old Asian woman, explains that when she arranges to meet clients at her house, the neighbours assume they are family because they are also usually Asian:

They [clients] will come to the flat as it is discreet and because they come in a van, it is like family visiting or something. Where I used to live is a quiet road and because there are Asian girls who are living there when the Asian punters come they think they are family, brothers and friends.

At the time of the interviews, Astrid and Krystal were in the process of finding new work premises. As a precaution they switch the location of their business every couple of months to avoid suspicion from neighbours. Working away from family households, schools and areas where children play is a self-imposed stipulation:

The neighbours are no problem because wherever I have worked because I am on my own and work alone, I am very quiet and discreet. I would never work where there was a family near. Although I know my clients and I trust them I would not like children around the location that I would be working. I would be looking for something similar to this or I wouldn't mind above a shop. If you are renting a decent place in a residential area the majority of people around are working during the day when I am working. So by the time they are coming home I am going. You have to respect other people. Nobody complains because most of the time they do not know that you are here anyway (Anita, working premises).

Informing roles

Owners, managers and workers from indoor establishments create collaborative relationships with the police as a trade-off for lenient policing. As Nemitz (2001: 101) documents, this relationship is characterized by an exchange of information in return for reduced police attention: 'He [police officer] comes here all the time for a cup of tea. He tells us what is going on, who has been raided and when to close' (Astrid, working premises). 'I think people don't appreciate the police's attitude now and they are completely on your side from what I hear' (Esther, escort).

Owners and managers of saunas explain how they inform the police of criminals that pass through the sex industry, if the police guarantee to turn a blind eye. Sylvia was offered a bribe: 'They did say that if I would tell them about other saunas then I wouldn't have to go to court. But I said no, I prefer to go to court.' Some months later, Sylvia decided to collaborate with the police to apprehend a suspected criminal who visited the sauna. Cooperation had earned Sylvia a reputation as a fair businesswoman with strict moral boundaries, firmly cementing the sauna's relationship with the police as one of allies, not enemies. The sauna has not been raided since. Maureen, another sauna owner, recounts a similar experience:

> I mean the police do come here often. I have seen the police here on several times but it is mainly when there is a murder on the streets and they want to know. Recently we had a punter who murdered his baby, and they came here and I have got to go to court about it actually to be a witness because he was coming here spending money. And obviously paedophiles, once or twice I have reported people who have said about young girls.

By investing in police relations the two sauna owners said they were on the right side of the law and had few concerns for the future. However, as Astrid notes, friendly relations with individual officers does not mean that the police are wholeheartedly seen as the good guys:

> The copper that comes here tries to get the dirt. He is still bill and he is still after his stripes, I don't care what you say. But I have got him on camera coming out of an unmarked car, coming here when he is not supposed to. Got it all on camera. So if he ever tries to fuck with me mate. He is OK but he is still bill.

Although none of the respondents were registered informers, so did not receive payment, other benefits such as protection or leniency were considered a lucrative benefit. Drawing out the distinct moral codes that govern the organization of the markets, providing intelligence to the police was considered an obligation of citizenship as well as an exchange bargain. Sylvia and Maureen suggested there are moral reasons that encourage them to participate in police operations; namely whistle-blowing on sexual and violent crimes against women and children. Complying with the police gave sauna owners an opportunity to illustrate their own moral codes and values and to move away from the stigma and sleaze attached to running a sex business.

Displacing deviance

Evidence from this study and the accumulated research illustrates that the consequences of controlling prostitution have negative costs for individual sex workers. Of most concern is the impact of policing on the safety strategies that street sex workers adopt to minimize their vulnerabilities in an exposed environment. The consequence of heavy policing in known 'red light districts' unravels the work of other agencies such as arrest referral and health-promotion schemes that work tirelessly to reintegrate excluded individuals. Equally, continual discrimination against women who prostitute reflects wider inequities: 'policing prostitution in the UK has on the whole provided a graphic illustration of the double standard enshrined in English law' (Campbell and Storr 2001: 103). Current policing approaches are costly and do not achieve the long-term objective of removing commercial sex from visible public spaces because 'prostitution currently thrives under a regime of police harassment and public condemnation' (Zatz 1997: 299). Such a failure may be because law-enforcement strategies are based on social assumptions that policing will disrupt the market (Maher and Dixon 1999: 490). Kulick (2003) demonstrates that after Sweden criminalized the purchase of sex in 1999, street prostitution temporarily disappeared from the public eye, only to return two years later when it became obvious that such laws were unenforceable. In Birmingham, despite years of committed policing, significant State resources and community operations, prostitution continues to be readily available from the same streets. Such policies have limited success because, as Hope (1995) suggests, community crime-reduction strategies rarely achieve intended results because there is a profound misunderstanding of the social relations and conditions that sustain the crime. In an analysis of why policing measures have not succeeded in the fieldwork location, four social and economic dynamics of prostitution are relevant.

First, crime-reduction methods are applied to street prostitution on the premise of 'perpetrator displacement' (Pease 2003: 956): that the crime is made so unattractive by the increased likelihood of arrest or harsher punishments, for example, that the perpetrator will be deterred or respond by moving to another location. On the contrary, sex workers suggest that while some women will move indoors or to another stroll, there will always be risk-takers, novices or women from out of town to take up the street corners that now have a national reputation as the place to buy sex in Britain's second largest city. Sex workers rationalize that although moving from the locality may reduce the risk of arrest, the reliability of clients in the risk zone outweighs the costs of criminalization. Policing does not deter even those who risk breaching an ABSO because the commodity of value (the client and the dealer) continues to entice women to advertise their availability.

Second, the crime-prevention tactics such as formal surveillance through CCTV and natural surveillance including increased street lighting only encourage prostitution because in a somewhat volatile environment these measures offer a fragment of security. Increased police presence potentially creates a safer environment for women who are vulnerable from clients, pimps and dealers. In effect, strategies that are intended to increase the security of the 'legitimate' community are used by those excluded from regular protection to make their illicit endeavours marginally safer.

Third, policing a specific space and a sexual activity reaffirms the deviant and risky status of prostitution – the exact attraction for some clients that seek a cheap thrill not only from the sexual act but the social, political and moral circumstances that situate the purchase of commercial sex. The criminalization of buying sex could potentially encourage the client 'motivated by the mystery and excitement associated with the risky encounter' (Monto 2000: 77; also see O'Neill 2001: 173). The thrill-seeking motivations of the client who is attracted by the risks associated with seeking out public, commercial sex (Holzman and Pines 1982) may indicate that formal tolerance zones may not be entirely successful because legitimately facilitating commercial sex reduces part of the attraction for a certain group of customers, therefore always creating a demand for an illegitimate market.

Fourth, as established by Walter C. Reckless (1925: 1), 'vice areas . . . are natural areas'; the geographical positioning of the street market is not haphazard but is a direct response to its proximity to the city. Like many street beats, in Birmingham the street market is located close to the city's entertainment strip along a main artery road into the business district. The entertainment strip boasts hotels, conference halls, restaurants, casinos and lap-dancing bars for the tourist, business clientele and Friday night revellers alike. The street market is conveniently situated for the men who seek out or are opportunistically tempted to buy sexual services. Ultimately, the historical reputation of the 'red light district' that is perpetuated by the media and the specific features of the environment provide a steady flow of customers. This means that there is minimal likelihood of a permanent relocation or disappearance of the market no matter how many people protest, the number of officers deployed to the area or the lengthy hours spent debating the issues in multi-agency forums. Sex workers have traditionally been in opposition with agents of social control and yet have always found a way to continue their trade. New policy initiatives and moral panics led by community campaigns are simply responded to by elaborate and creative strategies that dodge the law and reduce the risks of criminalization so that sex workers and owners of sex establishments can continue with business as usual.

Note

1 This is a reflection of the situation in Birmingham during 2000–01. At the time of writing the Home Office (2004) 'Paying the Price – a consultation on prostitution' is taking place, promising significant changes to the legal framework and policing practice for street and off-street prostitution.

Chapter 7

Secrets and lies

> We underestimate often the pain of humiliation, being denied the value of your worth and identity, of how you earned your living and kept your commitments to your family and neighbours. (Zygmunt Bauman, *The Guardian*, 5 April 2003)

> Working is like a double life that I lead . . . just lies after lies and you have to remember what you say and I hate lying (Katrina, working premises).

The destructive images and attitudes that society holds towards women involved in prostitution were a daily hazard for respondents in my study. To avoid the 'whore stigma' and prevent their family, partner and children finding out about their activities, many women worked in secrecy. Secrecy is crucial because sex workers fear disapproval, rejection and shame if loved ones discover their involvement in prostitution. Commentaries on the stigma in prostitution have not paid separate attention to the strategies that sex workers use to resist and avoid stigma. My findings go beyond describing the effects of 'whore stigma' by asking how sex workers manage the consequences of stigmatization. This chapter adopts a sociological analysis of secrecy as a rational response and it reports strategies adopted by sex workers that include pseudonyms and creating job aliases, relying on geographical space between work and home and choosing a sex market with care. Women cover up their careers by telling lies, isolating themselves from friendship networks and also by disclosing variations of partial truths about their money-making activities. These findings are discussed with reference to Goffman's (1959, 1963, 1967) concept of stigma management, impression management and social rituals.

Sexual stigma

To understand why secrecy is so common among sex workers, it is important to briefly outline the stigma associated with prostitution. Women who sell sex are subject to derogatory images and myths. Several accounts of the fetishization, marginalization and victimization of women who sell sex contribute to an understanding of the 'whore stigma'.[1] Sex workers are assumed to be members of a 'high risk' group, associated with HIV/AIDS and drug use, disease and sexual deviancy (Lawless *et al.* 1996). Corbin (1990: 211) suggests that the stereotype of the prostitute is made up of five myths: that they smell bad, are socially inept, diseased, are exploited sexual objects and fulfil a natural, necessary outlet for male sexual urges. Nagel (1997) contextualizes such stereotypes that define female identity as a binary where the categories of 'good girl' or 'bad girl' assign an identity of either privilege or stigma. Bell (1994) notes that women who identify with lesbianism or prostitution threaten to destabilize the heteronormativity that determines the social ordering of sex acts and consequently are relegated to the margins as 'others'.

After a decade of researching the sex industry, O'Neill (1996b) concludes: 'Prostitution is accepted by the bourgeoisie (it is not illegal) but the prostitute, the whore is not accepted, she is perceived as immoral, a danger, a threat to "normal" femininity and as a consequence suffers social exclusion, marginalization and "whore stigma".' The consequences can be far reaching:

> Being a prostitute makes a woman vulnerable to the loss of social services, removal of her children and termination of parental rights, expulsion from social support systems, such as family or church, rape or other violence, and arrest. The stigma associated with being a prostitute may make it impossible for these women to return to more legitimate lifestyles. Thus, it is extremely difficult for women to identify themselves as prostitutes. Often, those who have made a disclosure have lost so much that they have nothing left to lose. The women who are unable to hide their status are often the most vulnerable. (Weiner 1996: 100)

Only three respondents in my study said that they were not overtly affected by stigma and therefore did not bother about secrecy. In contrast to other respondents, their family and friends were relatively accepting of their profession and in two cases, their mother was involved in the sex industry. All three women already had friends in the business: 'I don't give a fiddler flying fuck, everybody knows what I do. My local pub knows ... I mean my big daughter knows ... It is not taboo any more, things are completely different' (Astrid, working premises). These interviewees did not hide their real name from clients and did not try to keep their business secret. Rachel had no qualms about using her birth name:

I have stopped working under a false name. I find it is much easier not to as I used to go out clubbing and there would be people shouting my working name across the bar and it was not right as the friends I was with got all confused. So I started working under my real name as I thought that the majority of clients are not going to shout out 'prostitute', as it looks bad on them as well. More often than not they will be really shy about it and if they speak they will be nice to you.

In contrast, the vast majority of sex workers, owners and organizers said their lives were directly affected by society's negative view of prostitution and as a result had experienced significant material loss. Workers had received hate mail in the post; six respondents had been subjected to ousting campaigns by angry neighbours; fifteen had been the victims of false allegations regarding the care of their children, sparking investigations from child-protection agencies; two women had been photographed by the local media and humiliated by newspaper reports; thirteen had experienced discrimination by housing associations; at least sixteen women had been labelled as common prostitutes in court; and a further thirteen respondents said that attacks were not taken seriously by police, because of their job.

The quotation from Polly: 'People don't see that we are normal people; we are either dirty or we have got no brains to do anything else', summarizes how several women felt stigmatized even though few people knew of their activities. Powerful and insidious messages can become internalized and act as a form of self-stigmatization. Becker (1963: 31) explains how it is not necessary to be publicly labelled to experience stigma because often when people are involved in activities that are considered deviant, a process of self-stigmatization occurs: 'I just want to feel normal because you don't feel normal when you do this job. You can't sit down and say "Oh guess what happened to me today". There are too many people telling you, you are wrong' (Sharon, sauna).

Stigma affects women in different ways depending on their biographical details, future plans, expected career duration and family circumstances. Twenty-two women said they could never be free from the stigma even when they no longer sold sex, so have resolved to remain in prostitution because they could never shrug off the negative image of being a 'prostitute'. Despite such resolution, most women said it was important to keep their work secret and that any discovery would result in significant emotional and material loss. The emotion of shame deserves some attention in an attempt to understand why respondents prioritized 'being discovered' on the hierarchy of harms.

Shouldering the shame

The emotional consequences of stigma are a real concern for sex workers. If friends, family, children or partner discover their involvement in sex work, the effects could be devastating:

> Sometimes when I am at home, when I am lying in bed I just cannot believe what I am doing and the risks I am placing on my children and husband. I have to hide it all the time: my clothes, where I am going, my health, the way I look after my body. If he knew, then he would suspect and that would be it, marriage finished (Leigh, working premises).

Being stigmatized is not only an unpleasant indictment on one's character, but brings with it potential personal loss. Often, women were not overly concerned with the impact of stigma on their individual character because they knew they were not dirty or diseased and rejected criticisms of their mothering skills. Instead, the strategies of secrecy described in this chapter are motivated by the desire to avoid the consequences of stigma interfering with personal relationships and loved ones:

> I like to be discreet as people have stereotypes of working girls and if they [friends and family] knew I was doing this they would have nothing good to say about it. But basically for that reason I keep it secret. Sometimes, I would like to tell people what I did but if I told them then they would be so shocked. There is a lot of vindictive people out there and they could tell my mum but I have disguised it well enough (Katrina, working premises).

> It is just hard to explain to people where you are working, to make up stories and remember them. Besides the less people who know the better. A lot of girls go out of their way to make sure people don't know ... We have to protect everybody else really, our families, that is why we don't say anything, that is why girls keep it secret (Dora, sauna).

One of the main motivations for secrecy is shame: 'I used to cut myself off completely but it would still swim around in your head. You would feel ashamed that you have done it and can't believe it' (Nicky, maid). Although the emotion of shame is not detailed explicitly, much of

Goffman's work in *Interaction Ritual* (1967) places shame and embarrassment at the centre of social relations, which consequently determine how individuals present themselves to one another and themselves. Elster (1999: 143/9) defines shame as 'a negative emotion triggered by a belief about one's own character ... triggered by the contemptuous or disgusted disapproval by others of something one has done'. Elster (1999: 153) states the differences between shame and guilt are that shame needs the presence of others whereas guilt does not. An individual may feel ashamed because there is an audience to witness their behaviour and make a negative judgement about their character by expressing disapproval (Elster 1999: 149). On being discovered by a partner or relative, a sex worker would feel shame because they accept that their behaviour deviates from the norm and in doing so they identify with the audience's opinion. Others argue that an imaginary audience prompts shame or that an audience is not always necessary to trigger shame. Taylor (1985: 59) suggests that to feel shame, all one needs is to be conscious of one's behaviour and self. In this sense, the individual's own eyes become the audience, as she identifies with the opinions of those that would disapprove and therefore condemns her own deviation.

The fear of shame is an incentive for secrecy because of the probable personal rejection if family, friends or partner discover a woman's involvement in prostitution. Elster (1999: 156) highlights exactly how shame can affect behaviour: 'The role of shame in decision making depends on whether it is anticipated or experienced ... We would expect, therefore, people to be very careful not to get caught engaging in shameful activities'. Interviewees anticipate shame by creating strategies to avoid getting caught:

> Everybody here is in the same position as me – nobody knows in their family where they work. Most of the girls here, their families don't know and like me, it is a constant lie. I couldn't say to my aunts or brother that I own a sauna because they would think I was a really, really bad person. You class people like that like the Mafia (Sylvia, sauna owner).

Goffman (1963: 130) notes how 'stigma management is a general feature of society, a process occurring wherever there are identity norms'. Women who are considered to work outside the identity norms of acceptable female behaviour are most likely to be involved in processes of stigma management. Mattley (1998: 150) also found that women who work on fantasy phone lines did not tell their family or partner for fear of disapproval. In my study, receptionists and owners, to prevent any association with the stereotype of the 'prostitute' or 'pimp', also adopted stigma-management techniques.

The tensions of truth

Forty-four interviewees had husbands, long-term partners or boyfriends. At the time of the research, thirteen women did not tell their partner they worked in the sex industry and of the thirty-one women who currently did, twenty-six said that they had, at some point, not done so. Women feared that if their partner knew the truth then they would be contemptuous, disgusted and angry. Disgrace would be brought upon the relationship and it would be over:

I would be mortified if anyone knew that I was working. It would be devastating. It would be the end of my personal life and getting married and his relationship with my children. Sometimes you think why am I doing it if it is such a big risk and why when the loss would be so incredible? I know that I could not cope if he did find out (Eleanor, sauna).

The decision to be truthful was a preoccupation for most respondents who sold sex without their partner's knowledge. Several women describe how they judge potential reactions and evaluate the costs of honesty:

I have had relationships in the past where they have known and they just throw it back in your face. He [ex-partner] was going to a wedding and I was supposed to go and he said I am not taking a whore to a wedding, as whores are not allowed in churches. The mental torture of it was unbearable. So I decided the next relationship I have, I won't tell him ... There is no way that I would tell my fella now. You are joking. He doesn't know what I do. We don't live together and if we did it would be hard. I had a relationship with somebody before and he found out and gave me an ultimatum. He said the job or me and I chose the job (Katrina, working premises).

When I had been with my current partner for about a month this chap just walked up to him in a nightclub and handed him a picture [of Esther dressed as a dominatrix]. So I had to tell him about that and from the reaction I got I made the decision that I was not going to tell him about anything else. It didn't go down very well, so I told him about the web design instead. It is a bit of a double life but I just don't think about it too much (Esther, working premises).

These women engaged in a rational process of assessing the costs of revealing the truth by summing up the likelihood of disapproval.

The desire to keep their employment hidden from their partner can also be understood through the 'Groucho paradox'. Elster (1979: 199) re-phrases this parody in relation to romantic encounters: 'I would not dream of loving someone who would stoop so low as to love me'. Sex workers keep their job secret not just to avoid shame but also to avoid attracting the wrong type of partner. The 'wrong type' is described as a man who would accept that his girlfriend has sex with men for money. Kelly explains how she realized her boyfriend was the wrong type:

> I did start working back at the saunas, but I told him that I was only working there doing massage. I was hiding a bit of money and said I wasn't earning much because I was only doing massage and I didn't want to sleep with them [clients] because I was going out with him. And he said I know you want to earn more money so I don't mind if you sleep with them. The minute he said that I knew that I was kicking him out. He had no respect for me and none for himself and he was just using me.

As an example of how an imaginary audience creates the feeling of shame, interviewees did not tell relatives, mainly their parents, to prevent disapproval: 'Not one of my friends or family know about what I do and I am going to keep it like that' (Leigh, working premises):

> I wouldn't tell my parents as they are very old and I was brought up a strict Catholic. For me to tell them, they are very religious and it would destroy them. I would not tell them because they don't need to know. They know that I am a qualified nurse and I have left it at that which means I am not actually lying to them. The majority of my close friends know, as many of them are working as well, or have done. I will tell people on a need to know basis. I am very cautious who knows (Petra, working premises).

Petra describes how disclosure depends on the person, their values and the strength of the relationship. Disclosing on a 'need to know basis' was a familiar tactic to control information.

Forty of the fifty-five interviewees had children. Of these forty, sixteen had told their children the truth, while the others worked hard to prevent their children finding out. Respondents feared the impact of their activities on their children's reputation at school, with their peer group or in the local community. Why respondents try to protect loved ones, particularly children, can be understood by what Goffman (1963) describes as courtesy stigma: when the character of those associated with the stigmatized individual is blemished and they too receive similar hostile treatment. Diane has four teenage children and has made a living as a single mother by working in a sauna for the past ten years. She summarizes the difficulties of keeping her occupation hidden:

> I am not telling them. I do not want them to know. I think they would be disgusted and I think the oldest would never talk to me again and would probably move out. I think the things that I have heard him say, like when *Band of Gold* was on, he couldn't understand how anyone could do that. I just have to keep quiet. It is hard when there is something on the telly and you hear him talking with his mates about slappers and prostitutes and he would hate me if he knew. When there are programmes about prostitution on telly and the kids are there it makes me feel really self-conscious. My girl is thirteen now and she asks questions, like why do women go with men and want to get paid for it? I always say I don't know, it is just the way that it is sometimes. I have to answer the questions as her mother. It is not because I am ashamed of what I do because I do this because I want to do it (Diane, sauna).

> My stepson does not know. He is 25. That is not because I would be worried about him knowing because from talking about issues with him I don't think he would condemn me. The problem is with the stereotype of what a working lady is (Petra, working premises).

Mothers in my sample invented pre-planned stories to fend off gossip or explain why they were spotted entering a hotel or sauna. Often they felt like they were cheating their children, not being a 'respectable', 'normal' mother, yet this sat uncomfortably with the claim that they worked to provide a decent quality of life for their children:

> I can do what I want and I can afford to do what I want and if I was on the social I could not. My kids they are in designer clothes, they are spoilt. If I did not do this they would be scruffy. I did not have any money before I started this and the kid's dad stopped paying maintenance and I was in one big shit. So my friend done it already and I just followed her doing it. But my kids they have got a good life. I mean they holiday every year. But I wouldn't want my kids doing it. I suppose in my situation I did have a choice but it was breaking my heart, my children going scruffy (Laura, working premises).

For these reasons, secrecy became a preoccupation not only when women were at work, but also in their private lives.

Covering up

Goffman (1963) polarizes victims of stigma into 'the discredited' whose stigma is immediately visible (because they are physically impaired, mentally ill, etc.) and 'the discreditables' whose stigma is not visible or always known in public. Sex workers fall mainly into the discreditables category, as their involvement in prostitution is not obvious unless they are observed in a work environment. Goffman highlights that for this latter group their main preoccupation is the management of information about the stigma. To display or not to display, to tell or not to tell and in each case to whom, how, when and where are everyday dilemmas for women involved in prostitution. The management of undisclosed, discrediting information about the self is known as 'passing off' (Goffman 1963). Sex workers regularly 'pass off' by pretending they are someone or somewhere else.

Pseudonyms and job aliases

Pseudonyms are a universal feature of prostitution. Only three interviewees used their birth names while the other fifty-two interviewees adopted an alternative name specifically for work. It is not uncommon for different names to be used in different places for different purposes. Name aliases are common in various organizations and groups. Nicknames are given to criminal gang members (Gambetta 2001; Varese 2001), codenames are used by secret agents, and members of religious orders have both a birth name and a spiritual name (Vallely 2001). In situations where secrecy is paramount, switching names takes on extra significance. In the sex industry, the pseudonym, like other trade names, is used freely and openly advertised in newspapers and on websites. Pseudonyms are also semantically different from codenames. Gambetta (2001: 38) explains how codenames are neutral words (e.g. Mr Pink, Mr Brown). Sex workers are known by proper female names or feminine words (e.g. Heaven, Angel, Silky) which are allusive and sexually suggestive. In the sex industry, it is normally the case that colleagues and clients only identify a woman by her working name while birth names are not used at work, only in private.

Unlike nicknames, pseudonyms are usually chosen by individual sex workers rather than bestowed by peers as a teasing gesture. Also, the sex worker controls the use and application of the alias, as opposed to the lack of control the individual has over a nickname. Pseudonyms are not based on physical or behavioural traits, achievements or skills. Despite the differences between pseudonyms and nicknames, they have similar purposes. Gambetta (2001: 44) describes how nicknames enable identification in one arena but prevent true identification in another. Pseudonyms in the sex industry enable clients to identify a worker, but at the same time stop her real identity being known. The characteristics of pseudonyms do not explain the reason why they are universal. Real names are hidden from clients and sometimes colleagues, because women do not want their 'real' identity to be exposed for fear of harmful consequences, such as stalking: 'You want to keep your real name secret' (Diane, sauna). Ali works from home and stopped using her real name when a client turned nasty:

> In brief, I saw him one time when I first started and he became a stalker. He would follow me to the shops and even when I was with my parents and children he would come after me. He started coming to my door and asking my neighbours about me. Then I used my real name and he went to ask the neighbours about what I was like and if he could get my home phone number.

Pseudonyms not only limit access to real identities but act as a psychological barrier between professional and private life:

> I don't think I would like the idea of someone using my real name when they are in an intimate position with me. I think a different name psychologically keeps your distance from your real life (Eleanor, sauna).

> The first visit they are getting to know Esther. The name keeps things separate. Some people quite happily work under their own names. But for me it keeps things easier and it makes work and home totally separate (Esther, escort).

Leigh works in complete secrecy and manufactures stories to account for her daytime activities. An alternative name at work reduces emotional complications:

> Using a different name at work is essential to help you move from one world to the other. When we move from mummy mode to work mode, you have to make out that you are a different person. Being known by a completely different name helps to do that and makes sure no one knows who you really are.

Alongside the pseudonym, forty-seven participants created an alias occupation to conceal their sex work. The caring profession was a popular job alias among respondents: 'Most of the working girls say that they work in old people's homes' (Tracy, working premises). Several women had previously worked in nursing or as care assistants, so decided to continue this storyline, as there was some truth in the disguise. The job alias is not normally unrealistic or unusual but, instead, reflects part of the woman's career history or skills used in sex work. Esther tells her boyfriend and family that she is a web designer. In part, this is true because she manages her own website and designs web pages for colleagues. Mary and Katrina use their previous employment as chefs to account for the long hours they work. Women who do not work many hours often use cleaning or catering as a cover-up: 'My family think I work in the Clarendon Hotel washing up because I worked there before' (Tracy, working premises).

> My partner thinks I work with my friend as she has got her own business. You have to otherwise they will be wondering what you do all day and why they cannot get hold of you. Years ago I used to have my own cleaning business so I can talk about cleaning and it all sounds real. I spray a bit of polish on me now and again before I go home so he can smell it and it stops him questioning what I do (Leigh, working premises).

> A lot of my friends who I hang out with are straight and some of them know and some don't know so I have to introduce friends who are working girls as someone from the office. I tell them all the same job; that I am a credit controller (Beryl, working premises).

Interviewees employ strategies to keep stigmatizing information hidden by simply posing as someone who does not possess stereotypical attributes of the 'prostitute'. Respondents 'pass off' by pretending to work in one occupation as a way of concealing their prostitution, especially from their children. In line with her bohemian lifestyle, Natasha tells her children that she is a tarot card reader, which explains why she wears a wig and dresses up. Another sauna worker tells her teenagers that she works nights in a twenty-four-hour petrol station. To account for working at home Melinda tells her landlord and neighbours she is a freelance therapist. It is not only sex workers who adopt a job alias. Sylvia owns a sauna but has always claimed to be the proprietor of a clothes shop or hair salon.

Passing off is an everyday tool for sex workers who are in the position of having to reveal their stigmatizing identity to one set of people (clients) and yet conceal the stigma from another set (family, friends, partner, official agencies). Goffman (1963: 64) describes how 'stigma symbols' are signs that convey information that associate personal identity with a social stigma. Red lipstick, high heels, stockings and suspenders, mini skirts and condoms are symbols that identify the occupation (and stigma) of the prostitute. Symbols associated with selling sex are revealed to clients, sometimes as an advertising mechanism, yet concealed from others outside the sex industry.

When worlds collide

Despite strategies to remain anonymous, thirty-two women said they had accidentally met a client in public, outside work. Sex workers describe two types of difficult encounters with clients. In type one (T1) a stranger, who recognizes a woman from a sauna or escort agency, approaches her in public. In this situation, the man has no inhibitions about being identified as a client. In type two (T2) a sex worker encounters a man that she knows from her private life in the context of the sex industry, which identifies him as a client. Usually, no sexual encounter takes place but sensitive information concerning both parties' involvement in the sex industry is exchanged. Respondents described how T2 does not pose the same kind of threat as T1 because in a meeting with T2 there is a mutual exchange of compromising information. Dora puts this scenario into context:

> We were all sitting down in the lounge and this man walked through and he was actually a friend of my cousins. He picked me and I just froze. I knew his wife and everything and I said 'don't tell my cousin, don't tell my cousin'. He didn't and I just gave him a massage. He said he had chosen me because he could never choose someone else in front of me because I know his wife. He said he would never say anything because I come here for my needs and you come here for your needs and he has been fine with me. The first time I saw him I was a bit nervous because he was with his wife and I was with my husband.

Thirty-one respondents said that men they knew, as friends, acquaintances, neighbours or relatives visited sex workers. However, possession of this secret information was not one-sided as these men also knew of the clandestine activities of the woman. In this situation, the worker and the client implicitly trust each other because they both know sensitive information that could be used against each other. Secrecy is maintained only because imparting the truth would implicate each other. The following three accounts demonstrate how mutual information is managed:

> There have been two clients that have come here in the five years that I have worked here who I have known, who live by me. I used

127

to go to school with their children and they are much older than me, but I do know their wives. So it is mutual really – they could not say anything and nor could I. It is a secret between the two of us (Diane, sauna).

When I was at the sauna I was living in the same area. I met a couple of the dads whose kids went to my kid's school. That is why I had to move from there. But once they know they know. Nothing happened they just said hello or say nothing at all. I remember being with my sister one time and saw this one guy, he was a vet. But he was really polite, he didn't say names, neither of us said names, and we were like hello how are you. And my sister, well as far as my family was concerned I worked in an old people's home and I am sure I passed him off as one of the sons of one of the old people who lived there (Annabelle, sauna).

I had this one client who came to see me every week sometimes more. I went on holiday with my mother, friend and daughter and we got to the airport and this client was there with his wife. We got called through to departure and he was called through, got on the plane and he was on the same flight. Then got on the bus to go to our destination and he was on that too. He was staying at the same hotel. I just blanked him, and pretended I didn't know him. But on the coach me and my mum and friend we were having a laugh and drinking and that and his wife was joining in. When we got to the hotel in the bar he came up to me and I told him to get on with his life and not give himself away. When I am on holiday I did not want to be around my clients. Anyway, through the holiday his wife got on well with my mother as they were the same age. She told us that their children had clubbed together for this holiday for them as he had been made redundant and they were living on benefits. I felt so bad about all the money I had taken off that man. When I came back I told him I would never ever see him again. That was not nice (Anita, working premises).

Even though sex workers devise a separate set of strategies to cope with 'being recognized', Anita's experience highlights how the 'double life' of hiding prostitution from loved ones is a constant effort. Even on holiday, in another country, Anita could not escape her job: she was reminded of how she earns money and her professional role. There are few other occupations where meeting work associates in private would be as problematic and uncomfortable.

Location

Geographical distance

Similar to the reactive strategies of drug dealers who do not 'deal in one's own backyard' (Adler and Adler 1980: 453), the geographical location of the workplace is influenced by the desire among sex workers to reduce the risk of identification:

> Nobody knows what I do where I live. I come over here and no one knows, not my children or my family or nothing . . . I don't worry that my family are going to find out because it is not near to where they live. I have been working for ten years and they haven't found out (Diane, sauna).

> I always work in Birmingham and never Wolverhampton. Doesn't matter how skint I am I would never work in Wolverhampton because I never want anyone to find out what I do and that. Because I knew quite a few people in Wolverhampton and plus my family lives there as well so I wouldn't work in Wolverhampton (Zoe, sauna).

Eleanor travelled a 200 mile round trip, three times a week, to work in a sauna that was away from her home town. Rita first started selling sex twenty years ago in another city from her home:

> As my children got older and they started attending secondary school, I didn't want to work in Birmingham and because I brought them up on my own I wanted them stable and secure. To keep that stability I didn't want anything bandied around although I have never worked out of a sauna. So I went to London to work. Initially in a sauna and then a house. I used to commute every three days and I had a girl living in my house with my children.

Working in a different geographical area provides a psychological barrier for women who want to make a stark division between work and home. Most participants could not contemplate entertaining clients at home:

> It is important for me to not work at home. I did try it for two weeks before I moved in here and there is no line between when you are working and when you are not then, but some people seem to handle it perfectly well. It must be different strokes for different folks (Esther, escort).

I would never work near where I live. I would be worried that someone would find out. Once I am out of the area where I know people I feel safe that no one is going to find out. The distance is important to me to keep a barrier (Leigh, working premises).

Those who work from home use other strategies to keep their profession hidden. To minimize the chance of meeting someone she knows, Ali advertises to attract clients from other cities:

A lot of the people who come to see me travel from London, Coventry and Leicester and are not from my hometown so it means that I am not likely to meet anyone that I know. It would be so shocking to meet my neighbour or something. I was planning to go to other people's houses but I have decided not to just in case someone finds out.

However, working in a different geographical area from family and friends does not guarantee anonymity:

There was this one time when some friends of my dad from the army came to the sauna. I shit myself. They were all the way from down south and they are his army mates. They all recognized me but not from my dad from being at my wedding. I got married to a soldier and they were at my wedding and remembered my husband. I could not believe it. They are from down south and what are they doing in Birmingham? I thought I would be safe up here because it is completely safe from knowing everyone and that when I have finished I will be able to bugger off and no one will be any the wiser ... It was such a shock (Kelly, sauna).

Choosing a market

To limit the chance of exposure some respondents made a careful decision about which market to work in. The lucrative advantages that accompany escorting are offset by the visible, intrusive and unsociable nature of the work:

I have done escorting a few years ago but I could never do it now because you would be found out too quick really. Running in and out of places and getting phone calls all the time. My kids would find out. I do think about it sometimes thinking that I would be better off on my own ... But it is too risky and too inconsistent (Mary, sauna).

That is why I stopped it [escorting] because when they were taking you out to buy you a meal I was like 'Oh god, everybody knows'. I am sitting here and everyone is knowing that I am a prostitute because what is this young lady doing with this old man? And I always made sure that when I went out there I was dressed casual but smart, you know no short skirts, like trousers suits or a long skirt. I would never wear anything that I think would make me look like a tart (Annabelle, sauna).

Choosing a market is often based on the level of public exposure. When Rita moved her business from London to her home town she still wanted to keep her prostitution secret so carefully chose the type of market: 'The fact that I used to be a townie and my children used to go drinking with me, people know me in Birmingham. So I didn't want it to follow me around, and go to hotels where the people I knew run the hotels, so I couldn't do hotel bookings.'

Respondents also considered how advertising could increase the risk of being discovered. Seventeen interviewees did not advertise on the Internet because they felt it was uncontrollable: 'I wouldn't because my uncle has got a PC and the Internet is too revealing' (Seema, sauna). One respondent moved from the street to working from home during the fieldwork period and spoke of the dilemmas associated with advertising using a photograph in a specialist magazine or launching a web page. She decided against the Internet as it was an unknown entity and she felt unsure of its capacities.

Isolation

Although isolation from peer groups can be a consequence of prostitution, it can also be pursued as a strategy. As a way of limiting the spread of information about their profession, respondents managed their friendships in two ways: first they selected the people they wanted to associate with and, second, they reduced the number of people in their support network. Becker (1963: 38) explains 'solidification' as a process of accepting a character or lifestyle by reducing contact with conventional society. Several interviewees confirm that all of their friends are people they met through work: 'I mean I have a few friends but not many people know. I don't really mix with anyone else any more ... I had friends that didn't work and sometimes in conversation they would point to someone else and say "she's a prostitute" and I would think oh no, if only they knew' (Sharon, sauna). Goffman (1959: 238) offers a positive analysis of isolating strategies: 'Among members of the team we find that familiarity prevails, solidarity is likely to develop and that secrets that could give the show away are shared and kept.' I observed elements of solidarity among sex workers that bred trusting relationships, but making new friends outside the industry was difficult, as invariably people want to discuss occupations:

> I have no friends. Because the friends that I did have before I started the job . . . why do they not ring me up, why do they never come to my door, why do they never ask me to go anywhere with them, why am I totally excluded from their life now? Why is that? Because of my job. And as for making new friends it is impossible because you have got to lie anyway. Because that is one of the first things when you get talking. Like the other night, I went out to a nightclub and I was talking to different people in there and having a good night and then someone said to me about what do I do. Now earlier I had said that everyone I meet I am just going to lie and make something up because I need to make friends because I feel isolated. Then I thought no, fuck this, why should I lie? It doesn't matter what people think about me here, as I never have to see any of them again in my life. So I told them. I said 'I am a prostitute'. Their faces hit the floor. I sell my pussy I said. Suffice to say it was not mentioned again all night. They still talked to me all night, I went dancing and they went running round the club telling everyone (Kelly, sauna).

Tracy said she had few friends, not out of choice, but because friends had disassociated themselves: 'When you do this job you lose all your friends. If I go out the only friends I know are working girls.' Most respondents said they had experienced a loss of friends once it became apparent that they sold sex for a living. The absence of friendship among women involved in prostitution appears to be a recurring theme (also see Maher 2000: 39). Social withdrawal as a stigma-management technique is a consequence of the marginal place of prostitution in society and has implications for individuals and the wider sex work network (also see Letkemann 2002: 519, who describes this process among unemployed people).

For instance, nine respondents avoided socializing outside work with colleagues to limit the chance of sensitive information leaking out:

> There was one woman who knew I worked. She was actually someone I met through working and we stayed friends for a while. She lived in the same town and we used to socialise together. I met my partner and she was very loud about what she did working in massage parlours. I did not want to be associated with that, which is very hypocritical of me. But I did not want anyone to associate

me with what she was saying so I quickly let her go as a friend. It was too close to home (Eleanor, sauna).

These strategies of isolation have been noted among police officers in the Royal Ulster Constabulary (Brewer 1990: 665) who ignored colleagues outside work as a way of controlling their occupational identity. Both the women who concentrated friendships within prostitution and those who did not said their family was the main source of social and emotional support. This echoes wider themes of kinship networks summarized by Maher (2000: 33), who highlights the gender differences of social networks. There is a tendency for women's networks to be based with kinship or same-sex friendships that are intensified by working together.

Variations of the truth

In order to maintain secrecy, all of the respondents said they told lies about their daily activities: 'That was the worse thing about it all, lying to your family' (Annabelle, sauna). As an example of what Goffman (1963: 121) described as 'good adjustment' to prevent the stigma becoming known so that the individual does not challenge the 'world of normals', most women I spoke with sustained a complex process of lying. As Mitchell Jr (1991: 98) explains, 'secrecy is one aspect of a broader process of impression management that we may refer to as concealment'. Hiding both physical objects and personal information were a continual feature of interviewees' everyday life:

Working is like a double life that I lead. I have got used to it now, but I do think about all the lies I have got to tell. Like today I was going on to my mum about overtime and time in lieu and all this lies after lies and you have to remember what you say and I hate lying (Katrina, working premises).

And the lies that you have to tell your mum and people because my family doesn't know. My mum will phone me up. I have got to make up excuses for where I have been and make up imaginary friends. It is difficult, you have to be one step ahead all the time. My sister came and stayed for a month and when she would come home from school she would want to know where I am. She was like a little spy for my mum. I had to keep hold of my work bag in case I lost something from it. It was a real nightmare (Suzanne, escort).

I told that many lies – like my aunty would ask me what I was doing and I would say that I have got a hairdressers and the next time I would forget what I have said and it became one lie after another which I really really hated. Then my children, well their friends would ask me what I was doing for a living and they would get really embarrassed and I would get embarrassed and they would forget what they had said and they would be telling constant lies. Because my children knew, it made them have to tell lies about what I did for a living (Sylvia, sauna owner).

Few participants have been lucky, skilled or ruthless enough to keep their work secret from everyone. Friends and family came to know about prostitution in many different ways and some workers eventually confided their activities. However, rarely was it the case of simply telling the truth. This final section explores how respondents used various truth mechanisms to control the level and type of information shared with loved ones.

Closed subject

Several respondents said they have been involved in prostitution for so many years that they are sure their family were aware. Ten women commented that family, especially parents, were aware of their involvement in prostitution but it was rarely mentioned. Maureen is an ex-worker and for the past decade has owned a sauna. In her teenage years, her father attended court when she was charged with soliciting. However, her current method of earning a lucrative wage is never discussed:

My brother, my mum and dad know, I think. They don't talk about it; they try to block it out ... They know I am not working because they phone me up and say oh I need you to come and get this shopping or do this, and I can go on the spur of the moment and so they know I am not working. They are not stupid. I think they just don't want to know.

Rather than explicitly telling the truth, Leanne relied on her family making assumptions about how she earned a living:

Well my family does know. I told my sister and then I told her that I had stopped working. But I did have a big row with my mum a few weeks ago and she said 'at least I am not a bloody prostitute' and I ignored it. I think she does know but she doesn't talk about it ... She knew that I was maiding for years and she used to say it won't be long before you are doing it.

Mutual denial has also been recorded as a strategy among topless dancers who did not discuss their jobs with family or partners, yet they were sure that close relatives knew of their stigmatizing occupation (Thompson and Harred 1992: 302).

Half the story

Not telling the whole truth was a popular strategy to prevent stigma and shame. Often, versions of the truth connect an individual to the sex industry but exclude her from selling sex. Respondents described how they selected acceptable aspects of the job to explain their association with prostitution. For example, the role of the receptionist is often used as a cover story as there is little shame in admitting to answering the phone:

> I told him [husband] that I was just the receptionist. But it covered me if we ever got raided. He thought I didn't do extras and then when I changed jobs I said that the management said I could just do massage and I didn't have to do extras and when I did start [providing sex] I said the clients give really good tips and that would account for the money (Rita, working premises).

Workers also hide the truth by claiming to offer services (such as massage) that do not involve sex:

> Close friends know what I do, my friend Jed knows what I do. But I never tell them exactly what I do. I always say that I do domination and bondage and no sex . . . They don't discuss it now. They don't ask (Mary, sauna).

> I did stop working for about a year since I have known him [current partner] but I found it wasn't me, I had to be making money somewhere. So after a while I said I was going back to work. I didn't tell him straight away I told him slyly and I said I specialized in domination (Zoe, sauna).

Zoe calculated that her boyfriend would accept that she offered domination services so she constructed a story that was partially true but did not connect her to the image of promiscuity.

Honesty

Half of the respondents explained how they are honest with some people in their personal lives:

My parents know what I do. I have got nothing to hide and I am a normal person. People like me for who I am and not what I do. And if they have got a problem with that then they can get lost. I am up front enough to tell them how it is and I am not ashamed about it. I have never had any problems ever and I have been working six years (Rachel, sauna).

My best mates know and my family know and the people that are closest to me all know. The people that I think should know all know. It is not feasible not to tell them, because I can have time off when I want and work when I want and have time off for parents' evenings or plays. So rather than explain a lot I just tell the truth, sometimes it is best (Beryl, working premises).

Plummer (1995) documents people revealing their sexualities as a social process of storytelling. In a similar way, sex workers engage in a process of 'coming out'. For some women, honesty was inevitable because when prostitution became a permanent feature of their lives, the lies and stories were more cumbersome than the truth. Continually 'passing off' affects the individual because of the high levels of stress associated with having to continually cope with secret information.

The consequences of stigma and shame are a significant risk for women involved in prostitution. In the hierarchy of harms (see Chapter 3), some respondents considered these consequences more harmful than other occupational hazards, such as violence or criminalization. Workers explained how they could recover from being robbed or beaten, pay a fine in court or deal with harassment from vigilantes because these risks only implicated themselves and usually did not interfere with their personal relationships. In contrast, being discovered involved in prostitution would probably be met with devastating personal consequences.

Strategies of secrecy can be understood as a product of dramatic performance, an object of social ritual and strategic gamesmanship – the metaphors through which Goffman defined his thinking about social life and the self (see Brannen 1997: lxiii). The place of secrecy in the world of sex workers is part of the strategic planning of performance through which they manage the stigmatized role. There are few other occupational examples where earning money becomes a social drama consisting of the interplay between the segregation of social space, social roles and social truths as information is managed between competing audiences. Social rituals and secrecy strategies enable sex workers to maintain what Goffman (1967) calls 'face' in order to preserve social status and mutual acceptance in ordinary, everyday life.

Despite these comprehensive, intentional strategies of passing off, sex workers explain how the truth cannot always be hidden. Over half of the participants had met someone they know while at work, or had been recognized in public (their private life) by a client. Respondents conveyed how they had to be prepared for a confrontation in their private lives and were continually anxious that their professional role and personal world would collide. Sometimes the strategies were successful, but often, the pressure of living in a complex web of deceit meant that women often revealed the truth and faced the consequences of mistrust, upheaval and isolation. As Murphy (2003: 326) summarizes from her findings among striptease dancers: 'through her secrets and lies, the stripper is not only on stage while she is dancing, she is on stage in her private life as well'. Avoiding being discovered and bringing shame on oneself or 'courtesy stigma' on loved ones requires continual mental acrobatics that may lead to what Goffman (1963: 7) describes as 'self-derogation'. Managing sex work is partly concerned with pragmatic strategies but also requires women to understand, interpret and manipulate emotional responses. The extent to which emotion management is a key feature of sex work is the focus of the next chapter.

Note

1 These accounts can be found either in the personal life stories of sex workers (Delacoste and Alexander 1988; Jaget 1980; Levine and Madden 1988) or by revealing experiences through qualitative research (O'Connell Davidson 1998; O'Neill and Barbaret 2000; O'Neill 2001; Pheterson 1996; Phoenix 1999a).

Chapter 8

Staying sane

> Emotion, it has been argued, can be and often is subject to acts of management. The individual often works on inducing or inhibiting feelings so as to render them appropriate to a situation. (Hochschild 1979: 551)

> Conscious decisions are made all the time to stop any contact happening even though you are having sex. (Eleanor, sauna)

Although sociological theorists have indirectly focused on the emotions to develop theories of social behaviour and structures (for instance, Weber's emphasis on values is grounded in emotional beliefs, while Durkheim muses that the creation of social solidarity is built through moral communities), the centrality of emotions in social life has been neglected in the social sciences (Denzin 1983; Shott 1979). More recently, emotions have been recognized as fundamental to the structure of interpersonal relationships and therefore social interactions (Elster 1999; Layder 2004; Shilling 1997; Williams and Bendelow 1998). The role of emotions in the workplace, work relations and the organization of employment has received increasing attention as a major determinant of productivity and organizational structures (Ashkanasy *et al.* 2000; Fineman 2003; Hochschild 1983). In this account of the risks associated with prostitution, no evaluation would be complete without reflecting on the role of emotions in sex work: in particular, the way in which sex workers experience emotions at work and, more importantly, the strategies they develop to manage emotions and prevent, if possible, psychological and emotional harm.

Empirical studies have attempted to assess the psychological effects of selling sex. Farley *et al.* (1998) conducted a large-scale, cross-cultural survey of 475 sex workers in South Africa, Thailand, Turkey, the USA and Zambia and found that 67 per cent of respondents displayed symptoms of post-traumatic stress disorder. A comparative study between ex-sex workers and a group with similar biographical histories found that those previously involved in prostitution had an 80 per cent chance of suffering depression (Bagley 1999). Other links between prostitution and poor mental health have been established in relation to eating disorders (Cooney 1990), low self-esteem (deMeis 2002), and drug use (Sterk 2000). Although no causal inferences can be made directly from these studies, they indicate that for some women, prostitution contributes to psychological distress.

Empirical findings can also be supported by recent research that documents pragmatic, symbolic and psychological defence mechanisms used by sex workers to separate their private life from work.[1] Hoigard and Finstad (1992) found that the public and the private worlds of the female sex worker are divided by blanking-out techniques, retaining physical boundaries, keeping to time, hiding appearance and avoiding emotional relationships with (long-term) customers. In Glasgow, McKeganey and Barnard (1996: 84) noted rituals based on clothing, make-up and bathing were strategies women used to act in and act out of the prostitute role, while Brewis and Linstead (2000a: 86) raise the profile of 'soft drugs' as a method to numb the unpleasantness of sex work. Pateman (1988: 207) relates distancing strategies to the need for the woman to retain her sense of self, while Miller (1986: 115) likens distancing strategies of prostitutes to those adopted by sexual abuse victims. In short, there is already evidence that sex workers recognize that selling their bodies has detrimental emotional implications and that they are thereby led to divide the private and the professional spheres of their lives.

This chapter magnifies the negative emotions experienced through the processes of selling access to body parts and describes how they motivate sex workers to create a range of emotion-management strategies. Relying on the basic themes of symbolic interactionism, identity and impression management, combined with emotion labour theory (Hochschild 1979, 1983), this chapter develops and adds to some of the emotion-management strategies already documented in the literature. I explain the following complex system of defence mechanisms as 'tools of the trade': avoiding personal relationships; the meaning of sex as work; body exclusion zones; and rationalization narratives. In an effort not to 'over-rationalize' these strategies, I explore how many sex workers are not in a material, social or economic position to create such distancing techniques or because of the strain of continually applying the strategies, the effectiveness of the techniques is questionable. In conclusion, I argue that despite a comprehensive set of emotion-management strategies, sex workers in my study were least proficient in managing emotional risks, despite prioritizing this type of risk above other occupational hazards in the 'hierarchy of harms'.

Negative emotions as motive

Emotional experiences can act as a powerful incentive to engage in a certain form of behaviour. Humphreys (2000) explains that one reason why doctors are motivated to reach and maintain clinical excellence is because of the small moments of emotional interactions they have with sick patients. The work practices that sex workers construct are also motivated by emotional experiences in relation to the commodification of their body parts. Thirty-seven of the fifty-five interviewees said that negative feelings such as guilt, disgust and shame are a consequence of selling sex. This section explains how these negative emotions prompt sex workers to construct a set of emotion-management strategies to prevent the body work and emotional labour they perform for clients producing undesired effects on their well-being.

Guilt

Guilt is an internal feeling that can be generated without reference to someone else's response. Annie summarizes how guilt is not dependent on someone else's reaction: 'In a way you feel guilt whether you are caught or not'. In contrast, Eleanor feels guilty because she knows she is deceiving her partner:

> I remember when on Valentines my partner took me out for the evening and just sitting looking at him and thinking what I do at work was really painful and guilt rushes over you.

Guilt is an emotion which does not necessarily need an actual audience but is often created using a hypothetical audience: 'Feelings of guilt often occur when we have violated a *principle* that we view as binding' (Elster 1999: 151). Despite only Eleanor's colleagues and clients knowing of her involvement, she still feels guilty because selling sex violates her own principles of fidelity, loyalty and honesty. Taylor (1985: 86–7) argues that guilt is a 'moral emotion' produced by the thought of harming others or committing acts that are considered forbidden or wrong. He describes guilt as an:

> Emotion of self-assessment . . . the person concerned believes herself that she has deviated from some norm and that in doing so she has altered her standing in the world. The self is the 'object' of these emotions, and what is believed amounts to an assessment of that self. (Taylor 1985: 1)

For many sex workers, even when work is hidden, they still feel guilty, not because they are harming anyone, but because they believe their behaviour is wrong. Polly admits: 'Sometimes I have gone through stages when I haven't worked and then the guilt has all come and then I have cried "What the fuck am I doing, what have I done?" It can just get too much.' Such consequences could have damaging effects:

> I used to go home and people would say what have you been up to and I would have to lie, but you know what you have done and you feel guilty and dirty as well. Plenty of times I have gone and got bottles of bleach and scrubbed my skin so bad that I have brought blood to it (Annie, street).

Several respondents made the relationship between guilt and morality: 'It [guilt] hits something inside of you and you deal with it but you are left questioning your own morality' (Sarah, sauna); 'I make myself feel fine about what I am doing because there is so much out there telling me that it is not. In certain circles it makes me feel like what I am doing is wrong' (Beryl, working premises). Such emotions are rarely felt in isolation.

Disgust

Thirty-seven respondents described emotions of disgust, normally as a result of physical contact with the client's body, in particular the genitalia and semen. Reflecting on why she stopped working as a dominatrix, Nicky recalls how some of the acts repulsed her: 'I walked out twice crying, not through pain, but through disgust at some of the things. It [domination] was so much harder than just a bonk. That is why I came out of it.' Others emphasized how difficult it was to confront negative feelings: 'If you stop and think about it you do feel dirty and disgusted' (Sharon, sauna).

Respondents described how the irony of experiencing negative emotions was that such feelings generated appropriate emotional responses. For some sex workers, the sight, smell and touch of a client's body is repulsive. A stranger's flesh is regarded as inferior, out of place and violates principles of privacy and intimacy. This is because intimate actions are, for most sex workers, as they are for those who are not in the business, usually associated with meaningful or pleasurable relationships. Because the commercial sexual relationship threatens this meaning, experiencing disgust enables an individual to mentally discriminate between what is enjoyable and what is not. Repulsion is a reminder that the flesh-to-flesh contact with unfamiliar men is confined to a commercial context and therefore different from bodily contact with sexual partners they chose. Sex workers described how the body fluids of male clients are contaminating and would infect their mind as well as their body:

> There was a girl here before, she would do everything and it was like she was saving nothing for herself. It is that mixing of bodily fluids, that skin to skin contact that is damaging (Eleanor, sauna).

Freud (1949) uses the concept of 'reaction formation' to describe how feelings such as shame, disgust and morality control or invert unacceptable impulses that may lead to the actualization of sexual desires. Women often commented that it was 'right' or 'natural' that they should feel repulsed by touching a stranger's genitalia or a stranger touching their body because such behaviour ruptures established codes of acceptability. This 'display of disgust' reinforces the understanding that for some women, sex with clients is not physically pleasurable or remotely satisfying. The group who said they enjoy sex with clients were not repulsed because they did not need to separate boundaries. However, the majority of women felt disgust and adopted complex strategies to organize their emotional experiences. Sex workers' identities are a complex relationship between desire and disgust (Epele 2001) that influence the external organization of the sex trade and the internal world of emotions.

Emotion management

Hochschild (1983: 7) offers two concepts of how emotions are managed: emotion work and emotional labour:

> I use the term *emotional labour* to mean the management of feeling to create a publicly observable facial and bodily display; emotional labour is sold for a wage and therefore has *exchange value*. I use the synonymous terms *emotion work* and *emotion management* to refer to these same acts in a private context where they have *use value* (original italics).

Emotional labour is the process of managing the responses of others. That is, the outward manifestation of feelings that sex workers display during interactions with clients are intended to create a desired positive response in the customer. One aspect of emotional labour is defined by Hochschild (1983: 10) as 'surface acting', where emotions are displayed to give the desired impression. This has been well documented in empirical studies on service work.[2]

Elsewhere I have argued that sex workers are involved in a form of 'service work' that engages in emotional labour for the paying customer (Sanders forthcoming). O'Neill (2001: 89) argues that 'emotional labour is a central aspect of the women's relationship with the client and involves them in manipulating, suppressing and falsifying their own feeling life in order to do the intimate work'. Emotional labour for male clients occurs not only through physical relief but pampering, frivolity and empathy. Kempadoo and Doezema (1998) and Chapkis (1997) have already argued that when women engage in sexual or erotic activities in prostitution it should be understood as selling a form of emotional labour. The nature of this labour has already been recognized: 'prostitution is extraordinarily stressful work . . . it calls for emotional labour of a type and on a scale which is probably unparalleled in any other job . . . the self-employed prostitute must keep herself in a constant state of readiness for tasks that are emotionally demanding and intrusive' (O'Connell Davidson 1998: 4). Emotional labour includes 'body work' (Wolkowitz 2002) that provides a display of the heterosexual female stereotype that matches the client's stereotypical ideal. The display includes what I have described elsewhere (Sanders, forthcoming) as a 'manufactured identity' that manipulates the cultural ideals of sexualized femininity to attract and maintain custom and make financial gain.

However, most of these arguments concentrate on how workers produce the desired response for the client, giving little attention to the emotion work that women perform on their own feelings. Hochschild (1979: 561) describes this as: 'the act of trying to change in degree or quality an emotion or feeling . . . the act of evoking or shaping, as well as suppressing, feeling in oneself'. In the context of prostitution, emotion work is an internal activity that concentrates on certain emotions during interactions with clients by preventing others occurring. Emotion work is carried out on feelings in private: women work on their internal feelings to separate, change and revise one set of feelings that are appropriate for professional work while reserving another set for private interactions. Emotions are managed internally by what Hochschild terms 'deep acting' – shaping an inner feeling to change the emotion. For example, a sex worker who is sexually aroused by an attractive client may try to turn this unwanted emotion into something more acceptable by concentrating on the emotion of disgust. Brewis and Linstead (2000a: 84) recognize the internal processes that sex workers perform on themselves:

Such occupations where the person(ality) of the worker is an important part of the service on offer, often threaten to 'consume' them in the process . . . This may require the prostitute to engage in the emotional labour necessary to maintain a sense of self-identity

... Prostitutes, due to the intensity and intimacy of their physical involvement in their work, do not necessarily find the distancing process easy, and a variety of styles and methods are employed by working girls (and boys) to sustain the mask, or series of masks, which make earning a living through the sale of sex possible.

One interpretation of prostitution argues that sex work is qualitatively different from other forms of labour on two accounts: first, that the client has control over the female body and, second, that because sexual identity and self are intertwined, selling sex necessarily means selling oneself. Pateman (1988: 203) argues that similar to the control an employer has over a worker, the client has control over the 'prostitute's person and body'. Pateman (1988: 207) goes on to state that prostitution is not simply about purchasing sexual services because when 'a prostitute contracts out use of her body, she is thus selling *herself* in a very real sense'.

This argument claims that selling sex can never be the same as ordinary labour power because prostitution specifically involves 'the direct use of one person's body by another' (Pateman 1988: 208). Casting prostitution as a consequence of patriarchal ideology is relevant to the discussion of emotion work: 'The integral connection between sexuality and sense of self means that, for self-protection, a prostitute must distance herself from her sexual use' (Pateman 1988: 207). Although there are important theoretical issues raised in this argument, such a linear understanding of what is for sale (i.e. the woman's body) ignores conceptualizations of self-identity or sexual identity, while at the same time rejecting any recourse to agency or decision-making.

Simmel (1955) introduced the notion of the modern 'self' constituting multi-faceted identities that are acted out in as many different roles, while Plummer (1995) speaks of identity as meanings that individuals construct about their lives and the stories they tell about themselves. Sex is a crucial aspect of social life and the forming of identities and sexual interactions become meaningful 'in the context of symbolically dense discursive terrains' (Oerton and Phoenix 2001: 388). This understanding of the forming of self and sexual identity provides the opportunity for no fixed sense of self but a more fluid reflection of how identities are dependent on many different contexts and understandings. Epele (2001: 162) argues that in prostitution women's gender roles are not 'static and frozen' but are part of a 'dynamic process, always open to challenge and contestation'. Therefore sexual identity is not fixed but there are 'fractured constructions of the sexual Self' (Hubbard 2002b: 366) created in response to the desire to separate working identities from other roles. The separation of identities is exemplified through the strategies sex workers construct to differentiate sex as work and sex that is associated with other meanings. Shrage (1999) illustrates this with her account of how women who are lesbians sell sex to men by defining the difference between active and passive engagement in intimate bodily contact. Oerton and Phoenix (2001) explain how 'discourses of meaning' map how women experience sex and sexuality as both public and private embodied experiences. The strategies sex workers adopt contradict the strict association of sex with bodily practices as 'sex can be de-coupled from the body' because sex workers are able to 're-inscribe different meanings of sexuality and space' (Oerton and Phoenix 2001: 391/2). Further, Hubbard (2002b: 365) propagates that the making of sexual identities is 'encoded in representations of space' that determine different types of sexual experience. This chapter demonstrates that through emotion work, women who experience prostitution under certain social and material conditions are able to control and order their feelings to achieve emotional distance from sex work. Emotion-management strategies limit the extent to which the self is commodified, enabling individuals to sell sex on their terms.

The exceptions

Having made the argument for sexual fluidity and plurality of identities, a minority of women in my sample did not perform extensive emotion work on themselves. From in-depth interviews with sex workers, Brewis and Linstead (2000: 206), McKeganey and Barnard (1996: 86) and McLeod (1982) found that for some women it is not necessary to place a rigid differentiation between work sex and non-work sex because they sometimes receive sexual pleasure from the commercial transaction. Six interviewees in my study revealed that sometimes sex with clients is enjoyable:

> Katrina: Sometimes you switch off, but sometimes you can't and you do think it is a punter and he is paying me to come, and it is turning you on.
> Leigh: When they are doing oral on you they are going for gold. They are sucking left overs from last week's chicken bones. They don't care. Your man would give you five minutes of oral pleasure at home. Of course you are gonna get turned on.
> Katrina: You try and think of everything, like shopping and then you just think sod it, I will just enjoy this. But sometimes when you come and they are wrinkled old farts, you think God what is happening to me? (Katrina and Leigh, working premises).

Anita explained that because she decided against having personal relationships while selling sex, it was an added benefit that she enjoys sex with some clients: 'When I came into this business I had been married for seventeen years and only had one man. So when I came into it I found that I enjoyed it and it was like a fantasy that had been fulfilled.' Echoing Warr and Pyett's (1999: 298) findings, seven respondents in my study had formed relationships with clients and crossed the boundary between the commercial into the personal:

> The guy I am seeing was an ex-client . . . he knows how it works and he knows that work is work and a relationship is different from being a punter. It works out well for me personally, he knows it is work and he is looking at it from the other side of the screen. He has a regular job so he is not dependent on me. I can talk to him after work about the clients (Krystal, working premises).

> TS: You mentioned about your partner knowing. How did that come about?
> Petra: He didn't have much choice really as he was a client. At the end of the day if you click with someone then it is an automatic thing no matter where you meet them. He knows what I do for a living and he sees the business side. I love my husband, I am married and I have a couple of kids and I love my family. I have a perfectly sound relationship with my husband and I have a normal married life (Petra, working premises).

For Petra and Krystal, personal relationships co-exist alongside selling sex precisely because their partners are also aware of the difference between commercial and private sex. However, my study provides ample evidence of how most women recognize that selling sex is emotionally risky. The majority of respondents are aware of the possible psychological damage of selling access to their vaginas, breasts and mouths but not their feelings, thoughts, personalities and minds:

> I will give physically, spiritually, advice, caring whatever, I will dish it all out. But there is one thing that they cannot have and that is a piece of my soul. And that includes anything to do with my private life (Sarah, sauna).

> I think working does damage you mentality wise. It does wreck your mentality because it is the trust. Before you start working you trust, but when you start working you don't trust [men] (Seema, sauna).

Below, I concentrate on the most popular types of emotion-management strategies that were evident among respondents in the indoor markets:

avoiding intimate relationships; the meaning of sex as work; body exclusion zones; and rationalization narratives.

The strategies

Avoiding intimate relationships

Ten interviewees decided to forfeit private sexual relations while they were involved in prostitution to prevent emotions in their professional world colliding with those in their private world: 'I could not work if I was in a relationship as I have done it before and it didn't work. It is too confusing and there is also never any time for me' (Melinda, works from home); 'I haven't really got a regular boyfriend because it interferes with work' (Katrina, working premises). Others explain why intimate relationships are inadvisable when selling sex:

> If I had a man in my life now and he knew what I did then he wouldn't love me. It would destroy him to think that I was going with six men a day, and you cannot say you don't enjoy the job as you would not do it (Anita, working premises).

> You get the ones who haven't got a problem with the job but they take liberties with the money or there are ones who have got a problem with the job and make your life hell. Or they have not got a problem with the job while you are making money. Most of them can't take it and you have to be on your own (Sammy, sauna).

Participants constructed the narrative around avoiding intimate relationships by referring to the moral condemnation associated with prostitution, maintaining that it was unreasonable to expect a partner to accept that his girlfriend has sex with other men, even in a business context: 'There won't be another relationship for me while I am working because no man would take it and I would not expect them to' (Lesley, sauna). 'No man who truly loves you would allow you to do this' (Beryl, working premises). Providing an alternative to the discourses reported by Phoenix (2000) with regard to sex workers making sense of their involvement in prostitution through relationships with men and money, the women in this subgroup were concerned that men they become romantically involved with will exploit them financially. Some respondents reflected on past experiences where boyfriends only tolerated their employment because it enabled them to be financially dependent. To avoid secrecy, emotional confusion, questions of trust and potential financial exploitation, this group of women rejected intimate, private relationships while they are involved in prostitution.

The meaning of sex as work

O'Neill (2001: 89) asks the question: 'How do women "make out" in conditions where they must separate body from "self" to do the intimate work of fulfilling clients' sexual needs/desires and, at one and the same time, how do they manage to suppress their own feeling life?' One way of resisting the threat to personal relationships and self-identity is to create separate meanings for sex at work and sex at home: 'Keeping boundaries are important in this business to keep your personal life separate' (Petra, working premises). 'Consumed bodies' are not determined by the client but are decided by the individual workers' parameters of what sex acts are acceptable in the 'economy of desire' (Epele 2001). Acts women perform on or for paying customers are desexualized in the same way that male sex workers perform fellatio as a business and not emotional investment (Reiss 1961). Desexualizing the commercial act is achieved by divorcing the meaning and experience of sex with a male client from that with their lover, partner or husband:

> When you are working you are having sex, you are not making love you are having sex ... so when you go back in your personal relationship you are doing the same but you are putting feelings to it, so it is not the same. I could not kiss a punter; I would not want anything to do with their mouth because I have to kiss my baby. And you would not want to kiss your man. Sex is with durex so you are not really touching them (Seema, sauna).

> My fella hasn't been home for three weeks. That is when I last had sex. It is personal at home, in here it is clinical. At home it is for my pleasure. I swear to god it [sex work] is like something you hate doing but it comes to me like washing up, like, it has got to be done. When you are with a punter you are thinking of something, and that is it, done (Astrid, working premises).

For some women it was essential that certain feelings are associated with paid sex while others are reserved for private experience. Beryl makes a conscious effort not to enjoy sex at work: 'If I let my mind go then I would enjoy it but I can't. I have to be in total control and I have to blank it.' Kelly described sex at work as a mechanical function: 'It is like acting, like I am a totally different person because to me sex is just a function. For me in my own life the person I am outside, away from work, sex is making love ... it is a completely different ball game.' A process described as 'switching off' 'indicates a body/self demarcation ... separate from their real/authentic-selves' (Oerton and Phoenix 2001:

398) and illustrates the shifting sexual identities that are apparent in different social settings.

To preserve the spontaneity, emotionality and integrity of the sexual experience, the worker constructs an alternative interpretation and consistently reproduces the meaning each time sex is sold. This process can be understood through Goffman's (1974: 319) 'reframing of experience'. Levi (1981: 48) summarizes the process of reframing as negating feelings, neutralizing and adopting a 'framework'. Goffman (1974: 319) claims that experience is divided into different 'tracks' or types of information. By placing information in different tracks and constructing a central storyline, the sex worker is able to define sex in different contexts. For those who decide to gain no pleasure from clients but want to maintain a 'normal' sex life in private, sex at work is interpreted as an economic unit, devoid of traditional associations of intimacy and affection (Browne and Minichiello 1995; Day 1994: 174; O'Neill 1996b; Scambler and Scambler 1997). Sex-as-work becomes disembodied from the emotions and bodily pleasures associated with sex-for-pleasure.

Respondents 'reframe' the sex work experience by comparing different types of sexual behaviour. Katrina believes that selling sex is more respectable than countless one-night stands:

At the end of the day I would rather be a working girl than be a slapper. At least I get paid for it rather than giving it away. Like I have got mates who don't work who go out every Friday and Saturday and pick up someone and she wasn't even using protection. Oh my god! In that sense, in my personal life I am very careful about sleeping around when I am working.

Further psychological processes are required to successfully reframe sex-as-work from private sex. Levi (1981: 58), in his paper *'Becoming a hitman'*, describes how killing becomes routine for the hitman because he 'negatively conditioned' himself to avoid certain features of the victim. The sex worker detaches herself from the client so she can sell sex without having to engage her personal identity with the client. Often, clients are considered in economic terms and their personal features are ignored: 'When that doorbell rings you don't see a face, all you see is ching [cash register noise]' (Astrid, working premises); 'It is just a job and I never think about clients' (Diane, sauna). Framing sex work as a job enables sex workers to manage one aspect of their sexual identity that transgresses what is considered acceptable and therefore acts as a technique of neutralization (Matza 1969).

Another way in which the meaning of sex is differentiated from sex in private is the symbolic use of the condom as a psychological barrier. As argued elsewhere, the condom in sex work acts as a barrier to emotional closeness (Plumridge *et al.* 1997; Sanders 2002; Warr and Pyett 1999). The division between their own flesh and that of the client during sex strengthens and sustains emotional barriers:

> It is like when you are performing oral on someone, to me it is not like oral sex as there is that condom there. When you are having sex you have got a cap there and a condom there which stops the contact ... As soon as anything touches you it is like barriers are broken (Eleanor, sauna).

Just as there is a strict rule regarding the use of condoms at work, there is an equally powerful discourse surrounding the absence of condoms in private, sexual and romantic relations: 'I don't feel right wearing a condom at home as it feels like work and that is not right' (Sammy, sauna). The condom is often avoided in private relations because, for some, unprotected sex symbolizes a trusting relationship and indicates a separation from the clinical and sterile feelings associated with commercial sex (Rhodes and Quirk 1998; Rhodes and Cusick 2000). Yet, the emotional reasons for not using condoms with sexual partners in the romantic sphere actually increases health-related risks (Faugier 1994; Ward *et al.* 1999). These meanings are reinforced by strict codes that determine which body parts are available.

Body exclusion zones

Limiting access to certain body parts and sexual acts was a universal emotion-management technique among respondents: 'If I have done the same client a million times, they still get the same spiel: don't kiss, don't do anal and you can only kiss and touch on top [part of the body]' (Krystal, working premises). Strict exclusion zones enable specific body parts, acts and physical responses to be reserved for private relationships. Edwards (1993: 103) summarizes how certain body zones are sacrosanct: some body parts are commodified while others are preserved, enabling women to 'sell their body and keep their soul'. Respondents confirmed: 'I think you have to have something saved for your partner' (Petra, working premises). O'Neill (1996b: 20) emphasizes that the line between sex as pleasure and sex as work must be rigid due to the ambiguous state of the body as a commodity. All of the sex workers in my study place a clear boundary between what is exempt from purchase and what is available. Neesha tells each client her rules every time they visit: 'My rules are no kissing, I don't hug, can't touch me between the legs or the anal area. Don't do anal, everything is with a condom, don't do reverse oral unless they wear a dental dam.' Women apply these stringent rules to ensure that access to their bodies happens on their terms.

O'Connell Davidson (1996: 184–5) explains how entrepreneurial worker 'Desiree' practised a five-stage routine with all clients ('settling him in', 'getting him going', 'getting him to shoot his load', 'reassuring him' and 'normalizing and getting him out'). Respondents in my study confirm the importance of routine in their work: 'It becomes routine. Like every client who comes in, you say the same things and after the service I say the same things' (Krystal, working premises). Other service industries such as the role of waiting staff in a restaurant (Crang 1994: 677), report the routinization of service as a control strategy. Routine strictly controls the client interaction and increases the chance of a predictable encounter. Brewis and Linstead (2000a) discuss the importance of limiting time with the client as a strategy that 'frames the sexual encounter'. In my study, respondents used timing as a technique to control the sexual routine by spending the minimum amount of time earning the maximum amount of money.

Some women exclude certain sex acts because experiencing sexual pleasure in a work context was considered unacceptable. Kelly gets to the point:

> When I was seeing my fella, I would not let them pussy lick me anymore. I was not having their germs from their mouth on me when my fella was not using condoms with me. So I stopped doing that. There is no chance, let me tell ya, I have set my guidelines and I do not veer off that course.

The type of sex that is on offer is a direct result of decisions women make to prevent negative emotions and preserve private pleasure. During her twenty-year career, Beryl's rules regarding the availability of sex acts changed, reflecting the fluctuation of commitments in her personal life:

> When I worked in Balsall Heath I worked the whole time without doing oral. But it was because I had got a personal life and you respect your man and then a few years ago I thought I am not going to have another man. So I thought sod it, if you stick a condom on then you are OK. I now make most of my money doing oral.

When Beryl decided to stop having serious male partnerships, oral sex was no longer 'special' or associated with intimacy, so was relegated to the realms of economic earning power. Sex workers shape the meaning of sex acts according to personal and economic needs. This also means that some acts are never for sale. Beryl continues:

Personally I don't kiss because it is very intimate and it has got to be with someone that I love and not with anyone. And at the end of the day I have got kids and I have got family and if I was kissing every single guy I saw kissing would mean nothing to me. Like sex, to me that can mean nothing so when I kiss someone it really means something. So that is why I won't kiss. Kissing is for me.

Kissing, and sometimes the mouth, is a sacred bodily orifice used only for loved ones. Carrie, a twenty-eight year old sauna worker, sums up the sentiment of most respondents:

If I kiss customers and then kiss my boyfriend I cannot see any difference between my boyfriend and the customer – there is no difference. For me not kissing is for personal reasons ... I have to keep things for myself. I can say that I am selling my body but I am not selling everything.

However, at the more lucrative end of the market, where women acted into a 'manufactured identity' to perform the 'prostitute role' as the ideal male fantasy, kissing is often on the menu because entrepreneurs realized that this was a commodity for which men would pay a high price. There are some men who want to experience what is known on the Internet chatrooms as 'the girlfriend experience' because, for the customer, these experiences go beyond physical satisfaction to include intimacy in the form of kissing, caressing and touching. Yet, for some sex workers, kissing is never acceptable at work:

Occasionally some of them will try to kiss and I tell them I don't do that and they are fine. Kissing I think is drawing a level between home and work. Alot of the Internet escorts do as they want to offer the 'girlfriend experience' but for me it is a line I draw (Esther, escort).

Among the sex work community there is a distinction between sex acts that should be sold and those that should not: 'Oral without [a condom] to completion, anal ... the girls are getting more degrading. I see me as a worker and them as dirty prostitutes. How can you have sex without, anal without? You are playing Russian roulette with your life' (Katrina, working premises). Maher (2000: 136-9) found among street-level drug-using sex workers that a code of acceptability existed where 'non-normative' acts would not be sold. In my study, none of the respondents admitted offering sex without a condom; only six included kissing and two women offered anal sex. There was bitter disapproval of women who offered these services that reflect wider cultural and social attitudes towards anal sex (Miller 1997). Some workers described those who sold anal sex as 'dirty', 'unhygienic' with 'no self-respect'. Such distinctions serve to stratify sex workers on the basis of their conformity to the community's code of sexual conduct.

Rationalization narratives

Jackman *et al.* (1963) refer to the 'social anathema' that women in prostitution experience as a result of disapproving social attitudes, and in response there is a recognition of the beliefs created by sex workers to counteract such negativity. Emotions such as guilt, shame and disgust are an extension of the consequences sex workers bare for conducting 'anti-social sex' (Polsky 1967: 186), but as argued throughout this book, disapproval is not accepted without a counter-offensive. Although other empirical work has identified how some sex workers have specific relationships with men and money that constitute a powerful aspect of their identity (Phoenix 2000), sex workers also define their identity in terms of providing functional services for men and society. A distinct set of rationalization narratives was evident among sex workers that justified why they were involved in prostitution and the important functions of prostitution.

Reminiscent of Davis' (1937) functionalist perspective, participants justify prostitution as a useful occupation through five narratives. First, forty-nine of the fifty-five respondents recognized their role as counsellors for men's emotional problems. Prostitution has already been described as a therapeutic service: 'Prostitution is not unlike being a counsellor or psychologist' (Arline, in Delacoste and Alexander 1987: 134); 'Sex work is nurturing, healing work' (Carol, in Delacoste and Alexander 1987: 124). In my study, women said that sometimes clients pay money just to talk with an empathic female, and evaluated that this made their job similar to that of a counsellor, therapist, social worker or psychiatrist: 'I see this as being a physical social worker. Ten per cent of the job is sex. Ninety per cent of the job is chatting, therapy' (Sarah, sauna); 'You are like a mixture of a social worker, a friend and a sexy sultry siren' (Esther, escort). Occasionally no sexual services are exchanged, or if they are, they occupy a small proportion of the transaction (Lever and Dolnick 2000: 95; Webb and Elms 1994).

Second, women explained how their job expands into health education, disease prevention and as therapists for sexual dysfunction. Embarrassed by medical professionals or their own female partner, men visit sex workers in the hope that sexual problems can be reversed or reduced: 'they think that we are doctors' (Diane, sauna). 'In terms of their body men don't know much. They have no idea about how diseases spread. That is where we come in' (Sarah, sauna). Explaining sexually transmitted infections and the dangers of unprotected sex is a daily feature of their job: 'What I find is an advantage from my nursing training is that when they come in and go on about having sex unprotected I can give them the advice to stop them from doing that' (Petra, working premises). The identity of prostitutes in Brazil has also been explained in terms of AIDS prevention and has been described as an important narrative women use to make sense of their 'social place' (deMeis 2002).

Third, some women argue that they provide a valuable service for men with disabilities. A quarter of the interviewees had been nurses or care assistants, so were accustomed to dealing with bodies, disabilities and ill health in legitimate, but nevertheless feminized, occupations. These women saw sex work as an extension of their caring role, and believed that sex work provides as valuable a service as mainstream medical care. Understanding their work as 'helping others' or 'care in the community' reframes the reality of exchanging sex for money. In this sense women conflate their role as sex provider on a similar plane to nurses and health-care workers who deal with the intimate bodily functions of patients while also engaging in sexualized discourses (O'Brien 1994). As Agustin (2004) argues, sex workers, like babysitters, domestic workers, nannies and carers, may pretend to care as part of the emotional labour performance, when they are actually divorced from any personal emotional investment.

Fourth, the majority of respondents describe how their profession offers an alternative to adultery and enables matrimonial relations to continue: 'Although thirty per cent of the men who come here just want normal stuff, the other seventy per cent I see are domination clients and it is something they could not ask their wives to do. I think this means their need to dress up as a woman say, is met and I believe it saves a lot of marriages' (Anita, working premises). Respondents maintain that buying sex rather than having extra-marital affairs reduces the likelihood of family breakdown: 'I always think they are coming to the right place ... They could be having affairs on their wives and this is just a bit of extra pleasure on the side, which probably that man needs. It prevents break ups and getting children involved in all that mess' (Diane, sauna).

Fifth, and most problematic, some respondents believe that the ability to buy sex reduces violent crime against women and children: 'We see a lot of strange men and you think how far would they take this if this service wasn't available' (Katrina, working premises). Sex workers said that the facility to act out fantasies in the confines of a consensual commercial transaction allows some men to enter into worlds that would be criminal and morally outrageous in real life. The rationalization of behaviour, and in particular the avoidance of self-blame, has been documented as a mechanism to justify actions in relation to deviant and criminal activities (Sykes and Matza 1957). Levi (1981: 47) adopts Goffman's (1974) theory of frame analysis and argues that where detachment is a prerequisite of the profession, a neutralization process of 'reframing' is necessary. This brief review of some of the rationaliz-ation narratives, coupled with extensive emotion work on internal feelings, provides some insight into the emotion management that sex workers, like other female service workers, perform every time they do business.

When emotion management fails

The majority of respondents I spoke with adopt some or all of the strategies described in this chapter to manage their emotions and protect themselves from the negative psychological consequences of selling sex. Although it was not an objective of this study to explore the success or failure of these strategies, there is evidence to suggest that defining meanings, reframing experience and maintaining distance is so exhaus-tive that even those skilled in emotion work found it difficult:

> I nearly had a nervous breakdown ... I went away for a month and left my children with my sister and had to go out of the situation and look at myself, a little bit like when someone says when they die. I had to look at the situation because I couldn't cope anymore (Rita, working premises).

> I have been working for a year now and I need a break. I am getting unprofessional about it and then you risk selling your soul, if you are not careful. You have to take care of yourself outside of here, spiritually and intellectually (Sarah, sauna).

McLeod (1982: 41) evaluates how continually engaging in separation techniques produces 'strain in maintaining [this] emotional self-protec-tion'. Loewenthal (2002: 151) asks: 'do people sometimes submit to carrying out emotional labour that is detrimental to them, for economic reasons?' For sex workers who devise coping strategies, sometimes the strategies become displaced by a failure in the technique or simply because of the continual amount of effort needed to sustain them. In the words of peep-show worker, Vicky Funari (1997: 28): 'I have no feelings, but I know their absence means they are hiding beneath the shell I must build and then demolish every time I work a shift. It's hard work, maintaining this shell.' The intensity of emotion work could alienate the worker: 'Beneath the differences between physical and emotional labour there lies a similarity in the possible cost of doing the work: the worker can become estranged or alienated from an aspect of self – either the body or the margins of the soul – that is *used* to do the work' (Hochschild 1983: 7).

This study came into contact with women who were not coping with their role as sex workers. They were often young women, working the street with poly-drug addictions, under the pressure of a pimp and with little inclination, liberty or energy to speak to a researcher. Those who do not adopt separating strategies leave their emotions and identity exposed: 'I do get down. It is hard and you get low days. Some days I hate what I do, I try and block it out. It is hard sometimes . . . I don't talk to anyone about it, it is better that way. The less I talk about it the less real it is' (Louise, street). Strong negative emotions have dangerous consequences: 'Last year I did go through a bad patch when I was drinking a lot just to get away' (Kelly, sauna). Other studies confirm that some women use drugs and/or alcohol to cope with selling sex.[3] Guilt and drug use appeared to be linked:

TS: What do you do to get over the feeling of guilt?
Annie: 'Buy more drugs. With heroin you smoke it and you are in a world of your own; and chilled out ain't the word. That is why I do it. When I started this job I used to just smoke weed. But when you go out there with the customers you don't feel right. But with the heroin you just smoke the heroin and you are with the customers and you don't have to think because you are lying there and I am like I am sleeping, in a gauge because of the drugs. Some of the customers have said that it is like sleeping with a dead person' (Annie, street).

Epele (2001: 164) reveals from the 'hotel stories' of drug-using sex workers in San Francisco how the consumption of drugs can make women lose control and consciousness, creating the conditions for 'drug-related sexual slavery'. Yet, as Wincup (2000: 417) has argued from ethnographic data of women in bail hostels, substance misuse is also connected to the 'desire to manage pain' and ignoring women's agency in drug-use activities only replaces individual determinism with structural determinism.

The presence of emotion-management strategies is achievable only under certain social and economic circumstances. Epele (2001: 161) describes how economic resources and material conditions determine the 'bodily well-being' and 'body commitment' made during sexual transactions. Identities constructed under limited opportunities, insecure and volatile personal histories, estrangement from social capital and material resources such as housing, welfare services and mainstream labour prevent women controlling the work routine, or making decisions about which market and location to work, with whom and under what rules. Emotion-management strategies may well be reserved for those who have entered prostitution as a career and make clear decisions about how to manage the complexities of selling sex.

Those who remain in prostitution may well be those who perfect these strategies and find a way of balancing the complexities of commodifying their bodies, yet not selling themselves. Those who do not realize how to manage emotions, or confuse different spheres of sexual activity and identity, may find other, less taxing methods of making money, illegally or through mundane mainstream options. The common pattern of 'taking a break' in prostitution can also be accounted for by the pressure to maintain separation, avoid contaminating personal relationships, and continually engage in emotion work. These findings suggest that often sex workers are more proficient at managing the physical risks involved in selling sex rather than the more complex emotional and identity-related consequences.

The women in this study that described emotion-management strategies firmly prioritized emotional risks in the 'hierarchy of harms'. Many of the respondents remained violence-free or rarely encountered physical attacks at work and considered their strategies coherent and successful. However, when it came to managing the emotional side of selling sex, respondents were less proficient, and because of the continual strains associated with emotion work and labour, they often experienced negative emotional consequences. Nevertheless, sex workers I spoke with did make decisions to organize, control and manage their own behaviour and emotional experiences as part of the complex web of risk-management strategies. They were also aware that any attempt to rationally reduce emotional risks was continually under threat while the relationships that surround the selling of sexual services remains illegal and the conditions of work are left unregulated and exposed to dangers.

Notes

1 See Boynton (2002: 8); Brewis and Linstead (2000a); Day (1994); O'Neill (2001: 89); Phoenix (2000); Warr and Pyett (1999).
2 For example, in the leisure and tourism industry (Adkins 1995); the airline industry (Bolton and Boyd 2003; Mills 1998; Williams 2003); 'care' work and nursing (O'Brien 1994); policing (Rattue and Cornelius 2002); hairdressing and beauty therapy (Black 2004; Furman 1997; Kang 2003; Sharma and Black 2001); and the image consultancy business (Wellington and Bryson 2001).
3 See Boynton (1998); Brewis and Linstead (2000a); Maher (2000: 13); McKeganey and Barnard (1996); Scambler and Scambler (1997).

Chapter 9

Professionalizing prostitution?

> There is no likelihood that sexual freedom will ever displace prostitution. Not only will there always be a set of reproductive institutions that place a check on sexual liberty, a system of social dominance which gives a motive for selling sexual favours, and a scale of attractiveness which creates the need for buying these favours, but prostitution is, in the last analysis, economical. (Davis 1937: 755)

Prostitution is considered by some to be an activity that signals a failure in individual morality, a breakdown of cohesive institutions such as marriage and the family. Prostitution is considered an indictment on female gender expectations and appropriate behaviour placing it, among other sexual behaviours, at the bottom of the social order of sexualities (Jackson and Scott 2004). This perspective fuels the belief that because prostitution symbolizes a transgression of acceptability, the relationships that facilitate the sale of sex must also be chaotic and capricious, without internal coherence or structure. There is some justification for this view because, as this book demonstrates, external legal constraints put strains on relationships forming between organizers and workers, leaving limited opportunity to collaborate on business interests or conflicts. Lines of communication are complicated by competition and 'dirty hustling' (Heyl 1979: 122), resulting in a fragmented indoor commercial sex economy. Reflecting Albini's (1971) model of independent enterprise, some saunas, brothels and independent escorts are isolated entrepreneurial units, loosely structured and positioned outside coordinated networks. Isolation is perpetuated by the risks created from policing (discussed in Chapter 6) and the need for most workers (and organizers) to hide their money-making activities and operate a double life.

Despite evidence of this disorganization, I observed a distinct degree of conformity between workers and establishments. Echoing Sutherland's (1937) exposure of the intricate skills and abilities of deviant and criminal groups, a substantial level of coherence and continuity was identified between the internal organization of sex establishments, the practices surrounding sex work and colleague relations. This chapter draws on the conclusions made throughout the book to explore how an irregular economy is actually structured by similar mechanisms and systems that are apparent in mainstream occupations. First, this chapter summarizes the rules, rituals and routines sex workers and organizers use to govern commercial sex. The competitive nature of selling sex determines both social norms and sanctions for those who stray from the expectations. Codes of conduct and moral hierarchies are borrowed from the official labour market and straight society, to self-regulate the illegal marketplace. Second, I describe a set of 'mechanisms of transmission' to demonstrate the complex networks and relationships through which individuals learn the trade. Mechanisms include modifying behaviour after making mistakes, transferring skills from other life experiences, apprenticeships and mentoring, formal allies in the shape of health organizations in addition to familial and occupational networks. Third, combining a meso-structural perspective of the organization of social deviance and a micro-structural perspective that centres on the context of the deviant sex work act, I re-focus the analysis to illustrate how risk can be regulated through unionization and collaboration, arguing that some aspects of prostitution are undergoing a process of professionalization. Concluding comments suggest there is a greater need to include clients' perspectives in the analysis of the organization of prostitution and I propose further ways to develop this research field.

Rules, rituals and routines

Throughout this book there has been a heavy emphasis on the strategies that sex workers apply to minimize dangers from violent men who pose as clients, techniques to protect their identities from exposure and manage psychological issues relating to selling access to their body parts. Much of this discussion has necessarily focused on individual efforts in order to convey the types and levels of rational evaluation that produce strategic responses. In addition, collective practices and expectations determine roles and maintain regularity in the industry. This section describes overarching norms and methods of regulation that influence the organization of prostitution in the indoor markets.

Norms and sanctions

From my analysis, it is clear to me that social norms exist among sex workers, organizers of businesses and male clients. The norms among sex workers are social rather than individual norms because they do not always maximize individual advantage but they are designed to foster collective interest. If we are to analyse prostitution as a non-normative career, the norms and values that structure commercial sex reflect that of the legitimate world of work. A set of competencies and work-based expectations have been identified that form a 'social code' (Sharpe 1998: 80) accompanied by 'etiquette and rules' (Hart and Barnard 2003: 36).

The consistent use of condoms in the sexual service and a fixed price code are good examples of social norms. It could be the case that offering sexual services without a condom benefits an individual financially, yet not practising safe sex would make business difficult for other workers because clients would expect all women to forfeit condoms. Equally, 'price-busting' (O'Neill and Barbaret 2000: 129) may be beneficial for one woman because she would receive increased custom but other workers stand to lose out as they too would be expected to offer lower fees and eventually all prices would plummet.

Despite the competitive nature of prostitution and the common situation where providers outnumber customers in the fieldwork site, there was evidence of a cohesive set of expectations of behaviour. For example, poaching regular customers was considered against the rules of fairness: 'Sharking is when they [other workers] go to the door with their tits hanging out and tell the clients that you are busy when you ain't. That shows the girl is not really a team player but is just out for herself and you have to be wary' (Kelly, sauna). Encouraging girls under eighteen to work, using drugs and staying in an exploitative romantic relationship also create ill-feeling between workers. Not only were these behaviours considered morally unacceptable because they are disrespectful to the individual or unfair play, they are frowned upon because they put others in danger. Overall compliance can be accounted for primarily because within this cut-throat business the rite of passage to be included in the local network was established through mutual cooperative sharing.

Where there are norms there are sanctions to reinforce behaviour and act as a deterrent for those who may be tempted to act differently. It was not often that norm breaking was observed and when women did protest and complain about rule-breakers there were distinct repercussions for the deserter. Sanctions take different forms but usually centre on ostracizing or excluding an individual from the workplace and network. Often this is signalled through 'humour [used] against each other to challenge, incite competitiveness, oust women from establishments, taunt and humiliate' (Sanders 2004a: 280). Gossiping, spreading ru-mours, folklore and urban myths are part of the oral culture that is used to create divisions between workers. Equally, as humorous banter signals inclusion and exclusion, silence is a powerful tool to distinguish those who are accepted and those who are unwelcome. For example, if there is one outlaw among the workers then 'in-house' procedures and information are sometimes withheld in the hope that the unwanted worker will make mistakes and be dismissed: 'We never told her the price for each room had gone up, so the boss thought she was undercharging. She was sacked. Result' (Letisha, sauna). I observed how such collective strategies were used against new workers who threatened the stability of the long-term workers and the philosophy of teamwork: 'Us girls have worked together for a long, long time. We trust each other because we have been through it all together. No need for anyone else' (Astrid, working premises).

Another reason for compliance rests with owners and managers of brothels, saunas and escort agencies that are enforcers of acceptable and unacceptable behaviour. With the reputation of the establishment at heart, strict rules prevent the business being brought into disrepute by a violent incident or robbery that could spark unappreciated gossip. Soothill's (2004b: 49) exposure of clients' perspectives on how establish-ments are measured for quality confirm that customers prefer to visit saunas and working premises that hold a reputation for, among other criteria, efficiency and safety. A sauna that has been robbed several times, or is unscrupulous about the type of client it accepts would discourage trustworthy customers. Although it was rarely spoken about, I observed how workers and owners among the licensed saunas in Birmingham constructed a hierarchy based on reputation. Poor reputa-tions motivated other owners and managers to preserve a good reputation by strictly enforcing norms and punishing those who ignore the standards.

It is worth noting at this point that when a client decides to purchase sex from the street, call out an escort or visit a sauna, although the interaction is a private sexual experience, the client is buying into a set of expectations and practices that are cogent with similar commercial transactions available throughout the regional, local and even interna-tional market. The client has most probably had several other commer-cial encounters with different women in a range of establishments and will be accustomed to the general trend of negotiating the contract, the process of payment and the sexual code. Clients learn the 'etiquette of the market' (Hobbs 1997: 60) because they become socialized into practising consistent rules. Evidence of the 'strictly scripted' routine (Murphy 2003: 320) can be found in the detailed arrangements such as the worker specifying the sexual position, keeping to the time paid for and only allowing the client access to certain spaces. Whatever the market, there are norms that govern the expectations of behaviour not only for the insiders, but the purchasers, who become temporary insiders, when they enter the illicit marketplace. By clients sharing knowledge through lively and frank discussions on the Internet (see Soothill 2004b) and popular manuals such as 'McCoys Guide to Adult Services', acceptable behaviour is repeated and purchasers become transmitters of norms, values and codes of practices.

Moral hierarchies: old versus new order

The social norms of any group are not static but subject to social, cultural and political change. This was evident in my study because the stories and experiences from across three generations of sex workers (the youngest respondent was eighteen while the oldest was fifty-five) suggested that a new and an old order of prostitution existed. In Birmingham the old order was characterized by a tightly knit, compact and smaller number of women who, over twenty years, had entered a rigid occupation based on a strict hierarchy of seniority. From my sample, those who entered the industry in the 1970s usually defined themselves as career women, rather than the new recruits who appeared to use sex work opportunistically alongside other scams, acquisitive crimes, part-time official employment or educational pursuits. Traditionally, markets were geographically fixed with limited mobility between establishments.

Older women I spoke with attributed the changes to the industry on the increase in drug use in younger women's lives. On the street, experienced women said the prevalence of drug-using sex workers affected the organization of sex work in several ways. First, as established by the literature (see Chapter 1), drugs have implications on the price of sex that in turn pressurizes non-users to lower the fee for sexual services. The drug culture that was beginning to seep into the indoor sex markets was highlighted as the culprit for a change in motivations among new recruits. Sarah, who had recently returned to working in a sauna after a three-year break, explains:

> Thirteen years ago, when I started here I had one main objective and that is the same reason I am here now, to get money and to get out. A lot of the girls these days don't have a plan. Years ago it would be like to get a house and everybody encouraged this . . . get a house and a mortgage, try and find a straight job . . . The issues of drugs means that there is no planning and it all becomes really short term. I wouldn't do this job to stick drugs up my nose, as it is too hard to earn it.

Second, the older women were concerned that blackmail and violence from a pimp or dealer normally accompanied drug use. Coercive relationships that marred the lives of street workers were in contrast to the subtle but strong feminist attitudes of independence and solidarity among the veterans. Third, in what can be described as the post-traditional prostitution industry, novices were described as less in-hibited, willing to provide an extensive variety of sexual services and specialize in a niche market for what was sometimes considered peculiar fantasies. Altogether, the old order of prostitution was said to be fading as newcomers, armed with sophisticated entrepreneurial skills and information technology such as computer-mediated communication, were rapidly reshaping the 'new ecology of sex work' (West and Austrin 2002: 496).

The influx of younger women creates competition for others who rely on their long-term regulars because attracting new custom is difficult. A concern among the older workers and organizers was that the new workforce, especially women who did not speak English as their first language and were migrant workers, did not enter the business under the traditional guidance of experienced workers. The concern was that flitting in and out of the business diluted the standards of the trade, threatening the homogeneity of working practices. Established workers and organizers considered it their responsibility to pass on tricks, standards and skills to the sex work community yet they felt their influence was dwindling despite their vision to continue to work as a loosely organized group of women: 'They don't want to know – the young ones. More interested in working on their own and using the web rather than sitting in here all day' (Wilma, sauna). However, suggestions of an old order of prostitution can be critiqued by what Bauman (1992: 138) describes as 'retrospective unity'. Threatened by ageing bodies and the pressure to keep up their appearance, older women talked about their early prostitution careers with nostalgia, reflecting similar narratives among the post-industrial working-class labour force (Lash 1994).

In support of a changing prostitution structure, I observed a distinct group of sex workers who were dislocated from the networks and uncommitted to the life of prostitution. Colleague relationships were characterized by what Monaghan (2002) describes as 'cool loyalties': indifference, psychological distance and shallow ties. An absence of integration was notable in larger saunas and brothels. Women were cautious not to disclose personal details about their 'real' lives to each other, preferring to hide behind their pseudonym, earn cash and return to their private lives untainted by their deviant dealings: 'You don't go to town with these girls, it's just work. Safer that way' (Kelly, sauna). Here, relations with colleagues were determined by 'commercial rather than ethical frontiers' (Hobbs 1997: 66), obeying the rules because they benefited the collective but showing little camaraderie or group affiliation. Often women did not want to become experts in the business, preferring to perceive their involvement in the sex industry as a temporary money-making stop-gap before their next plan got off the ground: 'I know it is short term for me to the end of the year. As soon as I get married I would never work and next month I am going to drop another day ... I am setting up two businesses – one in health and the other unrelated' (Esther, escort).

Reminiscent of Ruggierio's (1995: 132) 'deskilling of the criminal workforce' hypothesis, many of the novice sex workers simply 'go to work', with little commitment to developing skills, becoming self-employed or making the transition to manager or owner. Despite the changes in the structure of prostitution observed in this one city over a relatively short period of time, a moral framework was still apparent among organizers, purchasers and providers of commercial sex. As the drug industry plays by ethical rules regarding good practice with customers (Denton and O'Malley 1999: 520), a moral framework exists within the sex industry which is embedded in codes of practice.

Codes of practice

The preceding chapters have argued that in the indoor commercial sex industry there are codes of practice that determine how business should be conducted, the nature of relationships between colleagues, and the role of the management. I have described how a code of practice is evident in relation to minimizing risks of danger by regularizing screening strategies, accepting general working rules, precautionary measures, deterrents and if necessary remedial protection (see Chapter 5). 'Organized understandings' (Reiss 1967: 204) exist between women who often do not know each other but recognize the crucial importance of maintaining secrecy and preventing the exposure of real identifiers. For example, a code of sexual practices regulates behaviour among sex workers and clients. This code establishes what is acceptable as a sexual service and what is considered 'deviancy within deviancy'.

Generally kissing and anal sex are considered unacceptable practices in the commercial transaction but for different reasons. Although there are exceptions (see Sanders forthcoming) kissing was considered too intimate, far more than vaginal intercourse, and something to be saved for personal romantic relationships. In accordance with popular discourses (Middlethon 2002; Miller 1999: 100), receiving anal penetration from a client was considered disgusting, contaminating and humiliating. To a lesser extent, it was considered non-professional, rather than outright disgusting, to actually enjoy sex with clients or have orgasms.

'Golden rules' suggest romantic relationships with clients dangerously blur boundaries and rarely succeed. This moral sexual code is reinforced by a vehement display of abhorrence towards other explicit and often criminal forms of sexual deviancy such as paedophilia, incest and bestiality. Violent and overtly derogatory sex acts towards women such as the infliction of pain, fantasies that involve rape or children are considered outside the realms of acceptability:

> There was one man whom I could not see again as he talked about children and I stopped him there and then and asked him to get dressed and told him to leave. We are providing a service for fantasies but there are limitations and you need to protect your own sanity and the other girls as well (Eleanor, sauna).

Despite recognizing a new order of prostitution, the presence of sex codes is consistent over time. McLeod (1982: 40) interviewed sex workers in Birmingham in the 1970s and found a similar pattern of unacceptable sexual behaviour where anal sex was considered 'a nasty, dirty thing'. Although an area where little empirical data has been gathered, Soothill (2004b: 51) documents the moral integrity of clients in relation to sex with young females under the age of eighteen years, and suggested that a sex code and a moral code exist among the patrons of prostitution. Goffman (1983: 3) explains that within group interactions, through processes of social ritualization, there is a 'standardization of bodily and vocal behaviour through socialization'. This strict, consistent sex code is a clear example of the steadfast rules and moral standards that characterize parts of the sex work community in Britain and those who break the rules.

Mechanisms of transmission

Speaking directly about the sex industry, West and Austrin (2002: 490) state that 'the subject of how networks cross-cut markets and organizations is generally left unexamined'. This section details the connections between familial, collegial and social relationships that determine occupational networks in the sex markets I observed. Returning to the Chicago School's emphasis on studying the networks and contacts between deviants, these interlinking relationships between individuals and establishments are key mechanisms of transmission for learning the codes of practice, values and norms of the sex markets. Before this, however, it is important to analyse how individuals regularize sexual services through self-reflection on their own behaviours, especially when things go wrong.

Learning from mistakes

There was strong evidence to suggest sex workers engage in a process of evaluating their practices and make changes in relation to the risks they encounter and the mistakes they make. Sex workers in my study responded to mistakes in three ways. First, they re-evaluated the risks of the market and often moved to a safer environment. For example, when I met Amy she had worked on the streets for over twenty years. Shortly after, she experienced an attempted rape, so re-evaluated the risks of the street. As a direct result of this attack, Amy decided to accept only regular clients, at home or in their car. Also, I met Eleanor when she started working in a sauna. She said she would never work alone as an escort after a recent attack by a regular client in a hotel room. Eleanor described how changing from working alone to working in a sauna was a trade-off between secrecy and safety. Working in a collective environment increased the number of people who were aware of her involvement in prostitution but reduced the chance of a further attack. Not only their own mistakes but also incidents that happen to friends make women reassess where they work:

> I worked on the streets in 1993 and there was a girl killed by a punter. I knew her really well. I was only speaking to her a couple of hours before she was killed. I thought no, I better come off these streets (Katrina, working premises).

> I have a friend who was murdered in Chester by a client, in a building where there were other clients downstairs and the clients thought she was having kinky sex. This is one of the dangers of working alone, she was and it killed her. She should have been working with other people (Sarah, sauna).

Second, sex workers learn from mistakes by altering routines. Respondents spoke of a 'steep learning curve' when they entered prostitution and often isolated incidents changed their behaviour: 'I have had a client not pay but that was in a sauna. He asked me for a drink of water, went to get the water and he had gone. That was the only one. You don't do it again' (Rita, working premises).

Third, sex workers reflect on their mistakes by learning the importance of consistently applying procedures to all clients. Precautions and screening are only effective when applied to real-life decisions and interviewees confessed that when they did not follow the rules there was trouble:

> You have to learn as you go along and in the beginning I didn't care until some bad things had happened . . . When I went out there to

begin with I just used to get into any car, with two or three men and never used to check or anything. I got into quite a lot of trouble doing that . . . I was told the safety ropes by my mates but I would not listen as I thought they were just being racist. A couple of girls said not to go with black men, but I never listened and got into a lot of bother (Neesha, street but occasionally works indoors).

All the girls I know who are on the Internet and have met a bad customer have done it as they have needed an extra bit of money and have let one of their rules slip. They have accepted a booking without a mobile [telephone] number or have not checked up on the hotel (Esther, escort).

Transferring skills

Participants relied on skills they had acquired in mainstream occupations. Eleven of the fifty-five interviewees had trained and worked as either nurses in a hospital or psychiatric setting, or in care homes with the elderly and disabled. This kind of care work involves continually observing, monitoring and judging people's behaviour for signs that suggest aggression or agitation, as well as techniques to diffuse dangerous situations. Petra explains how the communication skills she was taught at nursing college are directly transferable: 'With regards to talking to clients you use the same skills that you would when you are with patients'. Also, Krystal's experience as a psychiatric nurse taught her to manage her emotions in the sex work setting: 'You see some really horrible sights as a nurse and you have to learn to switch off and do the job in hand. It is very much like that in the room; you have to switch off your feelings . . . it is very easy for me to switch off.' Learning to distance feelings by 'switching off' and making the job routine is essential in both the nursing profession (James 1989; Smith 1992) and sex work. Nicky, a maid for an entrepreneurial sex worker, made links between the skills she used in her current job and her previous employment as a bouncer in a nightclub. Both jobs involve assessing the credibility of strangers and judging people by appearance (Winlow et al. 2001).

Respondents also used their life experience to manage risks at work. Learning how to fight and retaliate are part of everyday life for some women: 'Being a little person and being picked on at school started me off on martial arts so I have been able to look after myself. Men do not frighten me and I have had loads of fights in clubs before' (Leanne, working premises). Controlling difficult situations is often embedded in respondents' personal histories. Anita did not find it hard to detach from work as she learned to live in two separate worlds from an early age: 'I am a very good actress to be honest. I have had to be as I was abused as a child. I learned to be two people from an early age and that is what

I do here.' The skills women learn to avoid danger and manage emotions in ordinary life are essential tools in the negotiations with clients.

Mobility and networks

A defining characteristic of the contemporary sex industry is the mobility of women at both a global and a local level (Agustin 2004). This movement has the potential to either strengthen or weaken the sturdy female networks that connect markets and workers. Although the majority of respondents I spoke to worked in Birmingham, twenty-six had worked in more than one other town and ten women had worked 'away days' in London, while a further six had worked in other cities such as Manchester, Leeds, Nottingham, Sheffield and Glasgow. Geographical mobility and mobility within markets are important mechanisms of transmission that provide an opportunity to pass on codes of practice. Although there was no report of a downward trajectory from the indoor markets to the street, an upward career move from the street to the indoor markets was common (Brewis and Linstead 2000a: 264, and Rickard 2001, also report this).

Movement between establishments is as popular: only seven of the fifty-five respondents had worked in just one establishment and two women with long career histories had worked in over forty different establishments. Like the networks created in mainstream labour markets, moving from job to job effectively creates an occupational network. The constant movement of workers, and to a lesser extent maids and managers, between saunas, brothels and escort agencies creates a strong localized female network often based on matriarchal family relations (Sharpe 1998: 41–9). As Lash (1994) describes, it is in the traditional communal forms of work patterns that shared identities are cemented and an exchange of knowledge is facilitated. As an example of the integrated networks that structure the indoor sex markets, the social, familial or occupational connections of eighteen women (all of whom were interviewed) can be traced to one sauna. Trying to make sense of these connections I noted in my fieldwork diary:

> Moonlights is a licensed sauna that has been in operation for over twenty years and for the last five has been owned by Sylvia and managed by Rebecca who have known each other socially for over a decade. Rebecca previously worked with Annabelle in another sauna, and when Rebecca became manager of Moonlights, Annabelle followed. Since then, Annabelle has left the industry full time but occasionally takes on escorting work. Recently Annabelle has befriended a young woman, Neesha, who has been working on the streets for four years and desperately wants to move indoors.

Because Neesha is not a drug user, Sylvia agreed to give her a trial at Moonlights. Rebecca manages the day to day running of the sauna and her sister also manages a sauna in another part of the city. To provide some variety for the clients or calm a quarrel, sometimes the managers swap staff. However, Sylvia prefers to keep a regular workforce: Zoe, who has been school friends with Rebecca for over twenty-five years, has recently returned to the industry and works in the sauna twice a week. Zoe also brought along her neighbour, Dora who is new to the industry. Permanent staff include Mary, Wilma and Letisha who work up to eight shifts a week and have been there for between three and five years. Eleanor is the newest recruit of six months. Rita was employed at Moonlights for over seven years but decided to rent her own apartment with another woman, Margaret, as the competition from younger women was too high. Astrid also did a brief stint at the sauna but found her own managerial flare and set up an apartment with her two school friends Krystal and Polly. Suzanne previously worked in Moonlights but found the hours too long and restrictive so, in partnership with her sister-in-law, Tracy, rented an apartment where they work together.

In contrast to the relatively solitary business of the street market (Dalla 2002), relationships indoors are often a mixture of fluid, transitory acquaintances centred partly on workplace relations, 'blood family' and close friendships that are grounded in historical and local times, places and events. The basis of any illicit business is trust, and loyalty is an expectation of primary kinship and kin-like relations (Denton and O'Malley 1999: 514). Emotional bonds guarantee a degree of loyalty because the obligation to conform becomes a reflection of the respect for the relationship rather than an overt commitment to the sex work culture. This is particularly important in groups where keeping identities and actions secret is paramount. Maher (2000: 161) suggests the street market also self-reproduces through a system of female fraternity: 'the existence of women-centred street networks [which] functioned as valuable conduits for information and the pooling of scarce resources'.

However, there is a tendency to romanticize the internal relationships between workers. Although team spirit and common interests facilitate learning, competition for clients creates tensions between workers:

You have to be careful where you are working, you get a lot of bitchiness. You get it out on the street, you get it indoors, everywhere. But the thing about the street is that you can move from it, you can move from that corner, you can work what corner you want to work. If you get bitchiness from one girl then move to another place. You get bitchiness from girls in the sauna best thing to do is ignore them or walk out (Neesha, street but occasionally works indoors).

Sometimes tensions trigger public arguments, even fighting, but more frequently workers leave or are sacked: 'There was a little bit of animosity because I became the favourite, so I left' (Rita, working premises); 'There was a girl here and she was a bitch so I left' (Seema, sauna). Despite the obvious tensions caused by market forces such as competition and an unequal ratio of supply and demand, there was a high level of cohesion and collaboration between women. Echoing findings in my study, Brewis and Linstead (2000a: 264) suggest street prostitution breeds low-trusting relationships characterized by pimps, drug use and sporadic customers, while indoor markets attract high-trusting relationships where workers support each other. Most of the interviewees said they found friendship and support from colleagues:

The other girls stop you going crazy. Because even if you don't particularly like the girls or particularly get on with the girls that well you are there for the same reason and you do understand each other because at the end of the day you are both selling your pussy. In terms of you both doing the same job you understand why you are both there. Sometimes it is nice to have that even if you don't like the person or you would never dream of speaking to them outside work. So it is better to have other girls around you (Kelly, sauna).

Below, Astrid and Polly discuss the loyalty and respect that develop between women who work in prostitution:

Astrid: I think with the trust, they [other working girls] know what you have to do for that money and they want to be the last person to take it from you . . . a lot of the girls are really really honest and they would really look after you and they know what you have had to do.
Polly: Like if you go out everyone takes care of everyone.
Astrid: We know quite a lot of people, because the girls travel around the saunas and the flats. They do help each other; if you are stuck one week they will try and get you work . . . If you are good to your girls they will be good back to you . . . the best friends that you can ever have. Everyone looks after everyone.

Some women spoke of a unique understanding with other sex providers that was not present with non-sex workers. This shared reality can motivate women to work in the interests of each other and not just for themselves. Brewis and Linstead (2000a: 264) suggest that there is a 'social community and kinship in sex work'. During my observations in saunas, working premises and the street there were continual examples of sharing information for the good of others not only between workers but also through the management. For instance, a group of independent escorts have created an Internet-based resource, 'Support and Advice for Escorts', that provides information to colleagues. The website includes extensive tips and case studies on topics such as 'paying tax', 'ways of working' and 'difficult clients', offering a shortcut to 'the learning process in a business where experience really does count' (www.saafe.co.uk).

Apprenticeships and mentoring

Unlike the State-controlled brothels of Nevada where training is compulsory and official (Campbell 1991: 1371), sex workers and organizers in Britain rely on a range of informal systems for passing on the tricks of the trade. Through a process of socialization, novices learn skills and techniques as well as a cognitive perspective that provides a 'scheme for understanding and making sense of their new, deviant world' (Best and Lukenbill 1982: 90). Similar to Bryan's (1968: 271) findings among 'call girls' in Los Angeles, the management has a role in distributing knowledge through philosophical training of the value structure as well as interpersonal training regarding customer relations, tips for problematic situations and in some cases, a sexual apprenticeship. I observed how three female managers (who were current or retired workers) implemented training: 'I have trained all my girls . . . they are good at what they do because I have personally trained them' (Astrid, working premises). The training equips the beginner with safety skills and aims to protect the business from trouble, official attention or tainting the establishment's reputation. Dora had been working in a sauna for eight months and recalled 'I have been learning off the manager really. I have been watching and learning from her as she taught me how to do everything. I show them [manager and owner] that I know what I am doing and when we work together I learn a little more each time.'

In addition, passive learning and imitation is a significant method of learning occupational norms. Described by Krugman and Hartley (1970: 184) as what is 'caught' rather than 'taught', sex workers learn the ropes simply by following others and practising the rules of the house. During the monotonous, inactive moments waiting for clients or carrying out the daily chores, learning is consolidated: 'You pick it up [screening clients] as you go along . . . from flats and saunas and the girls respect the rules'

(Polly, working premises). Leigh reports how she learnt the trade by combining skills from a variety of indoor establishments:

I have learnt the rules from the other girls in the sauna and working here with women who are really experienced. She [her colleague] knows it all as she has been working over twenty years. Stuff like getting the money off them first. I never used to do that and now I have changed the way that I work. You learn a lot when you are working with experienced women.

In indoor establishments much of the learning is taken for granted and accepted. Trying to understand why she rejected clients who are black, Suzanne demonstrates how exposure to regulations in a sauna often determines the procedures if individuals then become self-employed: 'I don't understand. It is just discrimination and habit. You don't really know why you have said no [to a black man] but you learn a lot from the saunas. That's what they do, so that's what you do.' Krystal confirms the informal, passive nature of learning through imitation: 'You pick up things all the time, especially when you are working with other girls'. Reiss (1967: 210) reflects on the organization of male prostitution and highlights the responsibility of the peer group for ensuring the novice is 'psychologically and socially prepared'. Saunas are physically organized around a large communal area, and women learn by observing each other working, competing for clients, diffusing situations and sharing gossip, humour and storytelling (Downe 1999; Sanders 2004a). Tracy recalls how her colleagues quashed her naïveté: 'The very first client I done, I come back out and said to the girls, where is the quilt . . . I thought I was gonna have to get into bed with him!'

Where there is no explicit training from seniors, friendship networks and 'buddy systems' (Murphy 2003: 323) form the main socialization methods. Through networks of friendships women are not only introduced to prostitution but continue to support each other after the initiation phase by literally working together, looking out for each other, passing over clients, exchanging condoms, cigarettes, clothes, make-up, alcohol, food, even childcare and daily chores. In the saunas and working premises I visited there was a sense of sisterhood between workers. Polly remembers when she first started working she had a mentor: 'I was seventeen when I met Katie and she looked after me . . . She took care of me and taught me everything I know.' Annabelle refers to how colleagues nurtured her: 'The women that worked there, they were a lot older and they sort of mothered you. They warned you of this punter, they would show you the ropes, what to use and what not to use, what to do and what not to do.' These informal, emotional bonds between workers also serve to create a 'predictable trading economy' (Hobbs 1997: 62) in an uncertain world, where reliable and trusting relationships can mean the difference between life and death.

Sympathetic allies

Government-funded health organizations, under the guise of harm reduction and HIV prevention schemes, provide expert services through over eighty-four statutory and voluntary projects in Britain (Cooper *et al.* 2001; Kirkpatrick 2000; Wilson 1999). Adopting various models of intervention, professionals pass on safety tips to minimize violence and health risks (Rickard and Growney 2001). Popular publications with titles such as *'How Safely Do You Work? A Step by Step Guide to Personal Safety'* are produced in consultation with sex workers. In other parts of the world, professionals also provide interventions to bring sex workers together and set standards for prices and safe sex (Rabinovitch and Strega 2004; Wojcicki and Malala 2001: 114).

One of the most effective methods of equipping sex workers with details of dangerous men is through local schemes known as 'Ugly Mugs' that are coordinated by health organizations. The scheme relies on workers reporting incidents (i.e. violence, harassment and robbery) to an outreach worker who records specific details including a description of the perpetrator. The information is recorded anonymously with the option of logging the details with the police. A report is then disseminated to as many women as possible as well as to other relevant agencies. Recently, the Ugly Mug scheme has been repeated by a popular website for escorts supplying sex workers with email addresses and telephone numbers of men who pose as clients.

Although the police are not formally involved with training sex workers, they are not excluded from the overall production of information that enables women to make critical judgements. O'Kane (2002b) visited tolerance zones in Glasgow where women can work a certain block of streets between the hours of 8pm and 4am free from arrest and with the safety of CCTV and adequate street lighting. Another scheme that promotes a safe space where women and men can engage in prostitution free from arrest is currently being piloted in Liverpool (www.managedzone.info), suggesting that some police and council officials are taking a proactive approach to assisting sex workers to operate in safer conditions. Official agencies that offer realistic solutions to managing the sex industry encourage a reciprocal flow of information between workers and law-enforcement agencies that provides a key framework for maintaining regulation.

Regulating a risky business

This book has concentrated on providing both a socio-structural analysis of the organization of sex markets and a socio-psychological perspective to explain how sex workers engage, manipulate and control the commercial sex act. Focusing on the 'significance of the local in the analysis of work' (West and Austrin 2002: 498) has established how sex workers rationally evaluate working conditions and act to minimize the risks inherent in prostitution. At a broader level, there are other mechanisms that manage the risks of prostitution by filtering the rational responses, strategies and tactics through the structures of the markets. This final section argues that the laws against the selling and purchasing of commercial sex and any changes in the law that would continue to criminalize and marginalize sex workers or clients are out of harmony with the comprehensive and largely regulatory mechanisms that are evident within the sex markets. Unionization and joint collaboration at a national level are highlighted as key mechanisms that are increasingly responsible for regulating, managing and professionalizing prostitution.

Unionization and collaboration

Mathieu (2003: 30) describes how there has been a global and especially European development in the politics of prostitution over the last decade, with the resurgence of a prostitutes' rights movement. Organizations like the International Committee for Prostitutes' Rights, the American based COYOTE ('Call Off Your Old Tired Ethics') established in 1973, and the 'Red Thread' Amsterdam-based group were initiated by sex workers, although the latter receives funding from the Dutch Ministry of Social Affairs and Employment. TAMPEP (Transnational AIDS/STD Prevention Among Migrant Prostitutes in Europe) receives European Community funding to provide active intervention with sex workers across Europe and favours peer educators and cultural mediators as distinct methods of communication (Wallman 2001). Other forms of collaboration are noted in Europe where laws, although growing increasingly conservative (Kilvington et al. 2001), enable prostitution to be offered as a legitimate career. For example, the 'Prostitution Information Centre' in Amsterdam offers a six-day training workshop in sex work techniques, fieldtrips to establishments, role plays with actors posing as customers and legal and tax information (Raymond 1999: 2). Although there are distinct barriers to mobilizing women involved in prostitution (see Mathieu 2003: 33), key activists have been at the forefront of collective organizations that aim to establish prostitution as valid work.

Although open to criticism of imposing internal logic on the sex industry by 'overationalizing' organizational features, there is evidence of an emerging professionalization process. Hosted in Britain, the International Union of Sex Workers (IUSW) advocates for 'sex workers' civil, legal and workers rights' and has successfully gained membership to a general workers' trade union (GMB) since 2002 (Lopes 2003). Arguing that sex workers' rights should be understood through a labour framework rather than a moral agenda, the IUSW offer free legal advice, training and development skills including career changes (for instance, from sex provider to striptease), table dancing workshops, taxation and employment advice (www.iusw.org). Since joining the GMB union the IUSW have gained some regulatory influence in the wider sex industry. Recently a code of practice was created between erotic dancers and managers of table dancing clubs to establish guidelines for safe working practices. Although membership remains low and activities depend on voluntary participation, there is a growing realization, especially among entrepreneurs who work alone and sex organizers, that quasi-official collaboration is a necessary step towards the legitimization of prostitution.

At a national level, the UK Network of Sex Work Projects (UKNSWP) is the main organizational body that represents the interests of sex workers and those who have a professional capacity within the sex industry. Consisting primarily of a network of agencies that provide services for sex workers, the UKNSWP works to 'promote health, safety, civil and human rights of sex workers, including their right to live free from violence, intimidation, coercion and exploitation' (UKNSWP Constitution 2002). Various working groups such as a subgroup that focuses on safety and policing issues facilitate up-to-date discussions and sharing of regional, national, European and international developments. The organization promotes a harm reduction model and provides education and training about sex work, a consultation and advisory service, and supports sex work networks. Among many of its aims, the network promotes sex workers' self-organization and provides a collective response to government proposals and changes in policy and legislation.

At a local level, self-regulation is also evident as insiders create their own mechanisms to formally organize the illegal enterprise. The first British forum of sauna owners, the 'Manchester Sauna Owners Forum', was set up in 2003. Initiated by the Manchester Health Promotion Specialist Service who are 'conscience constituents' (McCarthy and Zald 1987: 12) to the cause of regulating prostitution to improve the sexual and physical health of women, the aim of the Forum is to 'create a safe working environment . . . and the development of good practice guidelines' (www.msof.co.uk). The impetus for a formal network of sauna owners came because the 'industry lacks the sharing of information between saunas' and so the Forum sought to provide a space for 'useful information to be traded directly' (ibid.). The Forum regularly meets to discuss local issues, share advice on security and provide services such as a text alert system to pass on details of assaults and perpetrators. This is an example of how illicit enterprises mirror the same formal structures of legitimate businesses to develop a 'strategic knowledge of the market' (Hobbs 1997: 60) through an exclusive membership committee and transparent decision-making process that is standard practice in the business world. Options for licensed brothels or a registration scheme that could include mandatory health checks for workers (see Home Office 2004) need to take into account the existing frameworks of internal regulation and build on, rather than break down, the strong order of maintenance that already exists.

Professionalization

Sutherland (1937: 216) describes thieving as a profession because, firstly, thieves can make a living out of their illegal trade and, secondly, they share similar characteristics with the legitimate professions including 'technical skills, an exclusive group and immunity from punishment'. Throughout this book there is ample evidence to liken the structure of sex markets to other forms of occupational settings. At a meso-structural level this analysis of the organization of indoor prostitution markets identifies how prostitution is a 'socially ordered activity' that goes beyond mere honour among women and 'covers all the understandings and agreements necessary to their cooperative activity' (McIntosh 1971: 98). Placing the sex worker at the crux of the illicit interaction, a micro-structural perspective highlights how some women who work as prostitutes follow a strong business ethic and that the sex work community 'have followed the same trajectory as that of communities based upon traditional industries' (Hobbs 1997: 62–3). Yet the level of regulation in the sex markets should not be surprising if we take account of the history of both sexuality and sociology. Heap (2003: 460) describes how Thomas and Hendeson, early contributors to the Chicago School, set out in 1910, along with a team of twenty-eight others, to find out the underlying social conditions of female prostitution in the city. They discovered a 'unique urban community' of both 'casual and professional female prostitutes' organized around commercial sex (quoted in Heap 2003: 460).

In conclusion, I argue that the evidence presented in this chapter identifies that some forms of indoor sex work are entering a phase of professionalization. First, there is a steady increase in sex workers and pro-prostitution lobbyists organizing at a European, national and local level. As part of this collective movement, sex workers and organizers are reflecting traditional mechanisms of regulation and standardization by setting up representative bodies, decision-making organizations and affiliating to a mainstream trade union. Second, there is possibly a shift taking place from the old order of prostitution to a new economy of sex work. This is divided between those who are loosely connected to the sex industry and entrepreneurs who operate independent businesses, treating sex work as a professional job and often organizing their clients entirely on the Internet. As a commodity, prostitution could also be increasing in popularity within a growing secular society that, to some extent, nurtures the diversification of sexual behaviour, expression and identities. As a craft, the markets of prostitution (and the wider sex industry) have expanded and modernized in accordance with new media technologies, offering specialist services at a range of prices and qualities. These changes mean that a corporate approach to managing sex work is both necessary and appropriate if standards are to be maintained, workers are to be respected and treated fairly and customers are left with little option but to comply.

Finally, the self-regulation of indoor markets is subtly supported by official agencies that are sympathetic allies to the cause of providing a safe working environment for women. Rather than opt for a punitive approach, health-care professionals, and in some instances the police, are working with sex workers, managers and owners to promote public health, individual safety and anti-discriminatory practice. All of these changes to the indoor prostitution markets perpetuate the informal regulatory mechanisms such as codes of practice, norms and sanctions. The sex work community is beginning to straddle both deviant and conventional occupational structures by participating in prostitution politics, gaining legitimate representation and an increasing number of sympathetic allies that draw on official expertise, organizational skills and resources to benefit the cogency of the sex industry.

Any increase in legislation to prohibit or make an offence of non-coercive, consensual adult commercial sex would be in direct opposition to what is happening within some markets of the sex industry. There is strong evidence that the sex industry is a resourceful economy that can organize and transforms its activity from the shadows of the streets and back-alleys to a regulated, legitimate industry where women are safe and secure. The foundations of regulation that the industry have set out could be strengthened through institutional backing, comprehensive resources and legislation that prioritizes the safety of sex workers, while acknowledging the tensions prostitution causes communities without blaming individuals. Evidence of the professionalization of prostitution only renders attempts to abolish or curtail consensual prostitution as uninformed and unrealistic options for an industry that has never been prevented through legislation.

Colluding with clients

Throughout this book there has been minimal reference to the men who buy sex, partly because the research did not cover the purchaser's side of the deal and also because including the perspective of the client could overshadow the central focus of risk management in sex work. Failure to make a comparable analysis between the sex worker and client skims the detail of the commercial interaction, because prostitution, unlike most forms of deviance, requires more than one actor and subsequently involves a degree of organizational complexity and cooperation from reciprocal roles. The sociology of deviance must ask how deviants organize to reach their separate goals and question the patterns of relationships that coordinate a complex, sophisticated social interaction. Therefore men who buy sex should be analysed in the same depth as sex workers because at one level the buyer, like the seller, needs to acquire specialist knowledge, skills and understanding of the marketplace in order to become a competent actor. For instance, just as sex workers screen clients for trustworthiness, there is evidence that the purchaser engages in a process of checking the credibility of the indoor establishment or independent worker to wise-up on the latest scam and avoid 'clipping' (defrauding clients without providing a sexual service). The online sex work community is one such mechanism through which men gather information, share advice and describe their 'punting' experiences through 'field reports' (Sharp and Earle 2003). As Soothill (2004b: 52) concludes, 'An Internet site that is developed responsibly can help to ensure that the parlour game can continue without unnecessary conflict.'

Research on men who purchase sex has begun to explore some of the obvious questions such as the masculine commodified approach to sex (Jordan 1997; Monto 2000); justifications for kerb-crawling (Brooks-Gordon and Gelsthorpe 2003; Campbell 1997); and the contradictory 'rhetoric of mutuality' where clients create a fantasy relationship with sex workers (Plumridge et al. 1996). Despite these endeavours, there is still little known about the client's perspective of entering the deviant sex world, how he manages the stigma of being a 'punter' and the psychological consequences of paying for sex. Focusing on either party in isolation does not stretch or complete our understanding of the complex organizational structures of prostitution, or suggest how men understand their own roles and the place of prostitution in society.

Although it is apparent that the seller structures the trade in most commercial deviant interactions (Best and Lukenbill 1982: 132) and indeed the sex worker has 'control of these micro-encounters' (West and

Austrin 2002: 490), the behaviour of the buyer is a crucial aspect of the organization of the transactions in prostitution. The client and the sex worker purposely organize and generally behave according to the codes, practices and values set out in this monograph. There has been a lack of acknowledgement that although violence from men who pose as clients is high, most genuine clients cooperate in the informal regulation of sex work and are accomplices in passing on the value structure, the moral and sex codes of the commercial sex liaison. Previously blurred by the auspices of criminalization or anti-prostitution moralizing about the commodification of the female body, male clients have been denied social recognition and academic attention as legitimate actors in the deviant economy of commercial sex. Ultimately, it is the role of the client, the sex worker and the organizers of sex businesses that need to be analysed through an integrated approach in order to develop a theoretically informed debate on the nature of risk. This analysis can take forward the policy work that has put prostitution on the political agenda as an institution that is worthy of attention because of its steadfast nature that bridges the traditional and the modern, the local and the global. Only when these finer details are addressed will the business become less risky.

Bibliography

Abbott, S (2000) 'Motivations for Pursuing an Acting Career in Pornography.' Pp. 17–34 in *Sex for Sale*, edited by R. Weitzer. London: Routledge.

Adkins, L (1995) *Gendered Work: Sexuality, Family and Labour Market*. Buckingham: Open University.

Adler, P (1985) *Wheeling and Dealing: An Ethnography of an Upper-level Drug Dealing and Smuggling Community*. New York: Columbia University Press.

Adler, P A and P Adler (1980) 'The Irony of Secrecy in the Drug World.' *Urban Life* 8(4): 447–465.

—— (1991) 'Stability and Flexibility: Maintaining Relations Within Organized and Disorganized Groups.' Pp. 173–183 in *Experiencing Fieldwork. An Inside View of Qualitative Research*, edited by W. Shaffir and R. Stebbins. London: Sage.

—— (1994) 'Observational Techniques.' Pp. 377–402 in *Handbook of Qualitative Research*, edited by N. Denzin and Y. Lincoln. Thousand Oaks, CA: Sage.

Agustin, L (2004) 'A Migrant World of Services.' *Social Politics* 10(3): 377–396.

Albini, J L (1971) *The American Mafia: Genesis of a Legend*. New York: Appleton-Century-Crofts.

Altork, K (1995) 'Walking the Fire Line: The Erotic Dimension of the Fieldwork Experience.' Pp. 107–139 in *Taboo. Sex, Identity and Erotic Subjectivity in Anthropological Fieldwork*, edited by D. Kulick and M. Wilson. London: Routledge.

Anderson, E (2004) 'A Place on the Corner. Interview with Laurie Taylor' for *Thinking Aloud*, Radio 4 (5.5.04). www.bbc.co.uk/radio4/thinkingaloud.

Anon (1959) *Street Walker*. London: The Bodley Head.

Archer, J (1994) *Male Violence*. London: Routlege.

Ashkanasy, N, C Hartel and Q Zerbe (2000) *Emotions in the Workplace: Research, Theory and Practice*. Westport, Conneticut: Quorum Books.

Ashworth, G, P White and H Winchester (1988) 'The Red Light District in the West European City: a Neglected Aspect of the Urban Landscape.' *Geoforum* 19(2): 201–212.

Atkinson, R and J Flint (2001) 'Accessing Hidden and Hard-to-Reach Populations: Snowball Research Strategies.' *Social Research Update* 33.

Bacharach, M and D Gambetta (1997) 'Trust in Signs.' Department of Sociology, University of Oxford.

Bagley, C (1999) 'Adolescent Prostitution in Canada and the Philippines.' *International Social Work* 42(4): 445–454.

Bagely, C and Young, I (1987) 'Juvenile Prostitution and Child Sexual Abuse: A Controlled Study.' *Canadian Journal of Community Mental Health* 6: 5–26.

Bannister, J, N Fyfe and A Kearns (1998) 'Closed Circuit Television and the City.' Pp. 21–39 in *Surveillance, Closed Circuit Television and Social Control*, edited by C. Norris, J. Moran and G. Armstrong. Aldershot: Ashgate.

Barnard, M (1992) 'Working in the Dark: Researching Female Prostitution.' Pp. 141–156 in *Women's Health Matters*, edited by H. Roberts. London: Routledge.

—— (1993) 'Violence and Vulnerability: Conditions of Work for Street Working Prostitutes.' *Sociology of Health and Illness* 15(1): 5–14.

Barnard, M, G Hart and S Church (2002) 'Client Violence Against Prostitute Women Working From Street and Off-Street Locations: A Three City Comparison.' Violence Research Programme, ESRC.

Barrett, D (1997) *Child Prostitution in Britain*. London: The Children's Society.

—— (2000) *Youth Prostitution in the New Europe: The Growth in Sex Work*. London: Russell House Publishing.

Barry, K (1979) *Female Sexual Slavery*. New York: New York University Press.

—— (1995) *Prostitution and Sexuality*. New York: New York University Press.

Bartley, P (2000) *Prostitution, Prevention and Reform in England 1860–1914*. London: Routledge.

Barton, B (2002) 'Dancing on the Mobius Strip: Challenging the Sex War Paradigm.' *Gender and Society* 16(5): 585–602.

Bauman, Z (1992) *Intimations of Modernity*. London: Routledge.

Becker, H (1963) *Outsiders*. London: The Free Press of Glencoe.

—— (1965) 'Review of Sociologists at Work: Essays on the Craft of Social Research.' *American Sociological Review* 30: 602–603.

Bell, S (1994) *Reading,Writing and Rewriting the Prostitute Body*. Bloomington, IN: Indiana University Press.

Benson, C (1998) 'Violence Against Female Prostitutes.' Department of Social Sciences, Loughborough University.

Benson, C and R Matthews (2000) 'Police and Prostitution: Vice Squads in Britain.' Pp. 245–264 in *Sex for Sale* edited by R. Weitzer. Routledge: London.

Bernstein, E (2001) 'The Meaning of the Purchase: Desire, Demand and the Commerce of Sex.' *Ethnography* 2(3): 389–420.

Best, J and D F Lukenbill (1982) *Organizing Deviance*. New York: Prentice Hall.

Billingsley, R, T Nemitz and P Bean (2001) *Informers: Policing, Policy, Practice*. Portland, OR: Willan.

Bindel, J and J Kelly (2003) 'A Critical Examination of Response to Prostitution in Four Countries: Victoria, Australia; Ireland; the Netherlands; and Sweden.' Child and Woman Abuse Studies Unit, London Metropolitan University, London.

Bindman, J (1997) 'Redefining Prostitution as Sex Work on the International Agenda.' Anti-Slavery International, London.

Black, P (2004) *Gender and the Beauty Industry: 'Discipline and Pamper'*. London: Routledge.

Bloor, M, A Leyland, M Barnard and N McKeganey (1991) 'Estimating hidden populations: a new method of calculating the prevalence of drug-injecting and non-injecting female street prostitutes.' *British Journal of Addiction* 86(3): 1477–1483.

Bolton, R (1995) 'Tricks, Friends and Lovers: Erotic Encounters in the Field.' Pp. 140–167 in *Taboo. Sex, Identity and Erotic Subjectivity in Anthropological Fieldwork*, edited by D. Kulick and M. Wilson. London & New York: Routledge.

Bolton, S C and C Boyd (2003) 'Trolley Dolly or Skilled Emotion Manager? Moving on from Hochschild's Managed Heart.' *Work, Employment and Society* 17(2): 289–308.

Boynton, P (1998) 'Somebody's Daughters, Somebody's Sisters: A Reflection of Wolverhampton Working Women's Lives.' Aston University.

—— (2002) '"At the end of the day, it's a job": Discursive Practices around Sex Work.' Department of Psychiatry and Behavioural Sciences, Royal Free and University College Medical School.

Brannen, A (1997) 'Goffman's Social Theory.' Pp. xlvi–lxxxii in *The Goffman Reader*, edited by C. Lemert and A. Brannen. Cambridge, MA: Blackwell.

Brewer, J (1990) 'Talking about Danger: The RUC and the Paramilitary Threat.' *Sociology* 24(4): 657–674.

Brewis, J and S Linstead (2000a) *Sex, Work and Sex Work*. London: Routledge.

—— (2000b) ' "The Worst Thing is the Screwing" (2): Context and Career in Sex Work.' *Gender, Work and Organization* 7(3): 168–180.

—— (2000c) ' "The Worst Thing is the Screwing" (1): Consumption and the Management of Identity in Sex Work.' *Gender, Work and Organization* 7(2): 84–97.

Brooks-Gordon, B and L Gelsthorpe (2003) 'Prostitutes' Clients, Ken Livingstone and a New Trojan Horse.' *The Howard Journal* 42(5): 437–451.

Brooks-Gordon, B (forthcoming) *The Price of Sex. Police, Prostitutes and Their Clients*. Cullompton: Willan.

Brown, L (2000) *Sex Slaves: The Trafficking of Women in Asia*. London: Virago Press.

Browne, J and V Minichiello (1995) 'The Social Meanings Behind Male Sex Work: Implications for Sexual Interactions.' *British Journal of Sociology* 46(4): 598–622.

Bryan, J (1968) 'Apprenticeship in Prostitution.' Pp. 268–277 in *Deviance: The Interactionist Perspective*, edited by E. Rubington and M. Weinberg. London: Collier Macmillan.

Bryman, A and Burgess, R (1994) *Analysing Qualitative Data*. London and New York: Routledge.

Busch, N, H Bell, N Hotaling and M Monto (2002) 'Male Customers of Prostituted Women: Exploiting Perceptions of Entitlement to Power Control and Implications for Violent Behaviour toward Women.' *Violence Against Women* 8(9): 1093–1112.

Butcher, K (2003) 'Confusion Between Prostitution and Sex Trafficking.' *The Lancet* 361 (June 7): 1983.

Campbell, C (1991) 'Prostitution, AIDS, and Preventive Health Behaviour.' *Social Science and Medicine* 32(12): 1367–1378.

—— (2000) 'Selling Sex in the Time of AIDS: the psycho-social context of condom use by sex workers on a Southern African mine.' *Social Science & Medicine* 50(4): 479–494.

Campbell, R (1997) ' "It's Just Business, It's Just Sex": Male Clients of Female Prostitutes in Merseyside.' *Journal of Contemporary Health* 5: 47–51.

Campbell, R and Storr, M (2001) 'Challenging the Kerb Crawler Rehabilitation Programme.' *Feminist Review* 67 (Spring): 94–108.

Campbell, R, S Coleman and P Torkington (1996) 'Street Prostitution in Inner City Liverpool.' Liverpool Hope University College, Liverpool.

Campbell, R and H Kinnell (2001) 'We Shouldn't Have to Put Up with This: Street Sex Work and Violence.' *Criminal Justice Matters* 42 (Winter): 12.

Chan, W and G Rigakos (2002) 'Risk, Crime and Gender.' *British Journal of Criminology* 42(4): 743–761.

Chapkis, W (1997) *Live Sex Acts: Women Performing Erotic Labour*. New York: Routledge.

Church, S, M Henderson, M Barnard and G Hart (2001) 'Violence by clients towards female prostitutes in different work settings: questionnaire survey.' *British Medical Journal* 322: 524–525.

Clifter, S and S Carter (2000) *Tourism and Sex*. London: Continuum.

Cockington, J and L Marlin (1995) *Sex Inc.: True Tales from the Australian Sex Industry*. Sydney: Ironback Pan Macmillan.

Cookson, H (1996) 'Alcohol Use and Offence Type in Young Male Offenders.' *British Journal of Criminology* 32(3): 352–360.

Cooney, J (1990) 'Eating Disorders, Abuse and Prostitution.' *Irish Journal of Psychological Medicine* 7(1): 36–37.

Cooper, K, J Kilvington, S Day, A Ziersch and H Ward (2001) 'HIV Prevention and Sexual Health Services for Sex Workers in the UK.' *Health Education Journal* 60(1): 26–34.

Corbin, A (1990) *Women for Hire: Prostitution and Sexuality in France after 1850*. Cambridge, MA: Harvard University Press.

Crang, P (1994) 'It's Showtime: On the Workplace Geographies of Display in a Restaurant in Southeast England.' *Environment and Planning D* 12: 675–704.

Criminal Statistics for England and Wales (2003), Home Office, London.

Cusick, L (1998) 'Non-use of condoms by prostitute women.' *AIDS Care* 10: 133–46.

—— (1999) 'Social and Commercial Experiences of Glasgow Prostitutes Working in Different Sectors.' University of London.

Cusick, L, A Martin and T May (2004) 'Vulnerability and Involvement in Drug Use and Sex Work. Research Study 268.' Home Office, London.

Dalla, R (2002) 'Night Moves: A Qualitative Investigation of Street-level Sex Work.' *Psychology of Women Quarterly* 26: 63–73.

Davis, K (1937) 'The Sociology of Prostitution.' *American Journal of Sociology* 2(5): 744–755.

Day, S (1994) 'What Counts as Rape? Physical assault and broken contracts: contrasting views of rape amongst London sex workers.' Pp. 172–189 in *Sex and Violence: Issues in Representation and Experience*, edited by P. Harvey and P. Gow. London: Routledge.

—— (1996) 'The Law and the Market.' Pp. 75–98 in *Inside and Outside the Law*, edited by O. Harris. London: Routledge.

Day, S and H Ward (1990) 'The Praed Street Project: a cohort of prostitute women in London.' Pp. 61–75 in *AIDS, Drugs and Prostitution*, edited by M. Plant. London: Routledge.

——— (2001) 'Violence Towards Female Prostitutes.' *British Medical Journal* 323: 230.

Delacoste, F and P Alexander (1988) *Sex Work: Writings by Women in the Sex Industry*. London: Virago.

deMeis, C (2002) 'House and Street: narratives of identity in a liminal space among prostitutes in Brazil.' *Ethos* 30(1–2): 3–24.

Denton, B and P O'Malley (1999) 'Gender, Trust and Business. Women Drug Dealers in the Illicit Economy.' *British Journal of Criminology* 39(4): 513–530.

Denzin, N (1983) 'A Note on Emotionality, Self and Interaction.' *American Journal of Sociology* 89(2): 402–409.

Dodds, S (1997) 'Dance and Erotica: The Construction of the Female Stripper.' Pp. 218–233 in *Dance in the City*, edited by H. Thomas. London: Macmillan.

Dodsworth, J (2000) 'Child Sexual Exploitation/Child Prostitution.' University of East Anglia, Social Work Monographs.

Dorn, N and N South (1990) 'Drug Markets and Law Enforcement.' *British Journal of Criminology* 30(2): 171–178.

Douglas, J (1972) *Research on Deviance*. New York: Random House.

Douglas, J D, P K Rasmussen and C A Flanagan (1977) *The Nude Beach*. Beverley Hills, CA: Sage.

Douglas, M (1986) *Risk Acceptability According to the Social Sciences*. London: Routledge and Kegan Paul.

——— (1992) *Risk and Danger: Essays in Cultural Theory*. London: Routledge.

Downe, P (1999) 'Laughing when it Hurts: Humour and Violence in the lives of Costa Rican Prostitutes.' *Women's Studies International Forum* 22(1): 63–78.

Dunhill, C (1989a) *The Boys in Blue*. London: Virago.

——— (1989b) 'Working Relations.' Pp. 205–208 in *The Boys In Blue*, edited by C. Dunhill. London: Virago.

Durkin, K and C Bryant (1995) ' "Log on to sex": some notes on the carnale computer and erotic cyberspace as an emerging research frontier.' *Deviant Behaviour* 16: 179–200.

Dworkin, A (1981) *Pornography – Men Possessing Women?* London: Women's Press.

——— (1996) 'Pornography.' Pp. 297–299 in *Feminism and Sexuality*, edited by S. Jackson and S. Scott. Edinburgh: Edinburgh University Press.

Edwards, S (1993) 'Selling the Body, Keeping the Soul: Sexuality, Power and the Theories and Realities of Prostitution.' Pp. 89–104 in *Body Matters*, edited by S. Scott and D. Morgan. London: Falmer Press.

——— (1997) 'The Legal Relation of Prostitution: A Human Rights Issue.' Pp. 57–82 in *Rethinking Prostitution*, edited by G. Scambler and A. Scambler. London: Routledge.

Efthimiou-Mordant, A (2002) 'Sex Working Drug Users: out of the shadows at last.' *Feminist Review* 72: 82–83.

Elster, J (1979) *Ullysses and the Sirens: studies in rationality and irrationality*. Cambridge: Cambridge University Press.

—— (1999) *Alchemies of the Mind: Rationality and the Emotions*. Cambridge: Cambridge University Press.

English Collective of Prostitutes (1997) 'Campaigning for Legal Change.' Pp. 83–96 in *Rethinking Prostitution*, edited by G. Scambler and A. Scambler. London: Routledge.

Epele, M (2001) 'Excess, Scarcity and Desire among Drug-Using Sex Workers.' *Body & Society* 7(2–3): 161–179.

Evans, C and H Lambert (1997) 'Health Seeking Strategies and Sexual Health Among Female Sex Workers in Urban India: Implications for Research and Service Provision.' *Social Science and Medicine* 44(12): 1791–1803.

Farley, M, I Baral, M Kiremire and U Sezgin (1998) 'Prostitution in Five Countries: violence and post-traumatic stress disorder.' *Feminism and Psychology* 8: 405–426.

Faugier, J (1994) 'Bad Women and Good Customers: Scapegoating, Female Prostitution and HIV.' Pp. 50–64 in *Living Sexuality Issues for Nursing and Health*, edited by C. Webb. London: Scutar Press.

Faugier, J and M Sargeant (1996) 'Boyfriends, Pimps and Clients.' Pp. 121–136 in *Rethinking Prostitution*, edited by G. Scambler and A. Scambler. London: Routledge.

Ferell, J and S Kane (1998) *Ethnography on the Edge: Crime, Deviance and Field Research*: Northern University Press.

Fetterman, D (1991) 'A Walk Through the Wilderness: Learning to Find Your Way.' Pp. 87–86 in *Experiencing Fieldwork. An Inside View of Qualitative Research*, edited by W. Shaffir and R. Stebbins. London: Sage.

Fineman, S (2003) *Understanding Emotions at Work*. London: Sage.

Finnegan, F (1979) *Poverty and Prostitution: A Study of Victorian Prostitutes in York*. Cambridge: Cambridge University Press.

Frank, R (1991) *Microeconomics and Behaviour*. New York: McGraw-Hill.

Freud, S (1949) *Three Essays on the Theory of Sexuality* (translated by James Strachey). London: Imago.

Friedberg, M (2000) 'Damaged Children to Throwaway Women: from care to prostitution.' Pp. 72–85 in *Women, Violence and Strategies for Action*, edited by J. Radford, M. Friedberg and L. Harne. Buckingham: Open University Press.

Funari, V (1997) 'Naked, Naughty and Nasty.' Pp. 19–35 in *Whores and Other Feminists*, edited by J. Nagel. London: Routledge.

Furman, F (1997) *Facing the Mirror: Older Women and the Beauty Shop Culture*. London: Routledge.

Gambetta, D (2001) 'Conventional Signs.' Department of Sociology, University of Oxford, Oxford.

Gambetta, D, H Hamill and M Bacharach (2001) 'Signalling and Mimicking Trustworthiness. Taxi Drivers and Their Customers in Dangerous Cities.' Department of Sociology, University of Oxford, Oxford.

Garland, D (2001) *The Culture of Control: Crime and Social Order in Late Modernity*. Oxford: Oxford University Press.

Glendinning, C and J Miller (1992) *Women and Poverty in Britain: The 1990s*. London: Harvester.

Glover, E (1969) *The Psychopathology of Prostitution*. London: Institute for the Study and Treatment of Delinquency.

Goffman, E (1959) *The Presentation of Self in Everyday Life*. Edinburgh: University of Edinburgh.

—— (1963) *Stigma: Notes on the Management of Spoiled Identity*. Engelwoods Cliffs, NJ: Prentice Hall.

—— (1967) *Interaction Ritual*. New York: Anchor Books.

—— (1974) *Frame Analysis*. New York: Harper.

—— (1983) 'The Interaction Order.' *American Sociological Review* 48: 1–17.

Goldsmith, A (2003) 'Fear, Fumbling and Frustration: Reflections on doing criminological fieldwork in Colombia.' *Criminal Justice* 3(1): 103–125.

Goldstein, H (1990) *Problem-Oriented Policing*. Philadelphia: Philadelphia University Press.

Goode, E (2003) 'Sexual Involvement and Social Research in a Fat Civil Rights Organization.' *Qualitative Sociology* 25(4): 501–534.

Gould, A (1999) 'Punishing the Punter: The politics of prostitution in Sweden.' Department of Social Science, Loughborough University.

Green, A, S Day and H Ward (2000) 'Crack Cocaine and Prostitution in London in the 1990s.' *Sociology of Health and Illness* 22(1): 27–39.

Gulcur, L and P Ilkkaracan (2002) 'The "Natasha" Experience: Migrant Sex Workers from the Former Soviet Union and Eastern Europe in Turkey.' *Women's Studies International Forum* 25(4): 411–421.

Harras, R (1996) *Common Women: Prostitution and Sexuality in Medieval England*. Oxford: Oxford University Press.

Hart, A (1998) *Buying and Selling Power: Anthropological Reflections on Prostitution in Spain*. Oxford: Westview Press.

Hart, G and M Barnard (2003) "Jump on Top, Get the Job Done': Strategies Employed by Female Prostitutes to Reduce the Risk of Client Violence.' Pp. 32–48 in *The Meanings of Violence*, edited by E. A. Stanko. London: Routledge.

Hausbeck, K and B Brents (2000) 'Inside Nevada's Brothel Industry.' Pp 217–243 in *Sex for Sale*, edited by R. Weitzer. London: Routledge.

Heap, C (2003) 'The City as a Sexual Laboratory: The Queer Heritage of the Chicago School.' *Qualitative Sociology* 26(4): 457–487.

Heidensohn, F (1985) *Women and Crime*. London: Macmillan Press.

Hester, M and N Westmarland (2004) 'Tackling Street Prostitution: Towards a Holistic Approach.' Home Office, London.

Heyl, B (1979) *The Madam as Entrepreneur*. New Brunswick, NJ: Transaction Books.

Hobbs, D (1988) *Doing the Business Entrepreneurship, Detectives and the Working Class in the East End of London*. Oxford: Clarendon Press.

—— (1997) 'Professional Crime: Change, Continuity and the Enduring Myth of the Underworld.' *Sociology* 31(1): 57–72.

Hobbs, D, P Hadfield, S Lister and S Winlow (2003) *Bouncers. Violence and Governance in the Night-time Economy*. Oxford: Oxford University Press.

Hochschild, A (1979) 'Emotion Work, Feeling Rules and Social Structure.' *American Journal of Sociology* 85(3): 551–575.

—— (1983) *The Managed Heart*. Berkeley: University of Chicago Press.

Hoigard, C and L Finstad (1992) *Backstreets: Prostitution, Money and Love.* Cambridge: Polity.

Holdaway, S (1983) *Inside the British Police.* Oxford: Basil Blackwell.

Holzman, H and S Pines (1982) 'Buying Sex: The Phenomenology of Being a John.' *Deviant Behaviour* 4: 89–116.

Home Office (2004) *'Paying the Price: A Consultation Paper on Prostitution.'* London.

Hope, T J (1995) 'Community Crime Prevention.' In *Building a Safer Society,* edited by M. Tonry and D. P. Farrington. Chicago: University of Chicago Press.

Hopkins, N (1999) 'Oldest Profession Soldiers on in City Battered during Thatcher Years.' P. 9 in *The Guardian.* London.

Hubbard, P (1998) 'Community Action and the Displacement of Street Prostitution: Evidence from British Cities.' *Geoforum* 29(3): 269–286.

—— (1999a) 'Researching Female Sex Work: reflections on geographical exclusion, critical methodologies and "useful" knowledge.' *Area* 31(3): 229–237.

—— (1999b) *Sex and the City. Geographies of prostitution in the urban West.* Aldershot: Ashgate.

—— (2002a) 'Maintaining Family Values? Cleansing the Streets of Sex Advertising.' *Area* 34(4): 353–360.

—— (2002b) 'Sexing the Self: Geographies of Engagement and Encounter.' *Social & Cultural Geography* 3(4): 365–381.

Hubbard, P and T Sanders (2003) 'Making Space for Sex Work: female street prostitution and the production of urban space.' *International Journal of Urban and Regional Research* 27(1): 73–87.

Humphreys, R H (2000) 'The Importance of Job Characteristics to Emotional Displays.' Pp. 236–249 in *Emotions in the Workplace: Research Theory and Practice,* edited by N. Ashkanasy, C. Hartel and W. Zebre. Westport, CT: Quorum Books.

Jackman, N, R O'Toole and G Gilbert (1963) 'The Self Image of the Prostitute.' *Sociological Quarterly* 4(2): 150–161.

Jackson, S and S Scott (2004) 'Sexual Antinomies in Late Modernity.' *Sexualities* 7(2): 233–248.

Jacobs, K (2004) 'Pornography in Small Places and Other Spaces.' *Cultural Studies* 18(1): 67–83.

Jaget, C (1980) *Prostitutes: Our Life.* London: Falling Wall Press.

James, J and M Meyerding (1977) 'Early Sexual Experience and Prostitution.' *American Journal of Psychiatry* 134(12): 1381–85.

James, J (1974) 'Motivation for Entrance into Prostitution.' Pp. 177–205 in *The Female Offender,* edited by L. Crithes. London: Heath.

James, N (1989) 'Emotional Labour: skill and work in the social regulation of feelings.' *Sociological Review* 37(1): 15–42.

Jarvinen, M (1993) *Of Vice and Women: Shades of Prostitution.* Oslo: Scandinavian University Press.

Jeffreys, S (1997) *The Idea of Prostitution.* Melbourne, Australia: Spinifex Press.

Jenness, V (1993) *Making it Work: The Prostitutes Rights Movement in Perspective.* New York: Aldine de Gruyter.

Jones, H and T Sager (2001) 'Crime and Disorder Act 1998: Prostitution and the Anti Social Behaviour Order.' *Criminal Law Review* Nov: 873–885.

Jones, P and J Pratten (1999) 'Buying and Selling Sex: a preliminary examination of the service encounter.' *Management Research News* 22(12): 38–42.

Jordan, J (1997) 'User Pays: Why Men Buy Sex.' Australian and New Zealand Journal of Criminology 30(1): 55–71.

Kang, M (2003) 'The Managed Hand: The Commercialization of Bodies and Emotions in Korean Immigrant-owned Nail Salons.' *Gender and Society* 17(6): 820–839.

Kaplan, C, D Korf and C Sterk (1987) 'Temporal and Social Context of Heroin Using Populations: an illustration of the snowball sampling technique.' *Journal of Nervous Mental Disorders* 175(9): 566–574.

Kelly, L and L Regan (2000) 'Stopping Traffic: exploring the extent of, and responses to, trafficking in women for sexual exploitation in the UK.' Home Office Policing and Reducing Crime Unit, London.

Kempadoo, K and J Doezema (1998) *Global Sex Workers*. London: Routledge.

Kennedy, H (1993) *Eve was Framed: Women and British Justice*. London: Vintage.

Kesler, K (2002) 'Is a Feminist Stance in Support of Prostitution Possible? An Exploration of Current Trends.' *Sexualities* 5(2): 219–235.

Kilvington, J, S Day and H Ward (2001) 'Prostitution Policy in Europe: A Time for Change?' *Feminist Review* 67 (Spring): 78–93.

Kinnell, H (1991) 'Prostitutes' Perceptions of Risk and Factors Related to Risk-taking.' Pp. 79–94 in *AIDS Responses, Interventions and Care*, edited by P. Aggelton, G. Hart and P. Davies. London: Falmer.

—— (2004) 'Violence and Sex Work in Britain.' Pp. 179–197 in *Sex Work, Mobility and Health in Europe*, edited by S. Day and H. Ward. London: Kegan Paul.

Kirkpatrick, K (2000) 'Provider–client models of individual outreach and collective behavioural change: the delivery of sexual health promotion among sex workers.' *Health Education Journal* 59: 39–49.

Krugman, H and E Hartley (1970) 'Passive Learning From Television.' *American Sociological Review* 34(2): 184–190.

Kulick, D (2003) 'Sex in the New Europe: The Criminalization of Clients and Swedish Fear of Prostitution.' New York: New York University.

Kurtz, S, H Surratt, J Inciardi and M Kiley (2004) 'Sex Work and "Date" Violence.' *Violence Against Women* 10(4): 357–385.

Larsen, E (1992) 'The Politics of Prostitution Control: Interest Group Politics in four Canadian cities.' *International Journal of Urban and Regional Research* 16(1): 169–189.

Lash, S (1994) 'Reflexivity and its Doubles: Structure, Aesthetics, Community.' Pp. 110–73 in *Reflexive Modernization: Politics, Tradition and Aesthetics in the Modern Social Order*, edited by U. Beck, A. Giddens and S. Lash. Cambridge: Polity.

Lawless, S, S Kippax and J Crawford (1996) 'Dirty, Diseased and Undeserving: The Positioning of HIV Positive Women.' *Social Science and Medicine* 43(9): 1371–1377.

Layder, D (2004) *Emotions in Social Life*. London: Sage.

Lee, R (1995) *Dangerous Fieldwork*. London: Sage.

Letkemann, P (2002) 'Unemployed Professionals, Stigma Management and Derivative Stigmata.' *Work, Employment and Society* 16(3): 511–522.

Lever, J and D Dolnick (2000) 'Clients and Call Girls: Seeking Sex and Intimacy.' Pp. 85–100 in *Sex for Sale*, edited by R. Weitzer. London: Routledge.

Levi, K (1981) 'Becoming a Hitman: Neutralization in a Very Deviant Career.' *Urban Life* 10(1): 47–63.

Levine, J and L Madden (1988) *Lyn A Story of Prostitution*. London: The Women's Press.

Lewis, J and Maticka-Tyndale, E (2000) 'Licensing Sex Work: Public Policy and Women's Lives.' *Canadian Public Policy* 26(4): 437–449.

Liebling, A and B Stanko (2001) 'Allegiance and Ambivalence: Some Dilemmas in Researching Disorder and Violence.' *British Journal of Criminology* 41(4): 421–430.

Liepe-Levinson, K (2002) *Stripshows. Performances of Gender and Desire*. London: Routledge.

Light, I (1977) 'The Ethnic Vice Industry.' *American Sociological Review* 42(3): 464–479.

Loewenthal, D (2002) 'Involvement and Emotional Labour.' *Soundings* 20: 151–161.

Lopes, A (2001) 'Sex Workers of the World Unite.' *Feminist Review* 67: 151–153.

—— (2003) 'Building on the foundations of the union.' In *UK Network of Sex Work Projects Conference*. Birmingham, December 5–6.

Lowman, J (2000) 'Violence and the Outlaw Status of (Street) Prostitution in Canada.' *Violence Against Women* 6(9): 987–1011.

Lupton, D (1999) *Risk and Sociocultural Theory: new directions and perspectives*. Cambridge: Cambridge University Press.

Mackinnon, C (1982) 'Feminism, Marxism, Method and the State.' *Signs* 7: 3–13.

Maher, L (2000) *Sexed Work: Gender, Race and Resistance in a Brooklyn Drug Market*. Oxford: Oxford University Press.

Maher, L and D Dixon (1999) 'Policing and Public Health.' *British Journal of Criminology* 39: (4) 488–512.

Mahood, L (1990) *The Magdalenes: Prostitution in the Nineteeth Century*. London: Routledge.

Malbon, B (1999) *Clubbing: Dancing, Ecstasy and Vitality*. London: Routledge.

Manning, P (1977) *Police Work*. Cambridge, MA: MIT Press.

Mansson, S A and U Hedin (1999) 'Breaking the Matthew Effect-on Women Leaving Prostitution.' *International Journal of Social Welfare* 8: 67–77.

Mathieu, L (2003) 'The Emergence and Uncertain Outcomes of Prostitutes' Social Movements.' *The European Journal of Women's Studies* 10(1): 29–50.

Matthews, R (1986) 'Beyond Wolfenden? Prostitution, Politics and the Law.' Pp.39–48 in *Confronting Crime*, edited by R. Matthews and J. Young. London: Sage.

—— (1997) 'Prostitution in London: An Audit.' Department of Social Sciences, Middlesex University, London.

Mattley, C (1998) '(Dis) Courtesy Stigma. Fieldwork among Phone Fantasy Workers.' Pp. 146–158 in *Ethnography at the Edge*, edited by J. Ferrell and S. Kane. Boston: Northern University Press.

Matza, D (1969) *Becoming Deviant*. Englewood Cliffs, NJ: Prentice Hall.

May, T, M Edmunds and M Hough (1999) 'Street Business: the links between sex and drug markets.' Home Office Policing and Reducing Crime Unit, London.

May, T, A Harocopos and M Hough (2000) 'For Love or Money: Pimps and the Management of Sex Work.' Home Office Policing and Reducing Crime Unit, London.

McCarthy, J and N Zald (1987) *Social Movements in Organizational Society*. New Brunswick, NJ: Transaction Books.

McConville, M and D Shepherd (1992) *Watching Police, Watching Communities*. London: Routledge.

McCullagh, J, Q Syed and M Bellis (1998) 'Female Prostitution and Associated Drug Use in the North West of England.' Sexual Health and Environmental Epidemiology Unit, Liverpool University, Liverpool.

McHugh, P (1980) *Prostitution and Victorian Social Reform*. London: Croom Helm.

McIntosh, M (1971) 'Changes in the Organization of Thieving.' Pp. 98–133 in *Images of Deviance*, edited by S. Cohen. Harmondsworth: Penguin.

McKeganey, M and M Bloor (1991) 'Spotting the Invisible Man: the influence of male gender on fieldwork relations.' *British Journal of Sociology* 42(2): 195–209.

McKeganey, N and M Barnard (1996) *Sex Work on the Streets*. Buckingham: Open University Press.

McKeganey, N, M Barnard, A Leyland, I Coote and E Follet (1992) 'Female Streetworking Prostitution and HIV Infection in Glasgow.' *British Medical Journal* 305: 801–805.

McLeod, E (1982) *Working Women: Prostitution Now*. London: Croom Helm.

Middlethon, A-L (2002) 'Being Anally Penetrated: Erotic Inhibitions, Improvisations and Transformations.' *Sexualities* 5(2): 181–200.

Miller, E (1986) *Street Women*. Philadelphia, PA: Temple University Press.

Miller, J (1993) 'Your Life is on the Line Every Night You're Out There on the Streets: victimization and the resistance among street prostitutes.' *Humanity and Society* 17(4): 422–446.

—— (1995) 'Gender and Power on the Streets.' *Journal of Contemporary Ethnography* 24(2): 427–451.

—— (1997) 'Researching Violence Against Street Prostitutes.' Pp. 144–156 in *Researching Sexual Violence Against Women*, edited by M. Schwartz. London: Sage.

Miller, W Ian (1999) *Anatomy of Disgust*. Harvard: Harvard University Press.

Millet, K (1971) *Sexual Politics*. London: Sphere Books.

Mills, A (1998) 'Cockpits, Hangers, Boys and Galleys: Corporate Masculinities and the Development of British Airways.' *Gender, Work and Organization* 5(3): 172–188.

Mitchell Jr, R (1991) 'Secrecy and Disclosure in Fieldwork.' Pp. 97–108 in *Experiencing Fieldwork. An Inside View of Qualitative Research*, edited by W. Shaffir and R. Stebbins. London: Sage.

Monaghan, L (2002) 'Embodying Gender, Work and Organization: Solidarity, Cool Loyalties and Contested Hierarchy in a Masculinist Occupation.' *Gender, Work and Organization* 9(5): 504–536.

—— (2003) 'Dangers on the Doors: Bodily Risk in a Demonised Occupation.' *Health Risk and Society* 5(1): 11–31.

Montemurro, B (2001) 'Strippers and Screamers. The Emergence of Social Control in a Noninstitutionalized Setting.' *Journal of Contemporary Ethnography* 30(3): 275–304.

Monto, M (2000) 'Why Men Seek Out Prostitutes.' Pp. 67–83 in *Sex for Sale*, edited by R. Weitzer. London: Routledge.

—— (2004) 'Female Prostitution, Customers and Violence.' *Violence Against Women* 10(2): 160–188.

Monto, M and N Hotaling (2001) 'Predictors of Rape Myth Acceptance Among Male Clients of Female Street Prostitution.' *Violence Against Women* 7(3): 275–293.

Morgan-Thomas, R (2003) 'Impact of Closing Edinburgh 'Non-Harassment' Zone on World AIDS Day 2001: What's happened since?' in *UK Network of Sex Work Projects Conference*. Birmingham, December 5–6.

Muncie, J (1999) *Youth & Crime. A Critical Introduction*. London: Sage.

Murphy, A (2003) 'The Dialectical Gaze exploring the Subject–Object Tension in the Performances of Women who Strip.' *Journal of Contemporary Ethnography* 32(3): 305–335.

Nagel, J (1997) *Whores and Other Feminists*. London: Routledge.

Nemitz, T (2001) 'Gender Issues in Informer Handling.' Pp. 98–109 in *Informers: Policing Policy and Practice*, edited by R. Billingsley, T. Nemitz and P. Bean. Portland, OR: Willan.

Nencel, L (2001) *Ethnography and Prostitution in Peru*. London: Pluto Press.

Norris, C, J Moran and G Armstrong (1998) *Surveillance, Closed Circuit Television and Social Control*. Aldershot: Ashgate.

Norton-Hawk, M (2004) 'A Comparison of Pimp- and Non-Pimp Controlled Women.' *Violence Against Women* 10(2): 189–194.

O'Brien, M (1994) 'The Managed Heart Revisited: health and social control.' *Sociological Review* 42(4): 393–413.

O'Connell Davidson, J (1996) 'Prostitution and the Contours of Control.' Pp. 180–193 in *Sexual Cultures*, edited by J. Weeks and J. Holland. London: Macmillan.

—— (1998) *Prostitution, Power and Freedom*. London: Polity.

—— (2002) 'The Rights and Wrongs of Prostitution.' *Hypatia* 17(2): 84–98.

O'Connell Davidson, J and D Layder (1994) *Methods, Sex and Madness*. London: Routledge.

O'Connell Davidson, J and J Sanchez Taylor (1999) 'Fantasy Islands: Exploring the Demand for Sex Tourism.' Pp. 37–54 in *Sun, Sex and Gold: Tourism and Sex Work in the Caribbean*, edited by K. Kempadoo. Oxford: Rowman & Littlefield.

Oerton, S and J Phoenix (2001) 'Sex/Bodywork: Discourses and Practices.' *Sexualities* 4(4): 387–412.

Offe, C (1999) 'How Can We Trust our Fellow Citizens?' Pp. 42–87 in *Democracy and Trust*, edited by M. Warren. Cambridge: Cambridge University Press.

O'Kane, M (2002a) Prostitution: The Channel 4 Survey http: www.channel4.com/news/microsites/D/Dispatches/prostitution/survey.html

—— (2002b) 'Mean Streets.' September 18th in *The Guardian*. London.

O'Neill, M (1996a) 'Researching Prostitution and Violence: towards a feminist praxis.' Pp. 130–147 in *Women, Violence and Male Power*, edited by M. Hester, L. Kelly and J. Radford. London: Open University Press.

—— (1996b) 'The Aestheticization of the Whore in Contemporary Society: desire, the body, self and society.' in *Body and Organization Workshop*. Keele University.

—— (2001) *Prostitution and Feminism*. London: Polity Press.

O'Neill, M and R Barbaret (2000) 'Victimisation and the Social Organisation of Prostitution in England and Spain.' Pp. 123–137 in *Sex for Sale*, edited by R. Weitzer. London: Routledge.

Opperman, M (1999) 'Sex Tourism.' *Annals of Tourism Research* 26(2): 251–266.

Parker, H J, L Williams and J Aldridge (2002) 'The Normalization of "Sensible" Recreational Drug Use: Further Evidence from the North West England Longitudinal Study.' *Sociology* 36: 941–964.

Parry, O (1982) 'Campaign for Respectability: a study of organised British naturism.' M.Sc Econ, University College, Cardiff.

Pasko, L (2002) 'Naked Power: The Practice of Stripping as a Confidence Game.' *Sexualities* 5(1): 49–66.

Pateman, C (1988) *The Sexual Contract*. Oxford: Blackwell.

Pauw, I and L Brener (2003) ' "You are just whores – you can't be raped": Barriers to safer sex practices among women street sex workers in Cape Town.' *Culture, Health & Sexuality* 5(6): 465–481.

Pease, K (2003) 'Crime Reduction.' Pp. 948–979 in *Oxford Handbook of Criminology*, edited by M. Maguire, R. Morgan and R. Reiner. Oxford: Oxford University Press.

Peelo, M and K Soothill (2000) 'The Place of Public Narratives in Reproducing Social Order.' *Theoretical Criminology* 4(2): 131–148.

Perkins, R, G Prestage, R Sharp and F Lovejoy (1991) *Sex Work and Sex Workers in Australia*. Sydney: UNSW Press.

Pheterson, G (1993) 'The Whore Stigma.' *Social Text* 37: 37–64.

Phoenix, J (1995) 'Prostitution: Problematizing the Definition.' Pp. 65–77 in *Heterosexual Politics*, edited by M. Maynard and J. Purvis. London: Taylor and Francis.

—— (1999a) *Making Sense of Prostitution*. London: Macmillan.

—— (1999b) 'Prostitutes, Ponces and Poncing: Making Sense of Violence.' Pp. 261–289 in *Relating Intimacies*, edited by P. Bagguley and J. Seymour. London: Macmillan.

—— (2000) 'Prostitute Identities: Men, Money and Violence.' *British Journal of Criminology* 40(1): 37–55.

Pickering, S (2001) 'Undermining the Sanitized Account: Violence and Emotionality in the Field in Northern Ireland.' *British Journal of Criminology* 41(2): 485–501.

Pitcher, J and R Aris (2003) 'Women and Street Sex Work. Issues arising from an evaluation of an arrest referral scheme.' Nacro, London.

Plummer, K (1995) *Telling Sexual Stories. Power, Change and Social Worlds*. London: Routledge.

Plumridge, L (2001) 'Rhetoric, Reality and Risk Outcomes in Sex Work.' *Health, Risk and Society* 3(2): 199–215.

Plumridge, E, Chetwynd, S, Reed, A and Gifford, S (1996) 'Patrons of the Sex Industry: Perceptions of Risk.' *AIDS Care* 8(4): 405–416.

Plumridge, E, Chetwynd, S J, Reed, A and Gifford, S (1997) 'Discourses of Emotionality in Commercial Sex.' *Feminism and Psychology* 7(2): 165–181.

Poland, B and B Fischer (1998) 'Exclusion, "Risk" and Social Control – Reflections on Community Policing and Public Health.' *Geoforum* 29(2): 187–197.

Polsky, N (1971) *Hustlers, Beats and Others*. Harmondsworth: Penguin.

Porter, J and L Bonilla (2000) 'Drug Use, HIV and the Ecology of Street Prostitution.' Pp. 103–121 in *Sex for Sale*, edited by R. Weitzer. London: Routledge.

Porter, R (1994) *London – A Social History*. Oxford: Basil Blackwell.

Posner, E (2000) *Law and Social Norms*. Cambridge, MA: Harvard University Press.

Potterat, P, D Brewer, S Muth, R Rothenberg, D Woodhouse, J Muth, H Stites and S Brody (2004) 'Mortality in a Long-term Open Cohort of Prostitute Women.' *American Journal of Epidemiology* 159: 778–785.

Prus, R and S Irini (1980) *Hookers, Rounders, & Desk Clerks*. Canada: Gage Publishing Limited.

Punch, M (1989) 'Researching Police Deviance: A Personal Encounter with the Limitations and Liabilities of Field-work.' *British Journal of Sociology* 40(2): 177–204.

Pyett, P and D Warr (1997) 'Vulnerability on the streets: female sex workers and HIV risk.' *AIDS Care* 9(5): 539–547.

Rabinovitch, J and Strega, S (2004) 'The PEERS Story.' *Violence Against Women* 10(2): 140–159.

Radford, J (1987) 'Policing Male Violence – Policing Women.' Pp. 30–45 in *Women, Violence and Social Control*, edited by J. Hanmer and M. Maynard. London: Macmillan.

Raphael, J and D Shapiro (2004) 'Violence in Indoor and Outdoor Prostitution Venues.' *Violence Against Women* 10(2): 126–139.

Rattue, R and N Cornelius (2002) 'The Emotional Labour of Police Work.' *Soundings* 20: 190–201.

Raymond, J G (1999) 'Prostitution as Violence Against Women.' *Women's International Forum* 21(1): 1–9.

Reckless, W C (1925) 'The Natural History of Vice Areas in Chicago' PhD Dissertation, University of Chicago.

Reiner, R (1992) 'Police Research in the UK: A Critical Review.' In *Modern Policing*, edited by N. Morris and M. Tonry. Chicago: University of Chicago.

Reiss, A J (1961) 'The Social Intergration of Queers and Peers.' *Social Problems* 9: 102–120.

—— (1967) 'The Social Intergration of Queers and Peers.' in *Sexual Deviance*, edited by J. Gagnon and W. Simon. New York: Harper & Row.

Reynolds, H (1986) *The Economies of Prostitution*. Illinois: Charles C Thomas Publisher.

Rhodes, T and L Cusick (2000) 'Love and Intimacy in Relationship Risk Management: HIV positive people and their sexual partners.' *Sociology of Health and Illness* 22(1): 1–26.

Rhodes, T and A Quirk (1998) 'Drug Users' Sexual Relationships and the Social Organisation of Risk: The Sexual Relationship as a Site of Risk Management.' *Social Science Medicine* 46(2): 157–169.

Rickard, W (2001) ' "Been there, seen it, done it, I've got the T-shirt".' British Sex Workers Reflect on Jobs.' *Feminist Review* 67 (Spring): 111–132.

Rickard, W and T Growney (2001) 'Using Oral History in Peer Education for Sex Workers.' *Oral History* Spring: 85–91.

Roberts, J M (2001) 'Dialogue, Positionality and the Legal Framing of Ethnographic Research.' *Sociological Research Online* 5(4).

Roberts, N (1994) 'The Whore, her Stigma, the Punter and his Wife.' *New Internationalist* 252 (February).

Ronai, C (1992) 'The Reflective Self Through Narrative.' Pp. 102–125 in *Investigating Subjectivity: Research on Lived Experience*, edited by C. Ellis and M. Flaherty. Newbury Park, CA: Sage.

Ronai, C and C Ellis (1989) 'Turn-On's for Money: Interactional Strategies of the Table Dancers.' *Journal of Contemporary Ethnography* 18(3): 271–298.

Roseneil, S (1993) 'Greenham Revisted: Researching Myself and My Sisters.' Pp. 55–74 in *Interpreting the Field*, edited by D. Hobbs and T. May. Oxford: Oxford University Press.

Ruggiero, V (1995) 'Drug Economies: A Fordist Model of Criminal Capital?' *Capital & Class* 55 (Spring): 131–151.

Ryan, C and M Hall (2001) *Sex Tourism: Marginal People and Liminalities*. London: Routledge.

Ryan, C and R Kinder (1996) 'Sex, Tourism and Sex Tourism: fulfilling similar needs?' *Tourism Management* 17(7): 507–518.

Salamon, E (1989) 'The Homosexual Escort Agency: deviance disavowal.' *British Journal of Sociology* 40(1): 1–21.

Sanders, T (2001) 'Female Street Sex Workers, Sexual Violence and Protection Strategies.' *Journal of Sexual Aggression* 7(1): 5–18.

—— (2002) 'The Condom as Psychological Barrier: Female Sex Workers and Emotional Management.' *Feminism and Psychology* 12(4): 561–566.

—— (2004a) 'Controllable Laughter: Managing Sex Work Through Humour.' *Sociology* 38(2): 273–291.

—— (2004b) 'Researching the Online Sex Work Community.' In *Virtual Methods in Social Research on the Internet*, edited by C. Hine. Oxford: Berg.

—— (2004c) 'A Continuum of Risk? The Management of Health, Physical and Emotional Risks by Female Sex Workers.' *Sociology of Health and Illness* 26(5): 1–18.

—— (2005) 'Researching Sex Work: Dynamics, Difficulties and Decisions.' In *A Handbook of Fieldwork*, edited by D. Hobbs and R. Wright. London: Sage.

—— forthcoming. 'It's Just Acting: Sex Workers' Strategies for Capitalising on Sexuality.' *Gender, Work and Organization*.

Scambler, G, P Peswani, A Renton and A Scambler (1990) 'Women prostitutes in the AIDS era.' *Sociology of Health and Illness* 112(3): 260–273.

Scambler, G and A Scambler (1997) *Rethinking Prostitution*. London: Routledge.

Self, H (2003) *Prostitution, Women and Misuse of the Law*. London: Frank Cass.

Sharma, U and P Black (2002) 'Look Good, Feel Better: Beauty Therapy as Emotional Labour.' *Sociology* 35(4): 913–931.

Sharp, K and S Earle (2003) 'Cyberpunters and Cyberwhores: prostitution on the Internet.' Pp. 36–52 in *Dot Cons. Crime, Deviance and Identity on the Internet*, edited by Y. Jewkes. Cullompton: Willan.

Sharpe, K (1998) *Red Light, Blue Light: Prostitutes, Punters and the Police*. Aldershot: Ashgate.

—— (2000) 'Sad, Bad And (Sometimes) Dangerous To Know: Street Corner Research with Prostitutes, Punters and the Police.' Pp. 362–372 in *Doing Research on Crime and Justice*, edited by R. King and E. Wincup. Oxford: Oxford University Press.

Shilling, C (1997) 'Emotions, Embodiment and the Sensation of Society.' *Sociological Review* 45(2): 195–219.

Shott, S (1979) 'Emotion and Social Life: A Symbolic Interactionist Analysis.' *American Journal of Sociology* 84(6): 1317–1334.

Shrage, L (1994) *Moral Dilemmas of Feminism*. London: Routledge.

—— (1999) 'Do Lesbian Prostitutes Have Sex with Their Clients? A Clintonesque Reply.' *Sexualities* 2(2): 259–261.

Silbert, A and M Pines (1982) 'Victimization of Street Prostitutes.' *Victimology: An International Journal* 1–4: 122–133.

—— (1985) 'Sexual Abuse as an antecedent of Prostitution.' *Child Abuse and Neglect* 5: 407–411.

Simmel, G (1955) 'The Web of Group-affiliation.' In *Conflict and the Web of Group-Affiliations*, edited by R. Bendix. New York: Free Press.

Skilbrei, M (2001) 'The Rise and Fall of the Norwegian Massage Parlour: Changes in the Norwegian Prostitution Setting in the 1990s.' *Feminist Review* 67: 63–77.

Smart, C (1984) *The Ties that Bind Us: Law, Marriage and the Reproduction of Patriarchal Relationships*. London: Routledge and Kegan Paul.

—— (1995) *Law, Crime and Sexuality: Essays in Feminism*. London: Sage.

Smith, C (2002) 'Shiny Chests and Heaving G-Strings: A Night Out with the Chippendales.' *Sexualities* 5(1): 67–89.

Smith, C and E Wincup (2000) 'Breaking In: Researching Criminal Justice Institutions for Women.' Pp. 331–349 in *Doing Research on Crime and Justice*, edited by R. King and E. Wincup. Oxford: Oxford University Press.

Smith, J (1989) *Misogynies*. London: Faber and Faber.

Smith, P (1992) *The Emotional Labour of Nursing*. Basingstoke: Macmillan.

Soothill, K (2004a) 'Sex Talk.' *Police Review* 27 (February): 20–21.

—— (2004b) 'Parlour Games: The Value of An Internet Site Providing Punters' Views of Massage Parlours.' *The Police Journal* 77(1): 43–53.

Sprongberg, M (1997) *Feminizing Veneral Disease: the body of the prostitute in nineteenth century medical discourse*. Basingstoke: Macmillan.

Stanko, E (1990) 'When Precaution is Normal: A feminist critique of crime prevention.' Pp. 171–183 in *Feminist Perspectives in Criminology*, edited by L. Gelsthorpe and A. Morris. Milton Keynes: Open University.

—— (1996) 'Warnings to Women: Police Advice and Women's Safety in Britain.' *Violence Against Women* 2(1): 5–24.

—— (1997) 'Safety Talk: Conceptualizing Women's Risk Assessment as a "Technology of the Soul".' *Theoretical Criminology* 1(4): 479–499.

—— (1998) 'Warnings to Women: Police advice and women's safety in Britain.' Pp. 52–71 in *Crime Control and Women: feminist implications of criminal justice policy*, edited by S. Miller. London: Sage.

Sterk, C (2000) *Tricking and Tripping: Prostitution in the Era of AIDS*. New York: Social Change Press.

Storr, M (2003) *Latex and Lingerie: The Sexual Dynamics of Ann Summers Parties*. Oxford: Berg.

Sullivan, M and S Jefferys (2002) 'Legalization. The Australian Experience.' *Violence Against Women* 8(9): 1140–1148.

Surrat, H, J Inciardi, S Kurtz and M Kiley (2004) 'Sex Work and Drug use in a Subculture of Violence.' *Crime & Delinquency* 50(1): 43–59.

Sutherland, E (1937) *The Professional Thief*. Chicago: University of Chicago.

Swann, S (1998) *Whose Daughter Next?* London: Barnardos.

Swirsky, R and C Jenkins (2000) 'Prostitution, Pornography and Telephone Boxes.' Pp. 57–71 in *Women, Violence and Strategies for Action*, edited by J. Radford, M. Friedberg and L. Harne. Buckingham: Open University Press.

Sykes, G and D Matza (1957) 'Techniques of Neutralization: A Theory of Delinquency.' *American Sociological Review* 22(12): 664–670.

Tatum, B (2000) *Crime, Violence and Minority Youths*. Aldershot: Ashgate.

Taylor, D (2003) 'Sex for Sale: New Challenges And New Dangers for Women Working on and off the Streets.' Mainliners, London.

Taylor, G (1985) *Pride, Shame and Guilt. Emotions of Self Assessment*. Oxford: Clarendon Press.

Thompson, W and J Harred (1992) 'Topless Dancers: Managing Stigma in a Deviant Occupation.' *Deviant Behaviour* 13: 291–311.

Tomsen, S (1997) 'A Top Night: Social Protest, Masculinities and the Culture of Drinking Violence.' *British Journal of Criminology* 37(1): 90–102.

Travis, A (2003) 'Sex Laws to Get Major Overhaul' *The Guardian*, P. 1, 30 December. London.

Vallely, A (2001) 'Ambigious Symbols: Women and the Ascetic Ideal in Janism.' Pp. 131–144 in *Feminist (Re)visions of the Subject*, edited by G. Currie and C. Rothenberg. New York: Lexington Books.

van Maanen, J (1988) *Tales from the Field: On Writing Ethnography*. Chicago: University of Chicago Press.

VanBrunschot, E (2003) 'Community Policing and "Johns Schools".' *Canadian Review of Sociology and Anthropology* 40(2): 215–232.

Varese, F (2001) *The Russian Mafia: private protection in a new market economy*. Oxford: Oxford University Press.

Wacquant, L (1995) 'Pugs at Work: Bodily Capital and Bodily Labour Among Professional Boxers.' *Body & Society* 1: 65–93.

Walkowitz, J (1980) *Prostitution and Victorian Society: Women, Class, and the State*. Cambridge: Cambridge University Press.

Wallman, S (2001) 'Global Threats, Local Options, Personal Risk: Dimensions of Migrant Sex Work in Europe.' *Health, Risk & Society* 3(1): 75–88.

Walters, R (2003) *Deviant Knowledge Criminology, Politics and Policy*. Cullompton: Willan.

Ward, H, S Day and J Weber (1999) 'Risky Business: Health and Safety in the Sex Industry over a 9 year Period.' *Sexually Transmitted Infections* 75(5): 340–343.

Warr, D and P Pyett (1999) 'Difficult Relations: Sex Work, Love and Intimacy.' *Sociology of Health and Illness* 21(3): 290–309.

Warren, M E (1999) *Democracy and Trust.* Cambridge: Cambridge University Press.

Webb, L and J Elms (1994) 'Social Workers and Sex Workers.' Pp. 271–278 in *Sex Work and Sex Workers in Australia*, edited by R. Perkins, G. Prestage, R. Sharp and F. Lovejoy. Sydney: UNSW Press.

Weiner, A (1996) 'Understanding the Social Needs of Streetwalking Prostitutes.' *Social Work* 41(1): 87–105.

Weitzer, R (1996) 'Prostitutes' Rights in the United States: The Failure of a Movement.' *Sociological Quarterly* 32(1): 23–41.

—— (2000) *Sex for Sale.* London: Routledge.

Wellings, K, J Field, A Johnson and J Wadsworth (1994) *Sexual Behaviour in Britain.* London: Penguin.

Wellington, C and J Bryson (2002) 'At Face Value? Image Consultancy, Emotional Labour and Professional Work.' *Sociology* 35(4): 933–946.

West, J (2000) 'Prostitution: Collectives and the Politics of Regulation.' *Gender, Work and Organisation* 7(2): 106–118.

West, J and T Austrin (2002) 'From Work as Sex to Sex as Work: networks, "others" and occupations in the analysis of work.' *Gender, Work and Organization* 9(5): 482–503.

Westley, W (1953) 'Violence and the Police.' *American Journal of Sociology* 59(1): 34–41.

Whittaker, D and G Hart (1996) 'Research note: Managing Risks: the social organisation of indoor sex work.' *Sociology of Health and Illness* 18(3): 399–413.

Williams, C (2003) 'Sky Service: The Demands of Emotional Labour in the Airline Industry.' *Gender, Work and Organization* 10(5): 513–550.

Williams, S and G Bendelow (1998) *Emotions in Social Life: Critical Themes and Contemporary Issues.* London: Routledge.

Williamson, C and T Cluse-Tolar (2002) 'Pimp-Controlled Prostitution: Still an Integral Part of Street Life.' *Violence Against Women* 8(9): 1074–1092.

Wilson, J (1999) 'Outreach Programmes for Female Commercial Sex Workers.' *International Journal of STD and AIDS* 10(11): 697–698.

Wincup, E (2000) 'Surviving through Substance Use: The Role of Substances in the Lives of Women who Appear before the Courts.' *Sociological Research Online* 4(3).

Winlow, S, D Hobbs, S Lister and P Hadfield (2001) 'Get Ready to Duck. Bouncers and the Realities of Ethnographic Research on Violent Groups.' *British Journal of Criminology* 41(3): 536–548.

Wojcicki, J and J Malala (2001) 'Condom Use, Power and HIV/AIDS Risk: sex-workers bargain for survival in Hillbrow/Joubert Park/Berea, Johannsburg.' *Social Science and Medicine* 53: 99–121.

Wolf, D R (1991) 'High-Risk Methodology: Reflections on Leaving an Outlaw Society.' Pp. 211–223 in *Experiencing Fieldwork. An Inside View of Qualitative Research*, edited by W. Shaffir and R. Stebbins. London: Sage.

Wolfenden Report (1957) 'Commission on Homosexual Offences and Prostitution.' London, HMSO, London.

Wolkowitz, C (2002) 'The Social Relations of Body Work.' *Work, Employment and Society* 16(3): 497–510.

Wood, E (2000) 'Working in the Fantasy Factory: The Attention Hypothesis and the Enacting of Masculine Power in Strip Clubs.' *Journal of Contemporary Ethnography* 29(1): 5–31.

Zahavi, A and A Zahavi (1997) *The Handicap Principle. The Missing Piece of Darwin's Puzzle.* Oxford: Oxford University Press.

Zatz, N (1997) 'Sex Work/Sex Act: Law, Labour and Desire in Constructions of Prostitution.' *Signs* 22(2): 277–308.

Index

When added to the page number 'n' denotes a footnote.

abolitionist perspective 38, 95
acceptability, code of 152–3
acceptance, earning 28–9
addresses, revealing 69
adultery, prostitution as an alternative
    154
advertising 14, 21
    over the Internet 17
    by escorts 18
    and the risk of discovery 131
    see also calling cards
African-Caribbean men 51, 59–62
age
    of interviewees 47
        entry into prostitution 49
    as a screening strategy 62–3
    of street workers 19
age difference 62
aggression as a deterrent to violence
    85–7
alcohol
    clients under the influence 65, 66
    as a coping strategy 156
alias occupations 125–6
anal sex 152, 153, 164
ancillary industries 20–2
    within the industry 20–1
anti-massage parlour organizations
    104
appearance 57–9
apprenticeships 171–3

arrest
    attitudes to 109
    avoidance 105–12
        in the indoor markets 110–12
        in the street market 105–10
    risk 98
ASBOs (Anti Social Behaviour Orders)
    96, 98
    use on pimps and clients 101
assertiveness as a deterrent to
    violence 85–7
assessment
    importance 53
    over the Internet 68–70
    over the telephone 66–8
    see also visual assessments
attitude
    as a deterrent to violence 85–7
    and genuineness 58–9
    in telephone conversations 67

bags as suspicious items 66
'beats' 19
behaviour
    expectations 160
    suspicious 65–6
black men 51, 59–62
    image as pimps 59–60
    as partners of sex workers 60–1
'bodily capital' 87
'bodily' risks 44, 45

of fieldwork 35
body exclusion zones 150–3
'body work' 143
boyfriend-pimps
and violence 73
as deterrents to violence 80–1
boyfriends
revealing the truth to 121–2
the 'wrong type' 122
Brazil, prostitutes in 154
brothels 16–17
conduct 16
criminalization 89–90
drug use 16
licensing and regulation schemes 176
location 11, 16
in Nevada 171
opening hours 16
payment systems 16
staff 17
'buddy systems' 172–3
bulletin boards 27

Call Off Your Old Tired Ethics
(COYOTE) 174
calling cards 11, 96
card boys 21
CCTV 64–5, 83, 84
and the street market 84–5, 114
charges *see* payment systems
chatrooms 21
use for ethnographic research 27
checking consistency 67–8
'checking in' 83
children
and lying 134
revealing the truth to 122–3
choice 38–41
concept 37
risk-taking and 42–4
and women in developing countries
39
clients 178–9
criminalization 94, 95
and the 'etiquette of the market'
161–2, 179
monitoring 83–5
numbers 12

public encounters with 127–8
re-education 95
relationship between female
prostitutes and 40–1, 86, 91
romantic 146, 165
selection process *see* selection
process
thrill-seeking motivations 114
use of ASBOs (Anti Social
Behaviour Orders) 101
see also regular clients
'clipping' 178
close-circuit television cameras *see*
CCTV
closed subject 134–5
clothing
and avoiding detection 107–8
and safety 77
codes of practice 164–5
effect of policing 98
coercion of women 94
coercive relationships 163
cognitive mapping 71
collaboration 174
colleague relationships 163–4
collective work environments 78–80
'coming out', process of 136
commodity, the body as 150
'common prostitute' 94
communication in the trust game
56–71
community action 99–101
avoiding 106–7
effect on camaraderie and shared
code of practice 98
community policing 99
community safety 99
compliance and client honesty 68–9
condoms
as a psychological barrier 149–50
use 45, 67
as a social norm 160
conduct
in brothels 16
in licensed saunas 15
consistency, checking 67–8
contracts, breaking 54
costly signals

and being a regular 64
occupational status and identifying
features as 57–8
costly to fake principle 56, 68
courtesy stigma 122–3
courts, double standard 95
covering up 124–8
covert monitoring of meetings 83
COYOTE (Call Off Your Old Tired
Ethics) 174
Crime and Disorder Act (1998) 96, 99
Crime and Police Action Act (2001)
96
'crime shuffling' 98
'criminal diversifiers' 98–9
Criminal Justice and Police Act (2001)
95
criminal records 98
criminalization
of brothels and procuring 89–90
of sex workers and clients 94, 95,
114
see also 'quasicriminalization'
'cultural competence' 55

danger
and the sexual transaction 76
unpredictability 75
see also harms
'deep acting' 143
defence mechanisms 139
demeanour 57–9
depression 139
desexualization of sexual encouters
148–50
deterrents against violence 80–7
developing countries 39
deviance
displacement 113–15
social organization 43
deviant status of prostitution 114
directories 11–12
disabilities, service for men with 154
disclosure of the truth 121–3
discretion 110–11
disease
relationship between prostitution
and 10

role of the sex worker in prevention
153–4
disguising activities 110–11
disgust 141–2
displacement 98–9
of deviance 113–15
outcomes 98
see also 'national displacement';
'perpetrator displacement'
'display of disgust' 142
distancing strategies 139
doormen 82
'double lives' 33, 128
double standard in English law 95,
113
drink see alcohol
drivers 81–2
drug dealers and violence 73
drug use 10
amongst interviewees 49–50
in clients 66
as a coping strategy 139, 156
and guilt 156
in off-street prostitution 15
brothels 16
and prostitution
impact 162–3
links 139
in the street market 19, 20
and policing 109
see also heroin users

eating disorders and prostitution 139
email
ethnographic research through 27
as a screening method 68–9
emotion management 142–7
failure 155–7
strategies 139, 147–55
circumstances for achievability
156–7
motive 140–2
emotion work 142, 143–5, 155–6
exceptions 145–6
emotional consequences of stigma
119–20
emotional investment by researchers
36

emotional labour 142–3, 155
emotional problems, sex workers as
counsellors for 153
emotional risks 45–6, 138–9
emotions 138
see also negative emotions
employment
prostitution as 39–40, 44
see also work
'entrepreneurial' prostitution 17
escort agencies 17–18
fees 18
owners 25
escorts 17–18
fees 18
and the risk of discovery 130–1
services 18
and violence 78
precautions and deterrents 77–8,
81–2, 83
establishments 14–17
movement between 168
relationship between workers and
14
see also brothels; licensed saunas
ethical dilemmas of ethnographic
research 33–4
ethnicity
of interviewees 47–8
as a screening strategy 59–62
see also black men
ethnography 23–36
ethical dilemmas 33–4
interviewees 46–50
'layered access' 23–7
risks 35–6
straddling public and private
worlds 33
'etiquette of the market' 161–2, 179
exchange relationships 24, 27
experiential basis for trust 60
exploitation in prostitution 38, 94

'face' 136
face-to-face visual screening see visual
assessments
families
lying to 133–4

and mutual denial 134–5
revealing the truth 121–3
fantasies 14, 154, 165
provision in working premises 17
'fearless protagonist' 44
fees see payment systems
fellatio 14
charge
in licensed saunas 16
in the street market 19
feminist doctrines 39
'feminization of poverty' 39
field reports 70, 178
fieldwork
earning acceptance 28–9
and nakedness 32
rhythms 30–2
risks 35–6
straddling public and private
worlds 33
fines 94–5
'flourishing professional' 2
footwear and safety 77
frame analysis, theory of 155
'free choices' 38
friendship networks 131, 172–3
friendships 131–3
'front' 85–6
'functional camaraderie' 109

gendered power 41
'gentling' 77
genuineness 53–4, 71
attitude and 58–9
and ethnicity 59–62
and types of signal 56
geographical displacement 98, 99
geographical location
of the street market 114
and policing 97–8
of the workplace 129–30
see also addresses
geographical mobility
and avoidance of arrest 106–7
and the transmission of codes of
practice 168
'girlfriend experience' 152
'good adjustment' 133

good types 54
  signals from 56
government-funded health
    organizations 173
'Groucho paradox' 122
groups of men 65
guides to sexual services 11–12
guilt 140–1
  differences between shame and 120
  and drug use 156

'handicap principle' 56
health education, role of the sex
    worker 153–4
health organizations 173
  see also National Health Service
health risks 45
  see also physical risks
heroin users, and social displacement
    98
hierarchy of harms 44–6
home, working from see working from
    home
honesty 135–6
hotels 20
  visiting 77–8
hours of opening see opening hours
houses, visiting 77–8
husbands, revealing the truth to 121–2

identification, avoiding 107–8
identifying features 57–8
identity 144
  see also 'manufactured identity';
    sexual identities
illegal substances see drug use
imitation 171–2
imprisonment 94
indoor markets
  differences between the street
    market and 14
  drug use 15, 50, 162
  internal relationships 168–71
  location 11
  monitoring of clients 83, 84
  movement between establishments
    168
  organization 159–65

policing 97, 102–4
  guarding against 110–12
selection process see selection
    process
types 13–20
and violence 73
  attitudes to 88
  see also brothels; escorts; licensed
    saunas
information sharing 171
  by clients 178
initiation rituals in fieldwork 29
instincts in the selection process 52
intercourse 14
  charge
    in licensed saunas 16
    in the street market 19
International Union of Sex Workers
    (IUSW) 175
Internet
  advertising 12, 131
    by escorts 18
  as an ancillary industry 21
  assessment over 68–70
  information sharing 171
    by clients 178
  as a virtual fieldwork site 27
  working through 17
  see also email; field reports; websites
interviewees 46–50
interviews 30–2
intimate relationships, avoidance of
    147
isolating strategies 131–3

jewellery and safety 77
job aliases 125–6
'John's Schools' 95
justification for prostitution 153–5

Kerb Crawler Rehabilitation
    Programme 95
kerb-crawling, criminalization of 95
kinship networks 133
kissing 152, 164

labour, complexities 40–1
landlords 17, 20

lap-dancing bars 11
learning, passive 171–2
legal landscape 93–6, 177
   philosophies 94
legal risks in fieldwork 35
legitimate work
   selling sex as 38, 39–40, 44
   see also mainstream occupations
lesbians 145
levels of access in the ethnographic
   research 23–7
licensed saunas 14–16
   and drug use 50
   'house rules' 15
   location 11, 15
   opening hours 15
   owners 25
      formal network of 175–6
   payment system 15–16
   physical environment 15
      and safety 83
   policing 103–4
      collaborative relationships 112
   reputations 161
   services 16
   staff 15
   as a team environment 79
life experience, transfer of skill from
   167–8
location 11–12
   of brothels 11, 16
   and related ancillary industries 20
   of saunas 11, 15
   and secrecy 129–31
   the street market 11, 12, 19
   of working premises 17
lying 133–4

McCoy's Guide to Adult Services 11, 162
maids 20–1
   as a safety measure 82–3
mainstream occupations
   transfer of skills from 167
   see also legitimate work
male prostitution, organization of 172
managers of indoor agencies
   as enforcers of behaviour 161
   as a level of access 25

relationships with the police 111–12
   as a safety measure 82
'Manchester Sauna Owners Forum'
   175
'manufactured identity' 143
marginalization of sex workers 91, 101
markets 13–20
   ancillary industries 20–2
   characteristics 13–14
   choosing 130–1
   mobility within 168
   see also indoor markets; street
      market
massage, licensing for 14–15
'massage fees' 16
meetings, monitoring 83–4
men who purchase sex *see* clients
mental health and prostitution 139
mentoring 171–3
message boards 21
   assessing client reputation via 69–70
Metropolitan Police Vice and Clubs
   Unit 98
middle-aged men 62, 63
mimicry 54–5, 71
mistakes, learning from 166–7
mobility
   and avoiding criminalization and
      harassment 106
   and networks 168–71
   see also geographical mobility
monitoring clients 83–5
morality
   and prostitution 94, 158
   relationship between guilt and 141
   within the sex industry 164–5
murder of sex workers 73, 89
mutual denial 134–5

nakedness in fieldwork 32
'naming and shaming' 104
'national displacement' 106
negative emotions 140–2
   disgust 141–2
   guilt 140–1
   see also shame
neighbourhood groups 100
   see also residents

neighbourhood tensions
and the indoor markets 102
and the street market 99
see also vigilantism
networks
dislocation from 163
see also friendship networks;
occupational networks
Nevada, brothels of 171
'new ecology of sex work' 163
new order of prostitution 162–4, 177
non-contact sexual services 11
normalization of violence 73–5
norms 160, 162
see also occupational norms; social
norms
numbers
and safety 78–80
of sex workers 12–13

observable traits 55, 57–8
observation, participant 33–4
occupational hazards 10
occupational networks 165, 168
mobility and 168–71
occupational norms, learning 171–2
occupational status 57–8
offences related to adult prostitution 94
official agencies
support of 173, 177
see also policing
old order of prostitution 162–3
online sex market 27
see also Internet
opening hours
of brothels 16
licensed saunas 15
oral sex 14, 151, 152
organization see social organization
outcalls 17
overt methods of monitoring meetings
84
owners of indoor agencies
as enforcers of behaviour 161
as a level of access 25
relationships with the police 111–12
use of stigma management
techniques 120

parents, revealing the truth to 122
participant observation 33–4
partners
black men as 60–1
revealing the truth to 121–2
passers-by and violence 73
'passing off' 124, 136
passive learning 171–2
patriarchal ideology 38, 144
Paying the Price 13, 115n
payment systems
in brothels 16
escorts 18
fixed 160
in licensed saunas 15–16
street market 19
in working premises 17
peepholes 64–5
'perpetrator displacement' 113
personal risks of fieldwork 35–6
physical appearance 57–9
physical environment
of licensed saunas 15
manipulation 84–5
and safety 83
physical health 10
physical risks 44, 45
of fieldwork 35
see also violence
pimps 10
black men as 59–60
as deterrents to violence 80–1
relationship between street workers
and 20
use of ASBOs (Anti Social
Behaviour Orders) 101
see also boyfriend-pimps
policing 97–115
attitude towards protection 89–90
guidelines 96
the indoor markets 97, 102–4
collaborative relationships 111–12
and the promotion of safe space 173
reasons for lack of success 113–15
and the risk of violence 74–5
the street market 97–101
working relationships 108–10
see also 'self-policing'

politics of prostitution 174
post-traumatic stress disorder 139
power relations
    between sex workers and clients 41,
        86, 91
    in the researcher-respondent nexus
        28–9
precautions against violence 75–80
    consistency in application 166–7
    working practices 76–8
premeditated violence 74
price *see* payment systems
private lives
    co-existence of work with 146
    collision of work with 127–8, 137
    secrecy and 121–3
    separation of work from 33, 139,
        148–50
problem-orientated policing 99
procuring, criminalization of 89–90
professionalization of prostitution
    176–8
    process of 175
prostitutes' rights movement 39–40,
    174
protection against violence 87–90
    ambivalence of the police 89–90
pseudonyms 124–5
psychological effects of selling sex
    138–9
psychological strategies to prevent
    violence 77
public sexual health 94
punishment 94–5
'punter fees' 15
punters *see* clients

'quasicriminalization' of prostitution
    91

'rational choices' 38
rationalization narratives 153–5
re-identification 63–4
    see also regular clients
'reaction formation' 142
'receptionist fees' 15–16
receptionists 21
    as a safety measure 82

use of stigma management
    techniques 120
recreational drug use 49–50
'red light districts' 11, 19, 114
    impact of heavy policing 113
    movement between 106
    use of CCTV 84
'Red Thread' 174
'reframing of experience' 149
regular clients 63–4
    black men as 61
regulation 9, 174–8
    strengthening 177
    unionization and collaboration
        174–6
    see also state regulation
relationships
    avoidance of intimate 147
    between female prostitutes and
        male clients 40–1, 86, 91
    romantic 165
    between individuals and
        establishments 165
    coercive 163
    colleague 163–4, 168–71
    consequences of stigma 119
    effect of revealing the truth 121–3
    as a level of access 26–7
    with the police
        in the indoor markets 111–12
        in the street market 108–10
    see also exchange relationships
remedial protection against violence
    87–90
remote visual observation 64–6
rents for working premises 17
repulsion 141–2
reputation
    of clients 69–70
    of licensed saunas 161
'research bargains' 24
research sector 21–2
researcher-respondent nexus
    erotic and sexual dimensions 33
    power relations 28–9
residents, and the indoor street
    market 104
resistance 41

responses to violence 75–90
    deterrence 80–7
    precautions 75–80
    protection 87–90
revenue 13
risk
    of arrest 98
    avoidance 105–12
    concept 37
    of consequences of stigma and
        shame 136
    in prostitution 3, 10, 42–4
    hierarchy of harms 44–6
    re-evaluation 166
    in researching prostitution 35–6
    of violence 74–5
    responses 75–90
    see also emotional risk
risk management 10, 43
ritual as a distancing strategy 139
robberies 74
    guarding against 76
romantic relationships with clients
    146, 165
routines 151, 161–2
    altering 166

safety 72–92
    ancillary industry for 20
    code of female 43–4
    impact of policing 98, 113
    in numbers 78–80
    screening 70–1
sanctions to reinforce behaviour
    160–1
saunas see licensed saunas
screening mediums 56
    consistency in application 166–7
    Internet 68–70
    remote visual observation 64–6
    testing on the telephone 66–8
    visual assessment 57–64
secrecy 116–37
    covering up 124–8
    and isolating strategies 131–3
    and location of the workplace
        129–31
    reasons 117–23

and sex workers with black
    partners 60–1
and variations of the truth 133–6
selection process 51–71
    role of the client 71
    screening mediums see screening
        mediums
    trust game see trust game
self-esteem and prostitution 139
'self-policing' 92
self-regulation 175–6
    support by official agencies 177
self-stigmatization 118
separation strategies 139, 148–50, 155
    failure to adopt 156
service sector 21–2
    see also health organizations
service-provider role of researchers
    24, 25, 31
sex acts see sexual services
sex code 164–5
sex radicalism 39
sex as work 148–50
sex work, definition 10
sex worker-as-victim model 38
    criticisms 41
sex workers
    acting violently 87–8
    ambivalence of police protection
        89–90
    criminalization 95
    marginalization 91, 101
    murder of 73, 89
    numbers 12–13
    power struggle between clients and
        41, 86
    relationships
        between establishments and 14
        between male clients and 40–1,
            86, 91, 165
        with colleagues 163–4, 168–71
    roles 153–5
    'self-policing' 92
    stereotyping 117
'sexpolitation economy' 11
sexual deviancy 165
sexual dysfunction, role of the sex
    worker 153–4

sexual fantasies *see* fantasies
sexual health
  relationship between risk and 45
  see also public sexual health
sexual identities 144–5
sexual labour, complexities 40–1
Sexual Offences Act (1956) 94
Sexual Offences Act (1985) 95
Sexual Offences Act (2003) 96
sexual positions, safety of 76
sexual services 14, 152–3
  of escorts 18
  in licensed saunas 16
  shaping the meaning 151–2
  unacceptable 165
  in working premises 17
  see also anal sex; intercourse; oral
    sex
sexual transactions
  and danger 76
  desexualization 148–50
  social organization 43
sexuality, connection between sense of
    self and 144
shame 119–20
  differences between guilt and 120
sharking 160
'shift fees' 15
signalling theory
  application 54, 55
  costly to fake principle 56, 68
situational violence 74
skills, transferring 164, 167–8
'skills talk' 86–7
social displacement 98
social norms 160
  changes 162
  of the sexual transaction 76
  threatening of 94
social organization 158–65
  and resisting violence 72
  rules, rituals and routines 159–65
  changes 162–4, 177
  mechanisms of transmission
    165–73
social organization of deviance, theory
    of 43
social withdrawal 132–3

start-up costs for working premises 17
state regulation 53
stereotype of the prostitute 117
stigma 117–23
  of being a 'punter' 178
  effects 118–19
  emotional consequences 119–20
  management 116, 120
  of information about 124–8
'stigma symbols' 126–7
'street justice' 81
street market 10, 19–20
  avoiding arrest 105–10
  differences between indoor markets
    and 14
  and drug use 19, 20
  impact on organization of the
    industry 162–3
  geographical positioning 114
  location 11, 12, 19
  movement to the indoor markets
    from 105–6, 168
  payment system 19
  policing 97–101
  impact on safety strategies 98,
    113
  inconsistencies 97–8
  relationships 170
  coercive 163
  selection of clients 52
  use of 'front' 85–6
  and violence 73
  attitudes 88
  deterrents 84–5
Street Offences Act (1959) 94
street workers 19
  relationship between pimps and 20
Streetwatch 99, 100
subjective clues for selection 52
suburban neighbourhoods, brothels in
    11
'Support and Advice for Escorts' 171
'surface acting' 142–3
surveillance as an encouragement to
    prostitution 114
suspicious behaviour 65–6

'taking a break' 157

TAMPEP (Transnational AIDS/STD Prevention Among Migrant Prostitutes in Europe) 174
telephone conversations 66–8
  assertiveness in 85
  attitude 67
  checking consistency 67–8
thrill-seeking motivations of clients 114
time-wasters 55
timing as a control technique 151
'tools of the trade' 139
trafficking 10
training 171
traits 54–5
  based on appearance 58
'trapping factors' in street prostitution 19
trust 53–4
  experiential basis 60
  see also genuineness
trust game 53–6
  communication in 56–71
  costly to fake principle 56
  mimicry and traits 54–5
truth
  partial 135
  revealing 121–3
  variations 133–6

Uganda, sex trade 41
'Ugly Mugs' 173
UK Network of Sex Work Projects (UKNSWP) 175
unionization 175

vagrancy laws 94
verbal skills and prevention of violence 77
vice squads 102
victim model 38
  criticisms 41
vigilantism 99, 101
violence 40, 72–92
  by sex workers 87–8
  normalization 73–5
  reporting incidents to the police 109–10
  responses see responses to violence
  risk 74–5

types 74
violent crime, role of prostitution in reducing 154
visual assessments 57–64
  see also remote visual observation
voices, assessment 66–7

'walking beats' 19
weapons, carrying 87
websites
  assessing client reputation via 69–70
  sex workers' 18
  use in ethnographic research 27
white men 59
'whore stigma' 116, 117
women
  fear of sexual danger and 'fear of crime' 91
  prevention of exploitation or coercion 94
work
  difference between prostitution and 40, 144
  separation of private life from 33, 139, 148–50
  sex as 148–50
  see also legitimate work
work environments, collective 78–80
work model of prostitution 39–40
  criticisms 41
working alone 78–9
working from home 18–19
  disguising activities 110–11
working girls see sex workers
working practices
  importance of routine 151
  learning from mistakes 166–7
  that guard against violence and robbery 76–8
  to avoid arrest in the street market 105–6
working premises 17
workplace 17
  as the centre of the ethnography 31
  geographical location 129–30
  and the risk of violence 74–5

young men 62, 65